The Syntax of Arabic

CW00739869

Recent research on the syntax of Arabic
major syntactic phenomena found in the
provides an overview of the major syn
featured in recent linguistic debates, and
in the literature. A broad variety of topics
negation, tense, agreement phenomena,
topic sums up the key research results and provides new points of departure
for further research. The book also contrasts Standard Arabic with other Arabic
varieties spoken in the Arab world. An engaging guide to Arabic syntax, this
book will be invaluable to graduate students interested in Arabic grammar, as
well as syntactic theorists and typologists.

JOSEPH E. AOUN is President of Northeastern University, Boston, Massachusetts.

ELABBAS BENMAMOUN is Professor in the Department of Linguistics at
the University of Illinois at Urbana-Champaign.

LINA CHOUEIRI is Associate Professor in the English Department at the
American University of Beirut.

CAMBRIDGE SYNTAX GUIDES

General editors:
P. Austin, B. Comrie, J. Bresnan, D. Lightfoot, I. Roberts, N. V. Smith

Responding to the increasing interest in comparative syntax, the goal of the Cambridge Syntax Guides is to make available to all linguists major findings, both descriptive and theoretical, which have emerged from the study of particular languages. The series is not committed to working in any particular framework, but rather seeks to make language-specific research available to theoreticians and practitioners of all persuasions.

Written by leading figures in the field, these guides will each include an overview of the grammatical structures of the language concerned. For the descriptivist, the books will provide an accessible introduction to the methods and results of the theoretical literature; for the theoretician, they will show how constructions that have achieved theoretical notoriety fit into the structure of the language as a whole; for everyone, they will promote cross-theoretical and cross-linguistic comparison with respect to a well-defined body of data.

Other books available in this series

O. Fischer et al.:	*The Syntax of Early English*
K. Zagona:	*The Syntax of Spanish*
K. Kiss:	*The Syntax of Hungarian*
S. Mchombo:	*The Syntax of Chichewa*
H. Thrainsson:	*The Syntax of Icelandic*
P. Rowlett:	*The Syntax of French*
R. D. Borsley et al.:	*The Syntax of Welsh*
C.-T. J. Huang et al.:	*The Syntax of Chinese*

The Syntax of Arabic

JOSEPH E. AOUN
Northeastern University, Boston

ELABBAS BENMAMOUN
University of Illinois, Urbana-Champaign

LINA CHOUEIRI
American University of Beirut

CAMBRIDGE UNIVERSITY PRESS
Cambridge, New York, Melbourne, Madrid, Cape Town, Singapore, São Paulo, Delhi

Cambridge University Press
The Edinburgh Building, Cambridge CB2 8RU, UK

Published in the United States of America by Cambridge University Press, New York

www.cambridge.org
Information on this title: www.cambridge.org/9780521659864

First published 2010

Printed in the United Kingdom at the University Press, Cambridge

A catalogue record for this publication is available from the British Library

ISBN 978-0-521-65017-5 hardback
ISBN 978-0-521-65986-4 paperback

Contents

Abbreviations

1	First Person
2	Second Person
3	Third Person
s	Singular
p	Plural
m	Masculine
f	Feminine
Acc	Accusative
Nom	Nominative
Gen	Genitive
Dat	Dative
Asp	Aspectual Marker
Subj	Subjunctive
Ind	Indicative
Comp	Complementizer
Neg	Negative Marker
Fut	Future Marker
Prog	Progressive
FM	Focus Marker

1

Issues in the syntax of Arabic

1.1 The Arabic language(s)

Arabic belongs to the Semitic branch of the Afro-Asiatic (Hamito-Semitic) family of languages, which includes languages like Aramaic, Ethiopian, South Arabian, Syriac, and Hebrew. A number of the languages in this group are spoken in the Middle East, the Arabian Peninsula, and Africa. It has been documented that Arabic spread with the Islamic conquests from the Arabian Peninsula and within a few decades, it spread over a wide territory across North Africa and the Middle East. Arabic is now spoken by more than 200 million speakers excluding bilingual speakers (Gordon 2005).

Although there is a debate about the history of Arabic (including that of the Standard variety and the spoken dialects) Arabic displays some of the typical characteristics of Semitic languages: root-pattern morphology, broken plurals in nouns, emphatic and glottalized consonants, and a verbal system with prefix and suffix conjugation.

1.1.1 The development of Arabic

Classical Arabic evolved from the standardization of the language of the Qur'an and poetry. This standardization became necessary at the time when Arabic became the language of an empire, with the Islamic expansion starting in the seventh century. In addition to Classical Arabic, there were regional spoken Arabic varieties. It is a matter of intense debate what the nature of the historical relation between Classical Arabic and the spoken dialects is (Owens 2007).

Modern Standard Arabic emerged in the nineteenth century at a time when Arabic was gaining the status of official language in the Arab world, and coinciding with the emergence of Arab nationalism (see Suleiman (2003) and references therein). The process of modernization of the language started in the early twentieth century with Arab academies playing a crucial role in "preserving" the Arabic

1

language from dialectal and foreign influence, and adapting it to the needs of modern times. Unsurprisingly, in spite of the unifying work of those academies, one can still observe regional variations in Modern Standard Arabic.

1.1.2   The Modern Arabic dialects and Modern Standard Arabic

The linguistic space of the Arabic-speaking world, which spans a large geographical area from the Persian Gulf in Asia to the Atlantic Ocean in North West Africa, is shared by several language varieties, which include Modern Standard Arabic, and a number of Arabic vernaculars that remain mainly as spoken dialects. Those dialects differ from one another, with mutual intelligibility decreasing as the geographical distance between them increases. The main geographical linguistic groupings are the Maghreb (mainly North Africa), Egypt, the Levant, and the Gulf.[1] Modern Standard Arabic and the spoken dialects of Arabic exist in a diglossic situation (Ferguson 1959): the Arabic vernaculars are what people acquire at home, and thus, they are the native languages of the people in the Arab world. Modern Standard Arabic is the language for writing and for formal speaking and is only acquired at school. Thus, not all speakers of Arabic have equal command of the Standard dialect and their colloquial dialect. Language choice in the Arab world is not only determined by the factors that influence the functional distribution of the various Arabic varieties; it also has a political association, since Modern Standard Arabic has become a symbol of the unity of the Arab world (Suleiman 2003).

1.2   General characteristics of the syntax of Arabic

In this brief introduction to the sociology of Arabic we highlighted the complex relationships that exist between Modern Standard Arabic and the various Arabic vernaculars. This complexity can also be found in the variation observed between the grammars of the different Arabic varieties. In this book, we focus mainly on the description of grammatical structures in Standard Arabic, Moroccan Arabic, and Lebanese Arabic. However, to illustrate the range of variation that exists, we also use data from Egyptian Arabic, Palestinian Arabic, and the Gulf varieties.

---

[1]   There are also Arabic-speaking minorities in Sub-Saharan Africa (particularly Cameroon, Chad, and Nigeria) and Asia (Afghanistan, Turkey, and Uzbekistan) (see Versteegh 1997: chapter 13).

In the sections that follow, we introduce the key empirical generalizations that characterize the syntax of the various Arabic dialects under consideration, and which we develop in the present book, taking into consideration previous work in the area.[2]

1.2.1   The syntax of the A-domain

1.2.1.1   Clause structure

There are a number of issues that arise in the context of Arabic clauses. The first issue concerns the structure of the clause, particularly the categories, such as tense and negation, that occupy the space between the complementizers and the lexical predicates – the so-called A-domain. For example, it has traditionally been claimed that Arabic verbs carry aspectual or temporal morphology which is realized through verbal templates and agreement morphology. Thus, in the present tense, the verb in Standard Arabic may display a specific vocalic melody and discontinuous agreement (1a) while in the past tense it may display a different vocalic melody and suffixal agreement (1b).

(1)   a. ya-ktub-na
          3-write-fp
          'They are writing.'

        b. katab-na
          wrote-3fp
          'They wrote.'

The question we ask is whether tense (or aspect) is realized through the vocalic melodies or as part of the agreement morphology. To provide an adequate answer to this problem we must go beyond Standard Arabic to see how the dialects realize tense, and what role, if any, vocalic melodies play. The data that will be presented and discussed in chapter 2 suggest that tense in Arabic may not be realized through vocalic melodies or as part of the agreement morphology. This in turn raises the question of whether there is an abstract tense element/projection in the Arabic clause. Evidence from Case, temporal adverbs, and tensed negatives provide syntactic support for such a projection.

A related question that arises in the context of simple clauses concerns the structure of the so-called verbless sentences and whether they contain a null VP constituent (2).

[2] In this book we will deal only with the sentential syntax of Modern Standard Arabic and other Arabic varieties. Thus, we do not include a discussion of the Construct State and the syntax of DPs.

(2)   ?al-kitaab-u   žadiid-un
        the-book-Nom new-Nom
        'The book is new.'

In (2) there is no verbal copula and no element carrying tense. It has been debated in the literature whether a sentence such as (2) has the same structure as finite sentences with verbal predicates or whether it is a small clause. Again evidence based on Case – the Case assigned to adjectival and nominal predicates in Standard Arabic – argues for a full clause structure, but without a VP projection. This implies that a tense projection may not require the projection of a VP, a conclusion that is not consistent with most analyses that suggest that the presence of tense requires the presence of a verb (as its extended projection or feature checker).

1.2.1.2   Subjects and subject positions

A second issue concerns the status of the subject in Arabic varieties. Arabic subjects can occur in different positions: before the verb as in (3), and after the verb as in (4). This variability has led to debates about the underlying and surface positions of the subject and whether in some word order patterns (such as SVO) the so-called subject can indeed be characterized as such.

(3)   *SVO*
        a. Ɂomar kla   t-təffaaħa   *Moroccan Arabic*
           Omar ate.3ms the-apple
           'Omar ate the apple.'

        b. Ɂeħmad gaabal   mona   *Palestinian Arabic*
           Ahmed met.3ms Mona
           'Ahmed met Mona.'

(4)   *VSO*
        a. kla   Ɂomar t-təffaaħa   *Moroccan Arabic*
           ate.3ms Omar the-apple
           'Omar ate the apple.'

        b. gaabal   Ɂeħmad mona   *Palestinian Arabic*
           met.3ms Ahmed Mona
           'Ahmed met Mona.'

Chapter 3 takes up the discussion of subject positions in various Arabic varieties in detail. Contra proposals that have argued that the postverbal subject is in the specifier of the VP projection, we will discuss data that suggest that it is outside the VP. With regard to the preverbal subject, we will review the arguments which state that it behaves as a topic (see also chapter 8 of this book).

1.2.1.3   Agreement and agreement asymmetries

Standard Arabic is well known for its agreement asymmetries whereby the subject partially agrees with the verb under the VS order (5a) but fully agrees with it under the SV order (5b).

(5)   a. ?akal-**at** l-muʕallimaat-u
          ate-3fs   the-teacher.fp-Nom
          'The teachers ate.'

       b. l-muʕallimaat-u   ?akal-**na**
          the-teacher.fp-Nom ate-3fp
          'The teachers ate.'

The third issue we take up is the analysis of the agreement phenomena in Arabic. Various syntactic alternatives have been explored in the literature, but are shown to have fallen short of accounting for the full range of data. We will explore alternative ways of deriving the asymmetry from the interface of syntax and morpho-phonology.

Another intriguing agreement asymmetry concerns first conjunct agreement in coordination structures whereby the verb agrees with the first conjunct in the VS order but must agree with the full conjunct in the SV order. Moreover, number sensitive items seem to force full conjunct agreement in the VS order. The full set of facts will be discussed, as well as possible analyses, including a biclausal account for close conjunct agreement.

1.2.1.4   The syntax of sentential negation

The fourth issue we discuss within the Arabic simple clause is sentential negation, which presents a complex problem in Arabic syntax. In Standard Arabic, there are five main negative particles that realize sentential negation. Two of these particles, *lam* and *lan*, also carry temporal information (6).

(6)   a. T-Tullaab-u   lam   ya-drus-uu   *Standard Arabic*
          the-students-Nom Neg.past 3-study-mp
          'The students did not study.'

       b. T-Tullab-u   lan   ya-drus-uu
          the-students-Nom Neg.fut   3-study-mp
          'The students will not study.'

laa, by contrast, occurs only in imperatives and present tense sentences with verbal predicates.

(7)   a. T-Tullab-u   **laa**   ya-drus–uu-n   *Standard Arabic*
          the-students-Nom Neg   3-study-mp-ind
          'The students do not study.'

       b. laa   ta-drus
          Neg   2-study
          'Do not study!'

Another negative particle, *laysa*, occurs only in present tense sentences, accompanying verbal predicates as well as non-verbal predicates. However, unlike the other negatives, it carries agreement morphology.

(8)   laysat   fii l-bayt-i
       Neg.3fs in the-house-Gen
       'She is not in the house.'

The fact that negation can carry temporal information and agreement morphology argues for its head status and also, possibly, for locating it between the tense projection and the verbal projection.

On the other hand, in the spoken dialects, there are usually only two forms of negation whose distribution is also restricted by the tense of the clause and the category of the predicate. Though the spoken dialects and Standard Arabic differ in their negative particle inventories, the underlying syntax turns out to be similar in that the conditions that regulate the distribution of sentential negation in Standard Arabic also regulate its distribution in the spoken dialects. The main difference is that in Standard Arabic the negatives can carry temporal information but they cannot do so in the spoken dialects.

Another important aspect of sentential negation concerns the dependencies it enters into with negative polarity items and negative quantifiers. The NPI *ħədd* in Moroccan Arabic in (9) is restricted to the post-negative position. But another NPI, *ħətta+NP*, can occur in both the pre-negative and post-negative positions (10).

(9)   a. ma-ža   ħədd
          Neg-came.3ms one
          'No one came.'

       b. *ħədd ma-ža
          one   Neg-came.3ms

(10)   a. **ma**-ža   ħətta waħəd
          Neg-came.3ms even one
          'No one came.'

b. ħətta waħəd **ma**-ža
   even one   Neg-came.3ms
   'No one came.'

Word order, and more intriguingly, the category type of the negative polarity items
are critical to the distribution of those elements.

1.2.2   The syntax of the A'-domain: unbounded dependencies in Arabic

The various Arabic varieties under consideration make use of several
strategies for forming unbounded dependencies between a sentence or clause
peripheral element and a sentence internal position. In parallel with the canonical
unbounded dependency between a peripheral element and a gap in a sentence
internal position, certain constructions exhibit a phenomenon called *resumption*,
where the sentence internal position to which the peripheral element is related
is occupied by an overtly realized anaphoric element, called a *resumptive*.[3] Most

---

[3] It is generally pronouns that serve as resumptive elements (see McCloskey 2002, 2005);
although, it has been observed that certain noun phrases, like epithets, can also occur as
resumptives, as illustrated in the Lebanese Arabic example in (i) (see McCloskey 1990;
Shlonsky 1992; Aoun and Choueiri 2000; Aoun, Choueiri, and Hornstein 2001):

(i)   ħkii-na   maʕ l-bint   lli   ʔaal-o   ʔənno ha-l-mʕattara ħa-təSʔut
        talked-1p with the-girl that said-3p that this-the-poor Fut.-fail.3fs
        'We spoke with the girl whom they said that this poor one will fail.'

In addition, there is variability among the Arabic dialects as to whether they allow
strong pronouns as resumptive elements. Whereas in Moroccan Arabic strong pronouns
are excluded from the contexts of resumption, Lebanese Arabic strong pronouns are not.
Ouhalla (2001) provides relevant examples from Moroccan Arabic to illustrate this point
((iia–b) correspond to Ouhalla's (21a–b)).

(ii)   a. šmen Talib nsiti   fin   tlaqiti-h   (*huwwa)
           which student forgot-2s where met-2s-him (HIM)
           'Which student have you forgotten where you met?'

        b. šmen Talib saferti   qblma yTerdu-h   (*huwwa)
           which student traveled-2s before expelled-3p-him (HIM)
           'Which student did you travel before they expelled?'

The sentences in (ii) contrast with their equivalents in Lebanese Arabic, where the
sentence initial wh-phrase can bind the strong resumptive pronoun (iii).

(iii)   a. ʔayya tilmiiz nsiit-e   ween ltaʔay-te fi-i   huwwe
           which student forgot-2fs where met-2fs in-him HIM
           'Which student did you forget where you met?'

        b. ʔayya tilmiiz seefar-te ʔablma yišħaT-u   -u   huwwe
           which student traveled-2fs before expelled-3p him (HIM)
           'Which student did you travel before they expelled?'

In all Arabic dialects, weak pronouns can be used productively as resumptive elements,
and in this book we discuss only weak pronouns as resumptive elements.

Arabic dialects make productive use of the resumptive strategy, in parallel with the gap strategy.

One of the main questions that can be raised in that regard is: why do languages make use of more than one strategy to construct unbounded dependencies? In order to answer such a question, one needs to understand the properties of the gap strategy and those of the resumptive strategy and how the gap strategy and the resumptive strategy are related cross-linguistically and within a given Arabic variety.

1.2.2.1 Wh-interrogatives

Wh-interrogatives display the richest repertoire of strategies in forming unbounded dependencies. Thus, the various Arabic varieties make use of up to four different strategies in forming wh-questions: the gap strategy, the resumptive strategy, the Class II resumptive strategy, and the wh-in-situ strategy. Whereas in the gap strategy the variable position corresponds to an empty position inside the sentence, in both the resumptive strategy and the Class II resumptive strategy, it is occupied by a pronominal element. The in situ strategy involves a wh-constituent in the variable position inside the sentence.

Lebanese Arabic, for instance, makes use of all four strategies, as exemplified in (11):

(11)   a. ʔayya mmasil šəft   Ø b-l-maTʕam?   *Gap Strategy*
            which actor   saw.2ms   in-the-restaurant
            'Which actor did you see in the restaurant?'

        b. ʔayya mmasil šəft-o   b-l-maTʕam?   *Resumptive Strategy*
            which actor   saw.2ms-him in-the-restaurant
            'Which actor did you see in the restaurant?'

        c. miin (ya)lli šəft-o   b-l-maTʕam?   *Class II Resumptive*
            who that   saw.2ms-him in-the-restaurant   *Strategy*
            'Who is it that you saw in the restaurant?'

        d. šəft   ʔayya mmasil b-l-maTʕam?   *In-situ Strategy*
            saw.2ms which actor   in-the-restaurant
            'Which actor did you see in the restaurant?'

The wh-in-situ strategy is not available in Standard Arabic; the gap strategy doesn't seem to be available in Egyptian Arabic. However, each of the Arabic varieties under consideration seems to make use of at least two different strategies in forming its wh-interrogatives.

Table 1.1 *Wh-phrases that can be related to a resumptive*

Resumptive elements	
Yes	No
?ayy(a) NP 'which NP', *miin/man* 'who'	*šu/maaðaa* 'what,' *kam NP* 'how many NP,' *?addee(š)* 'how much,' *ween/?ayna* 'where,' *?eemta/mataa* 'when,' *kiif/kayfa* 'how,' *lee(š)/limaaðaa* 'why'

The different strategies impose different restrictions on (i) the type of wh-phrase that can be involved, and (ii) the distribution of the "variable" position within the sentence. The gap in wh-interrogatives can occur in simplex and complex sentences, but it is prohibited inside islands. The pronoun, whether in resumptive wh-interrogatives or Class II resumptive interrogatives, can occur in all contexts, including islands. Wh-in-situ elements can occur in simplex and complex sentences.[4]

There has been much discussion on the relation between the availability of a given strategy for forming wh-interrogatives and the nature of the wh-constituent involved. Thus it has been argued that, whereas all wh-constituents may be related to a gap in a wh-question, only a subset of those can be related to a pronominal in a resumptive wh-question. In Lebanese Arabic, this is illustrated in Table 1.1.

We will argue that the notions of referentiality/d-linking, however understood, are inadequate to characterize the set of wh-constituents which can form unbounded dependencies with a pronominal element. This is further complicated by the fact that within Lebanese Arabic, the same wh-constituent, namely *šu* 'what,' is prohibited in resumptive wh-interrogatives, but not in Class II resumptive wh-interrogatives.

The nature of the wh-constituent which occurs in the in situ strategy varies across the Arabic dialects. Whereas in Egyptian Arabic all wh-constituents may occur in situ, in Lebanese Arabic only a subset of those can occur in situ. The subset of wh-constituents which occur in situ in Lebanese Arabic does not coincide with that of those which occur in resumptive wh-interrogatives. Thus, *kam NP* 'how many NP,' which cannot occur in a resumptive wh-question (12a), can occur in situ (12b).

(12)   *Lebanese Arabic*
　　　a. *kam　　　kteeb ?ǝryuw-un　　t-tleemiz?
　　　　　how many book   read.3p-them the-students
　　　　　'How many books did the students read?'

---

[4] There is not much discussion in the literature on Arabic on the wh-in-situ strategy in island contexts.

b. ?əryo   t-tleemiz   kam   kteeb?
read.3p the-students how many book
'How many books did the students read?'

In chapter 6, we will examine various analyses which attempt to characterize, in general terms, the subset of wh-constituents which occur in situ, but will conclude that none of them account for the facts across the various Arabic varieties.

1.2.2.2   Restrictive relatives

The resumptive strategy is the default strategy for forming restrictive relative clauses in the various Arabic dialects. The investigation of those constructions in chapter 7 leads us to uncover further generalizations in the syntax of resumption. First, we show that a difference needs to be made between definite relatives and indefinite relatives. Definite relatives always occur with the complementizer *allaði*, the only complementizer available for relative clauses in Standard Arabic (13a); indefinite relatives on the other hand cannot occur with a complementizer (13b).

(13)   a. Daaʕa   l-kitaabu *(allaði) štaraytu-hu l-baariħata
           be-lost.3ms the-book that   bought.1s-it yesterday
           'The book that I bought yesterday is lost.'

        b. ?ufattišu ʕana kitaabin (*allaði) ?aDaʕtu-hu l-yawma
           look.1s   for book   that   lost.1s-it   the-day
           'I am looking for a book that I lost today.'

When the gap strategy is available in forming relative clauses (e.g. in Standard Arabic), it is only available for definite relatives and not for indefinite relatives. While non-referential NPs can be the antecedent in a definite relative, they cannot head an indefinite relative.

Second, a thorough investigation of the distribution of resumptive pronouns in definite relatives shows that, unlike what is generally argued for Arabic, resumption is selectively sensitive to islands. Thus, a resumptive pronoun related to a non-referential NP cannot occur inside an island, as illustrated in the Lebanese Arabic sentences in (14).

(14)   a. *s-sərʕa   lli   btinbəSTo laʔanno saami byištiʁil   fiy-**a**
           the-speed that pleased.2p because Sami works.3ms with-it

           hiyye l-maTluube
           she   the-required
           'The speed with which you are pleased because Sami works is the required one.'

    b. *n-narvaze   lli   btaʕrfo miin byiħke fiy-**a**   maʕ
      the-nervousness that know.2p who talk.3ms with-it with

    z-zbuneet   raħ bithaššəl-un
    the-clients fut. drives-away.3sf-them
    'The nervousness that you know who speaks with to the clients
    will drive them away.'

This selective sensitivity to islands shows that resumption cannot be said to be
a unitary phenomenon within a given Arabic variety.

1.2.2.3   The syntax of the left periphery

    The examination of focus fronting constructions, which use the gap strat-
egy in forming unbounded dependencies, and clitic-left dislocation constructions,
which make use of resumption in their unbounded dependencies, further confirms
two generalizations:

(15)   a. Gap constructions do not impose restrictions on the nature of their
        antecedents.
    b. The set of possible antecedents of a resumptive pronominal is not
        constrained by referentiality/d-linking.

While chapter 8 examines further differences between the syntax of focus
fronting and clitic-left dislocation, chapter 9 focuses on the interaction between
the gap strategy and the resumptive strategy, as exemplified in sentences which
involve both focus fronting and clitic-left dislocation. We observe that whereas
in a given sentence there can be multiple clitic-left dislocated elements, there can
be only one (fronted) focused constituent. Another important observation is that,
while some Arabic varieties impose an ordering requirement on focused elements
and clitic-left dislocated elements, other varieties don't.

We will conclude that clitic-left dislocated noun phrases need to be distinguished
from preverbal subjects, as well as broad subjects (Doron and Heycock 1999; and
Alexopoulou, Doron, and Heycock 2004). In light of all these generalizations we
argue that the "Split CP" hypothesis (Rizzi 1997) provides a plausible account for
the syntax of the left periphery in Arabic.

2

Clause structure in Arabic

2.1   Introduction

One of the distinguishing features of the Principles and Parameters framework is the fundamental assumption that syntactic configurations expressing hierarchical relations between heads and their surrounding constituents are key to capturing generalizations involving Case assignment, agreement relations, argument selection, polarity licensing, restrictions on displacement, and perhaps word order and other properties. However, there is no consensus as to how to account for the variation that clauses display cross-linguistically or even within the same language. Under some approaches, languages differ as to whether a particular element heads a syntactic projection in the syntax. This issue has been extensively debated in the context of categories such as agreement (Pollock 1989; Ouhalla 1991; Benmamoun 1992a; Iatridou 1990; Chomsky 1995; Cinque 1999). The same question arises in the context of tense and VP. For example, in some languages there is neither an overt tense marker nor a copula in the present tense, leading some approaches to claim that there is neither a TP (Tense Phrase) nor a VP projection in such constructions, which in turn implies that the TP and VP projections may not be universal. Arabic dialects are good testing grounds for this debate. They display a temporal system that is not easy to characterize morphologically and they do not have a verbal copula in the present tense.[1] In this chapter, we provide crucial data for this debate and argue that the most warranted conclusion is that Arabic has a TP projection in all the main tenses, i.e. past, present, and future, but no VP projection in present tense verbless constructions. We then discuss the implications of this conclusion. The chapter starts with a brief overview of the CP (Complementizer Phrase) layer and then turns to a more detailed discussion of the TP layer and its interaction with the verb. The syntax of the so-called verbless sentences is dealt with at the end of the chapter.

---

[1] Except in generic sentences where an overt copula is possible. See Moutaouakil (1987) and Benmamoun (2000).

2.2   The CP layer

There are two broad classes of complementizers in Arabic: complementizers that occur in the context of finite clauses (1) and complementizers that occur in the context of non-finite clauses (2).[2]

(1)   a. ʔaʕtaqidu ʔanna l-walad-a   ya-lʕabu   *Standard Arabic*
          believe.1s that   the-child-Acc 3-play
          'I believe that the child is playing.'

      b. ta-n-Dən   bəlli l-wəld   ta-y-lʕəb   *Moroccan Arabic*
          Asp-1-believe that   the-child Asp-3-play
          'I believe that the child is playing.'

      c. biftikir   ʔənno l-walad ʕam   byi-lʕab   *Lebanese Arabic*
          believe.1s that   the-child Asp-3-play
          'I believe that the child is playing.'

(2)   a. rafaDa   ʔan   ya-drusa   *Standard Arabic*
          refused.3ms Comp 3-study
          'He refused to study.'

      b. rfəd   baš   yə-qra   *Moroccan Arabic*
          refused.3ms Comp 3-study
          'He refused to study.'

      c. rafaD   ʔənno yi-drus   *Lebanese Arabic*
          refused.3ms Comp 3-study
          'He refused to study.'

In Standard Arabic, *ʔanna* heads finite clauses and *ʔan* introduces non-finite ones.[3] Moroccan Arabic, like Standard Arabic, has two different complementizers introducing finite and non-finite clauses, *bəlli* and *baš* respectively. Lebanese Arabic has only one complementizer, *ʔənno,* which may occur in both types of clauses. In contrast with Standard Arabic, which requires the complementizer *ʔan* to occur in non-finite complement clauses, Moroccan Arabic non-finite complement clauses are not always headed by the complementizer *baš* (3–5). In Lebanese Arabic, there are generally no complementizers in such contexts, but *ʔənno* can occur (6).

---

[2] We gloss the complementizers that occur in the context of non-finite clauses as Comp. Notice that when we use the term "non-finite" we mean that the sentence does not have an independent temporal interpretation. There is a widespread assumption that there are no infinitives in Arabic (see below).

[3] In line with Mohammad (2000), we characterize *ʔan* as a complementizer.

(3)   a. rafaDa   *(ʔan)   ya-drusa   *Standard Arabic*
         refused.3ms (Comp) 3-study
         'He refused to study.'

      b. rfəd   yə-qra   *Moroccan Arabic*
         refused.3ms 3-study
         'He refused to study.'

(4)   a. ħaawala   *(ʔan)   ya-drusa   *Standard Arabic*
         tried.3ms (Comp) 3-study
         'He tried to study.'

      b. ħawəl   (*/? baš) yə-qra   *Moroccan Arabic*
         tried.3ms (Comp)   3-study
         'He tried to study.'

(5)   a. waažib   (ʕalay-h) *(ʔan) ya-ʔtii   *Standard Arabic*
         necessary (on-him) (Comp) 3-come
         'He must come.'

      b. wažəb   (ʕli-h)   (baš)   y-ži   *Moroccan Arabic*
         necessary (on-him) (Comp) 3-come
         'He must come.'

(6)   *Lebanese Arabic*
      a. žarrab   (*/? ʔənno) yi-ʔra
         tried.3ms (Comp)   3-read
         'He tried to read.'

      b. rafaD   (ʔənno) y-fill
         refused.3ms (Comp) 3-leave
         'He refused to leave.'

      c. Daruure   (ʔənno) nšuuf-o
         necessary (Comp) see.1p-him
         'We must see him.'

An important difference between Standard Arabic and the modern Arabic dialects is that in the former the complementizer that takes finite clause complements assigns Accusative Case to the embedded "subject" as is evident from the Accusative Case marker on *l-walad* 'the child' in (7a) and the accusative clitic *-hu* attached to the complementizer in (7b).[4]

---

[4] See chapter 3 for a more detailed discussion of the syntactic status of "subjects" in Arabic and their syntactic distribution.

(7)   *Standard Arabic*
  a. ?aʕtaqidu ?anna l-walad-a   ya-lʕabu
     believe.1s that   the-child-Acc 3-play
     'I believe that the child is playing.'

  b. ?aʕtaqidu ?anna-hu ya-lʕabu
     believe.1s that-him   3-play
     'I believe that he is playing.'

The modern dialects have lost overt Case marking and we therefore cannot test whether the embedded preverbal lexical "subject" is assigned Case by the complementizer. However, the dialects do have accusative and genitive clitics. Interestingly, in Moroccan Arabic the embedded "subject" cannot be realized as a clitic on the complementizer (8), but it can be in Lebanese Arabic (9).

(8)   *ta-n-Dən   bəlli-h   ta-y-lʕəb   *Moroccan Arabic*
       Asp-1-believe that-him Asp-3-play

(9)   biʕti?id   ?inn-un   ʕam byi-lʕabo   *Lebanese Arabic*
       believe.1s Comp-them Asp- 3-play.p
       'I believe that they are playing.'

The fact that the complementizer assigns Case to the adjacent noun phrase raises an important question about the status of the so-called embedded "subject" with respect to Case Theory.[5] If the preverbal NP that is assigned Case by the complementizer is indeed a subject then, under standard assumptions, it is assigned Case by T. This results in the subject NP being assigned Case by two different heads, the complementizer (head of CP) and the tense (head of TP/IP). It is not clear however that the NP assigned Case by the complementizer is a subject and is overtly located in [Spec, TP]. It is plausible that it is located in an A′-projection between CP and TP, binding a resumptive pronoun in a lower projection in the A-domain of the clause, perhaps either TP or VP. This might provide a solution for the problem of double Case marking but this option is only viable for the contexts

---

[5] The main principle of Case Theory within the Principles and Parameters approach is the requirement – the so-called Case Filter – that NPs in argument positions must be assigned case (Chomsky 1981). Accusative Case is usually assigned by verbs while Nominative Case is assigned by tense or agreement under some versions of Case Theory. Nominative and Accusative Cases are considered structural. Cases assigned by nouns and some prepositions are considered inherent (Chomsky 1986), though this is a matter of debate within Semitic and Arabic syntax (Fassi Fehri 1993; Siloni 1997). The status of abstract Case within the Minimalist Program is not clear. (Structural) Case is a non-interpretable feature in the sense of Chomsky (1995), yet it is not clear what its syntactic role is. See Pesetsky and Torrego (2007) for a possible approach.

where the verbal head inflects for the full set of agreement features required to identify the putative null resumptive pronoun subject. It is a problematic solution for the so-called verbless sentences such as (10), where there is no overt verbal head that could be said to carry the agreement features to identify the putative null subject pronoun.

(10)   a. ?aʕtaqidu ?anna l-walad-a   fii l-bayt-i   *Standard Arabic*
           believe.1s that   the-child-Acc in the-house-Gen
           'I believe that the child is in the house.'

        b. ta-n-Dən   bəlli l-wəld   f-d-dar   *Moroccan Arabic*
           Asp-1-believe that the-child in-the-house
           'I believe that the child is in the house.'

        c. biʕti?id   ?ənno l-bənt b-l-beet   *Lebanese Arabic*
           believe.1s that   the-girl in-the-house
           'I believe that the girl is in the house.'

In (10) the embedded NP following the complementizer is assigned Accusative Case as shown by the Accusative Case marker in (10a).[6] However, the PP predicate does not carry the necessary agreement features to identify a null pronominal. Hence the subject in those sentences cannot be a null pronoun. The most plausible conclusion is that the embedded accusative NP is in the subject position, which again raises questions with respect to double Case marking. One possibility discussed in Mohammad (2000) is to assume that heads are endowed with Case features which they must discharge. Then, in (10), both T and C discharge their Case feature onto the NP subject. The Case feature that is overtly realized is the one assigned by the highest head; in (10), this head is C. If, on the other hand, the subject remains lower than the predicate and another NP occupies the position between the predicate and the complementizer, the subject gets Nominative Case from T and the other NP gets Accusative Case from C, as shown by sentence (11) from Mohammad (2000:108).[7]

---

[6] In the absence of an overt lexical NP in Lebanese Arabic, an accusative clitic appears on the complementizer, as illustrated in (i):

(i)   biʕti?id   ?ənn-a   b-l-beet
          believe.1s that-3fs.Acc in-the-house
          'I believe that she is at home.'

[7] If the idea that an NP can receive more than one Case is correct, then Case assignment by the complementizer needs to be constrained by locality, otherwise we would need to find a way to prevent a lower subject from getting Accusative Case from a higher complementizer.

(11)   qultu   ʔinna-hu waSala   l-ʔawlaad-u
         said.1s that-it   arrived.3ms the-children-Nom
         'I said that the boys arrived.'

In (11) the accusative expletive -*hu* is cliticized onto the complementizer *ʔinna* and the lexical subject *l-ʔawlaad-u* following the verb is in the nominative form. Thus, (11) clearly demonstrates that there are two structural Cases available in the functional domain delimited by TP and CP.[8]

As for the embedded non-finite clauses, one important observation to make about them is that they do not allow subject-to-subject raising (12).

(12)   *Standard Arabic*
         a. ya-žibu ʔan ya-drusa   l-ʔawlaad-u
            3-must that 3-study.subj the-boys-Nom
            'The boys must study.'

         b. *l-ʔawlaad-u   ya-žibuuna ʔan ya-drusuu
            the-boys-Nom 3-must.mp that 3-study.mp

As illustrated by the unacceptability of (12b), raising of the embedded subject in (12a) to the higher clause is blocked. On the basis of these facts Mohammad (2000) concludes that there is no subject-to-subject raising in Standard Arabic.[9] Mohammad attributes this generalization to the absence of infinitives in Arabic. That is, the embedded clauses in sentences such as (12a) can license the subject, which is assigned Nominative Case. This amounts to saying that, in Arabic, the non-finite TP is able to assign Case to a subject. The Case assignment abilities attributed to non-finite TPs in Arabic may be related to the fact that the verbs in these contexts are fully inflected for agreement features.

In brief, the ability to assign Case is one of the significant properties of the complementizers that take finite clause complements in Arabic, with important implications for the status of the preverbal NP and Case assignment in the grammar. Complementizers of non-finite clauses head sentences that can license a lexical subject and hence do not allow subject-to-subject raising.

---

[8] The Cases are structural, rather than inherent, under the assumption that inherent Case is restricted to elements that receive a thematic role from the Case assigner. This is not the case in (11).

[9] We have slightly modified the transcription used by Mohammad to be consistent with the transcription used in this book.

2.3   Tense in Arabic

As can be observed in many languages, the subject of finite clauses in Arabic takes Nominative Case. In Standard Arabic, this Case is realized overtly on the noun by the suffix -*u*:

(13)   daxala   l-walad-**u**   *Standard Arabic*
          entered.3ms the-child-Nom
          'The child came.'

In the modern dialects, where overt Case marking on lexical NPs has disappeared, the Nominative Case on the subject of finite clauses is only seen when pronouns are used. In Lebanese Arabic, for instance, only the independent form of the pronoun can be used in subject position (14).

(14)   huwwe b-l-beet   *Lebanese Arabic*
          he   in-the-house
          'He is in the house.'

These independent pronouns cannot be used in non-subject positions, as illustrated by the unacceptability of (15).

(15)   *šəft   huwwe
          saw.1s he
          'I saw him.'

The standard assumption within the Principles and Parameters framework is that Nominative Case is intimately related to the presence of a tense head. Tense heads a projection located between CP and VP, and Nominative Case is assigned in that projection.

2.3.1   *Projecting tense in Arabic*

Under those assumptions, we are led to posit a tense projection in Arabic, where the subject in (14) is assigned Case. There is also independent evidence for such a projection. First, expletive subjects, which are assumed not to be generated within the thematic shell (VP), but are rather required by the EPP, a property of the tense head, are possible in Arabic, as illustrated in (16) from Standard Arabic.[10]

---

[10] It is not clear what the EPP property really is. The proposals vary between the EPP being the requirement for a subject (Chomsky 1981), the requirement to check the nominal categorical feature [+D] of T (Chomsky 1995), or just the requirement that a category be in [Spec, T] (or C for that matter; Chomsky 2000).

(16)   hunaaka walad-un ya-drusu fii l-bayt-i   *Standard Arabic*
        there   boy-Nom 3-study in the-house-Gen
        'A boy is studying in the house.'

Second, as we will discuss in greater detail in chapter 5, in Standard Arabic, tense is realized on the sentential negative particle rather than on the verb. Thus, in (17a) past tense is realized on the sentential negative *lam* and in (17b) future tense is realized on the sentential negative *lan*.

(17)   a. lam   ta-ktub
           Neg.past 3f-write
           'She didn't write.'

        b. lan   ta-ktuba
           Neg.fut 3f-write
           'She won't write.'

These facts can be straightforwardly captured if tense occupies its own projection in the Arabic clause structure.

(18)

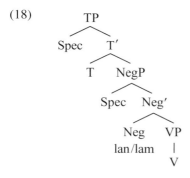

The host for tense is the closest possible host. Given the representation in (18), in the context of sentential negation, the closest host is the negative head. In the absence of sentential negation, the closest host is the verb. However, this analysis relies crucially on the notion that tense is projected separately from the verb, heading its own projection (Benmamoun 1992a).

2.3.2   *The morphology of tense*

As in other Semitic languages, verbs in Arabic dialects display two morphological patterns, the so-called perfective and imperfective forms. By way of illustration, we present these two forms in Lebanese Arabic, Moroccan Arabic, and Standard Arabic. As can be observed from the lists below, the dialects differ from each other with respect to the richness and degrees of syncretism in their paradigm.

(19)   *Lebanese Arabic*
    A. Perfective

Person	Number	Gender	Affix	Verb+Affix
1	Singular	F/M	-t	katabt
2	S	M	-t	katabt
2	S	F	-te	katabte
3	S	M	-0	katab
3	S	F	-it	katabit
1	Plural	M/F	-na	katabna
2	P	M/F	-to	katabto
3	P	M/F	-o	katabo

B. Imperfective

Person	Number	Gender	Affix	Affix+Verb
1	Singular	M/F	ʔ-	ʔəktub
2	S	M	t-	təktub
2	S	F	t—e	təkətbe
3	S	M	y-	yəktub
3	S	F	t-	təktub
1	Plural	M/F	n	nəktub
2	P	M/F	t—o	təktbo
3	P	M/F	y—o	yəktbo

(20)   *Moroccan Arabic*
    A. Perfective

Person	Number	Gender	Affix	Verb+Affix
1	Singular	F/M	-t	ktəbt
2	S	F/M	-ti	ktəbti
3	S	M	-0	ktəb
3	S	F	-at	kətbat
1	Plural	M/F	-na	ktəbna
2	P	M/F	-tu	ktəbtu
3	P	M/F	-u	kətbu

B. Imperfective

Person	Number	Gender	Affix	Affix+Verb
1	Singular	M/F	n-	nəktəb
2	S	M	t-	təktəb
2	S	F	t—i	tkətbi

Person	Number	Gender	Affix	Affix+Verb
3	S	M	y-	yəktəb
3	S	F	t–i	təktəb
1	Plural	M/F	n—u	nkətbu
2	P	M/F	t—u	tkətbu
3	P	M/F	y—u	ykətbu

(21)   *Standard Arabic*

A. Perfective

Person	Number	Gender	Affix	Verb+Affix
1	Singular	F/M	-tu	katab-tu
2	S	M	-ta	katab-ta
2	S	F	-ti	katab-ti
3	S	M	-a	katab-a
3	S	F	-at	katab-at
2	Dual	M/F	-tumaa	katab-tumaa
3	D	M	-aa	katab-aa
3	D	F	-ataa	katab-ataa
1	Plural	M/F	-naa	katab-naa
2	P	M	-tum	katab-tum
2	P	F	-tunna	katab-tunna
3	P	M	-uu	katab-uu
3	P	F	-na	katab-na

B. Imperfective

Person	Number	Gender	Affix	Affix+Verb
1	Singular	M/F	ʔa-	ʔa-drus(u)
2	S	M	ta-	ta-drus(u)
2	S	F	ta—iin(a)	ta-drus-iin(a)
3	S	M	ya-	ya-drus(u)
3	S	F	ta-	ta-drus(u)
2	Dual	M/F	ta—aan(i)	ta-drus-aan(i)
3	D	M	ya—aan(i)	ya-drus-aan(i)
3	D	F	ta-aa	ta-drus-aan(i)
1	Plural	M/F	na-	na-drus(u)
2	P	M	ta—uun(a)	ta-drus-uun(a)
2	P	F	ta—na	ta-drus-na
3	P	M	ya—uun(a)	ya-drus-uun(a)
3	P	F	ya—na	ya-drus-na

Starting with the perfective paradigm, this form occurs almost exclusively in the context of past tense sentences.

(22)   a. katab-uu   l-kitaab-a   ?ams   *Standard Arabic*
            wrote-3mp the-book-Acc yesterday
            'They wrote the book yesterday.'

        b. kətb-u   lə-ktab   lbarəħ   *Moroccan Arabic*
            wrote-3p the-book yesterday
            'They wrote the book yesterday.'

        c. katab-o   l-kteeb   mbeeriħ   *Lebanese Arabic*
            wrote.3p the-book yesterday
            'They wrote the book yesterday.'

There are at least two possible approaches to analyze the perfective form of the verb in Arabic. On one hand, one could advance the view that the suffix on the verb in the perfective realizes both tense and agreement.[11] On the other hand, one could argue that the suffix on the verb in the perfective realizes only agreement and that the verb in Arabic does not inflect for tense.

Under the analysis that the suffix in the perfective paradigm realizes past tense (in addition to agreement), the prediction is that the suffix should only occur in the context of the past tense. However, this prediction is not borne out. The suffix occurs on negative *laysa* in (23) and aspectual particles such as *laazaala* in sentences with present tense interpretation (24), as Benmamoun (1992a, 2000) shows.

(23)   lays-uu   fii l-bayt-i
        Neg-3mp   in the-house-Gen
        'They are not in the house.'

(24)   laazaal-uu fii l-bayt-i
        still-3mp   in the-house-Gen
        'They are still in the house.'

Notice that the negative particle *laysa* in (23) and the aspectual particle *laazaala* in (24) display all the forms of the perfective verb in Standard Arabic (21). (25) illustrates the observation for the aspectual particle.[12]

(25)   1 Singular   F/M   -tu   zil-tu
        2 S   M   -ta   zil-ta
        2 S   F   -ti   zil-ti

---

[11] There is also the view that the Arabic verbs encode aspect but not tense, leading to the characterization of Arabic as an aspectual language. As we will show below, the verbs in Arabic carry neither tense nor aspect.

[12] The aspectual particle consists of the negative *laa* and the verb *zaal*.

3	S	M	-a	zaal-a
3	S	F	-at	zaal-at
2	Dual	M/F	-tumaa	zil-tumaa
3	D	M	-aa	zaal-aa
3	D	F	-ataa	zaal-ataa
1	Plural	M/F	-naa	zil-naa
2	P	M	-tum	zil-tum
2	P	F	-tunna	zil-tunna
3	P	M	-uu	zaal-uu
3	P	F	-na	zil-na

The presence of the same suffix in the perfective paradigm in the context of the present tense clearly demonstrates that this suffix is not a realization of the past tense. The most reasonable characterization is that the suffix carries agreement only.

Note also the fact that the negative and aspectual particles inflect as in the verbal perfective paradigm militates against the view that the vocalic melody on the verb carries tense or aspect (McCarthy 1979). The vocalic melody of the root *zwl* of the aspectual particle *laazaala* in (24) is identical to the vocalic melody of the so-called hollow roots in Standard Arabic, i.e. roots with a medial glide. This is illustrated in (26) with the root *nwm* 'sleep,' where the correspondences between the forms can be clearly observed.

(26)	1	Singular	F/M	-tu	nim-tu
	2	S	M	-ta	nim-ta
	2	S	F	-ti	nim-ti
	3	S	M	-a	naam-a
	3	S	F	-at	naam-at
	2	Dual	M/F	-tumaa	nim-tumaa
	3	D	M	-aa	naam-aa
	3	D	F	-ataa	naam-ataa
	1	Plural	M/F	-naa	naam-naa
	2	P	M	-tum	nim-tum
	2	P	F	-tunna	nim-tunna
	3	P	M	-uu	naam-uu
	3	P	F	-na	nim-na

Moreover, as pointed out in Benmamoun (2000), Moroccan Arabic does not have a distinct vowel melody that one could associate with a particular grammatical tense or aspect. The only stem vowel available in Moroccan Arabic is the schwa /ə/, a vowel that occurs as a stem vowel (after the first root consonant) in a wide range of contexts: past tense (27a), present tense (27b), and on nouns (27c) and adjectives (27d).

(27)   a. lʕəb
           play.3ms
           'He played.'

       b. ta-yə-lʕəb
           Asp-3-play
           'He is playing.'

       c. nmər
           'tiger'

       d. zrəq
           'blue'

In short, the past tense in Arabic is expressed neither by the overt affixes of the perfective form, which seems to carry agreement only, nor by the vocalic melody on the verb. Rather, it seems to be an abstract morpheme located in tense which can be hosted by negation or by the verb, as we will discuss below.

The conclusion that the perfective form of the verb does not morpho-phonologically encode past tense can be extended to the imperfective form as well.[13] This form, too, seems to carry neither tense nor aspect. This conclusion is actually easier to establish for the imperfective, a form which occurs in such a wide variety of aspectual and temporal contexts that it is impossible to attribute a particular temporal or aspectual interpretation to it. For example, the imperfective occurs in the context of tensed negative sentences, as illustrated in (17), repeated here as (28).

(28)   a. lam   ta-ktub
           Neg.past 3f-write
           'She didn't
           write.'

       b. lan   ta-ktuba
           Neg.fut 3f-write
           'She won't write.'

The fact that the tense interpretation, past in (28a) and future in (28b), comes from the negative particle shows that the imperfective verb does not carry tense. The imperfective is also the form of the verb that occurs in the context of modals

---

[13] The imperfective paradigm in Standard Arabic displays a number of so-called moods (the indicative, subjunctive, and jussive). The issue is not directly relevant for this discussion, but see Benmamoun (2000) for a critical overview.

(29), future tense markers (30), non-finite embedded clauses (31), negative imperatives (32), and, in addition to those contexts, regular present tense sentences (33).

(29) a. qad   ya-drus   *Standard Arabic*
         may 3-study
         'He may study.'

      b. lazəm   yə-qra   *Moroccan Arabic*
         necessary 3-study
         'He must study.'

      c. leezim   yiʔra   *Lebanese Arabic*
         necessary 3-read
         'He must read.'

(30) a. sa-ya-drus   *Standard Arabic*
         fut-3-study
         'He will study.'

      b. ɣadi yə-qra   *Moroccan Arabic*
         will 3-study
         'He will study.'

      c. raħ yi-ʔra   *Lebanese Arabic*
         will 3-read
         'He will read.'

(31) a. ʔaraada   ʔan ya-drusa   *Standard Arabic*
         wanted.3ms Com 3-study
         'He wanted to study.'

      b. bɣa   yə-qra   *Moroccan Arabic*
         wanted.3ms 3-study
         'He wanted to study.'

      c. baddo   yi-drus   *Lebanese Arabic*
         want.3ms 3-study
         'He wants to study.'

(32) a. laa   ta-drus   *Standard Arabic*
         Neg 2-study.s
         'Do not study.'

      b. ma-tə-qra-š   *Moroccan Arabic*
         Neg 2-study-Neg
         'Do not study.'

　　　　c. ma ti-ʔra(š)　　　　　　　　　　　*Lebanese Arabic*
　　　　　　Neg 2-read.s(-Neg)
　　　　　　'Don't read.'

(33)　　a. ya-drus　　　　　　　　　　　　　*Standard Arabic*
　　　　　　3-study
　　　　　　'He is studying.'

　　　　b. ta-y-qra　　　　　　　　　　　　*Moroccan Arabic*
　　　　　　Prog-3-study
　　　　　　'He is studying.'

　　　　c. ʕam yi-drus　　　　　　　　　　　*Lebanese Arabic*
　　　　　　Prog 3-study
　　　　　　'He is studying.'

The fact that the imperfective occurs in different temporal contexts shows clearly that this form does not encode any tense, particularly not the present tense (Bahloul 1994; Ouhalla 1993); the present tense interpretation in (33) is just one context where the imperfective can occur. Thus, on a par with the past tense, the present tense seems to be a null abstract morpheme.[14] In short, tense in Arabic seems to be an abstract morpheme generated in T and the affixes observed on the verbs in Arabic are reflexes of agreement features.

We can come to a similar conclusion with respect to aspect in Arabic. This conclusion is easy to establish in the modern Arabic dialects, which have their own aspectual markers that may attach to the imperfective form of the verb. Thus, in Moroccan Arabic (34a) and Lebanese Arabic (34b) the progressive aspect is realized by the proclitic particles *ta-* and *ʕam* respectively.[15,16]

(34)　　a. ta-y-qra
　　　　　　Prog-3-study
　　　　　　'He is studying.'

　　　　b. ʕam yiʔra
　　　　　　Prog 3-read
　　　　　　'He is reading.'

The main difference to be noted between the perfective and imperfective forms of the verb in Arabic concerns how agreement is realized. In the perfective,

---

[14] Future tense in Arabic is realized by independent particles or proclitics.

[15] Standard Arabic does not have overt particles or clitics on the verb to express progressive or habitual aspect. The bare imperfective form of the verb is used in those contexts.

[16] Moroccan Arabic has another particle, *ka-*, that alternates with *ta-* in some dialects or even within the same dialect.

all agreement features are realized by a suffix on the verb. In the imperfective, agreement is realized discontinuously, with the prefix carrying mainly person and the suffix mainly number, a fact that will turn out to be significant when we try to analyze the relation between tense and the verb in the present and past tenses.

2.3.3   The syntax of tense

Starting with the observed interaction between tense and negation, we hinted that the fact that past tense in Standard Arabic occurs on the negative particle can easily be explained by generating negation between TP and VP ((18) is repeated below as (35)).

(35)

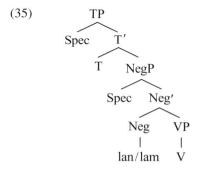

If the negative projection is absent, the verb can raise and merge with tense. On the other hand, if negation is present, verb movement across it would violate Relativized Minimality (Rizzi 1990) or the Head Movement Constraint of Travis (1984).[17] The fact that the past tense is realized on negation suggests that the abstract tense head needs lexical support, hence the inflected negative.

With respect to negation in the context of the present tense, we first notice that there is no negative form dedicated to the present tense. The negative that occurs in this context, *laa*, occurs also as constituent negation (36a), and on negative quantifiers (36b).

---

[17] The main idea behind Relativized Minimality is that licensing relations across c-commanding elements of the same type are not allowed. Thus, an NP cannot license a reflexive across another c-commanding NP; a wh-phrase, particularly if it is extracted from a subject or adjunct position, cannot license its trace across another intervening wh-phrase that c-commands its trace; a head, such as a verb, cannot license its trace across another head. The latter is essentially a recapitulation of the Head Movement Constraint of Travis (1984) which bans movement of a head across another intervening head.

(36)   *Standard Arabic*
    a. laa walada fii l-bayt-i
        no boy   in the-house
        'There is no boy in the house.'
    b. laa ʔaħad
        no one
        'No one'

The fact that there is no present tense form of negation may be explained if the present tense head in T does not need to be lexically supported and therefore does not force verb movement or merger with negation. Thus, though both the past and present tenses are abstract heads of T, only the former requires lexical support.

2.4 Verb displacement in Arabic

Independent evidence is available for the conclusion that, while the abstract past tense head requires lexical support in Arabic, the present tense head, also an abstract head, does not. There are a number of intriguing facts in Arabic, discussed in Benmamoun (2000), which seem to be consistent with the analysis that the past tense forces verb movement while the present tense head does not. First, let us return to the agreement morpheme paradigms in the imperfective and perfective. Recall that agreement in the perfective is exclusively realized by suffixes but in the imperfective the person feature is realized by a prefix and the number feature by a suffix. It is assumed within historical studies of Semitic languages such as Arabic that the person morpheme evolved out of a pronoun (Gray 1934). The number morpheme, on the other hand, may be a marker of agreement and concord. Confining our attention to the person morpheme, let us assume that the subject in Arabic may remain in a position lower than tense. If the past tense must attract the verb, we predict the pronominal subject to follow the verb in T, as illustrated in (37).

(37)

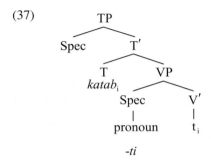

In the configuration in (37) the only form of cliticization that the pronoun can undergo is encliticization. Thus, the obligatory movement of the verb in the past tense accounts for the fact that the person agreement morpheme is a suffix in the so-called perfective paradigm.

On the other hand, if the verb in the present tense does not need to move to T, the verb should be able to remain lower than the subject, providing the latter with only one cliticization option, namely procliticization. Thus, what we get is person prefixation in the so-called imperfective paradigm.

(38)

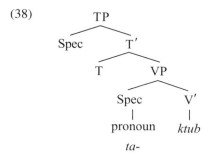

Another intriguing piece of evidence comes from idiomatic expressions or so-called God wishes discussed in Ferguson (1983) and Bahloul (1994). Consider the following idiomatic expressions from Moroccan Arabic.

(39)   a. raħm-u   llah
          bless.past.3ms-him God
          'May God bless him.'

       b. llah y-rəħm-u
          God 3-blessed-him
          'May God bless him.'

Notice that the past tense form of the idiom displays the VS order but the present tense form displays the SV order. This can be explained if in the past tense the verb must move to T, a position higher than the subject, yielding the VS pattern. On the other hand, in the present tense the verb does not need to move to T, resulting in the SV pattern.

In addition to the diachronic arguments given above, we find evidence for the syntactic asymmetry between verbs in past tense sentences and verbs in present tense sentences in the modern Arabic dialects as well.

In Egyptian Arabic, the past tense verb must merge with sentential negation (40) but it does not have to do so in the present tense (41). Merger with negation is indicated by the fact that the verb is sandwiched between the two discontinuous parts of the sentential negation *ma*, and *-š*, which do not have to be separated, as shown in (41b).

(40)   a. Ꜥomar ma-katab-š   ig-gawaab
                Omar Neg-wrote-Neg the-letter
                'Omar didn't write the letter.'

         b. *Ꜥomar mi-š   katab ig-gawaab
              Omar   Neg-Neg wrote the-letter

(41)   a. ma-biyiktib-š
             Neg-writing-Neg
             'He doesn't write.'

         b. mi-š   biyiktib
             Neg-Neg writing
             'He isn't writing.'

(42)

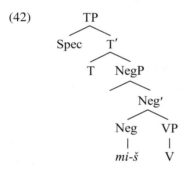

The facts in (40–41) (from Jelinek 1981:41) can be accounted for as follows. To avoid a violation of minimality, the verb in the modern dialects of Arabic moves to T in the past tense, by going through the negative head (Benmamoun 1992a), hence merger with negation. By contrast, in the present tense, tense does not force verb movement, hence merger with negation does not obtain and *maš* appears preceding the verb (42).[18]

It is highly plausible that the future tense projects a TP node above the VP, because future tense is realized either by a morphologically independent marker ((43a) and (44)) or by a proclitic (43b).

---

[18] If the verb moves in the present tense, it is most probably due to some property of negation. This property forces movement in Moroccan Arabic and Lebanese Arabic where merger with negation is obligatory, but not in Egyptian Arabic, as illustrated in (41).

(43)   *Standard Arabic*
   a. sawfa ya-drus
      fut   3-study
      'He will study.'

   b. sa-ya-drus
      fut-3-study
      'He will study.'

(44)   a. ɣadi yə-qra   *Moroccan Arabic*
         will   3-study
         'He will study.'

   b. raħ yi-drus   *Lebanese Arabic*
      will 3-study
      'He will study.'

   In Standard Arabic, given that future tense can be realized on the negative we are led to argue that there is a future tense feature generated in T, which is realized as *sawfa* or its clitic variant *sa-*.[19] In the context of negation, the negative merges with T and the complex is realized morphologically as *lan*. In the other modern dialects, it is not clear that there is a future tense marker in T. Let us consider the Moroccan Arabic and Lebanese Arabic "future" markers *ɣadi,* in (44a), and *raħ*, in (44b). Moroccan Arabic *ɣadi* is a participle form of the root of motion ɣd, which means 'go.' Lebanese Arabic *raħ* is the perfective form of the root of motion *rwħ*, which also means 'go.' These forms can be used as the main predicate of motion as illustrated in (45).

(45)   a. ʔana ɣadi l-d-dar   *Moroccan Arabic*
         I   going to-the-house
         'I am going home.'

   b. raħ   ʕa-l-beet   *Lebanese Arabic*
      went.3ms to-the-house
      'He went home.'

That the predicate of motion in Moroccan Arabic (45a) is the same as the marker of "future" tense is supported by the fact that unlike the future markers *sawfa* and *sa-* in Standard Arabic, *ɣadi*, when used in future tense contexts, may carry the

---

[19] The fact that the imperfective form of the verb is used in the context of future tense may indicate that the verb does not actually need to move to T. The cliticization of *sa-* on the verb in Standard Arabic may not necessarily require movement of the latter.

same inflections, such as the feminine marker in (46b) and the plural marker in (47b), as it does when it is used as a motion verb ((46a) and (47a)).

(46)   *Moroccan Arabic*
    a. hiya γady-a   l-d-dar
        she   going.fs to-the-house
        'She is going home.'

    b. hiya γady-a   tə-qra
        she   will-fs 3f-study
        'She will study.'

(47)   *Moroccan Arabic*
    a. huma γady-n   l-d-dar
        they   going.p to-the-house
        'They are going home.'

    b. huma γady-n   yə-qra-w
        they   will-p   3-study-p
        'They will study.'

Though the agreement inflection on γadi is optional when used to mark future tense, the fact that in future tense contexts it may inflect like a regular participle suggests that the sentences containing γadi are interpreted as future tense but syntactically they are present tense sentences with γadi heading a VP projection below TP (and negation). In other words, syntactically, the sentence in (44) is a prospective present tense sentence in the sense of Comrie (1976).

If this analyis is on the right track we predict that in dialects where the verb in the present tense does not move past the tense head, the "future" tense marker should occur below sentential negation. This prediction is borne out as the following Egyptian Arabic example from Brustad (2000:285) illustrates.[20]

(48)   miš ħa-yi-bʔa   ħilw ʕalayya   *Egyptian Arabic*
    Neg will-3-become pretty on-me
    'It won't look good on me.'

The "future" tense verb in Egyptian Arabic behaves exactly on a par with the verbs in the present tense, which do not move to T. Thus, past tense in Arabic can be said to project a TP node headed by an abstract past tense feature. Similarly, the present tense projects a TP node headed by an abstract present tense feature. However, the two tenses are radically different. The past tense triggers verb movement to T while

---

[20] We modified the transcription and the gloss slightly to be consistent with the conventions used in this book.

the present tense does not. Diachronically, this explains the contrast between the perfective verb and the imperfective verb with respect to the affixation of the person agreement morphology and word order in idiomatic expressions. Synchronically, the verb in the past tense merges with negation because it must move to T through the negative projection located between TP and VP. In the present tense, the verb does not need to move to tense (but it can move to negation), yielding the possible lack of merger of negation and tense in Egyptian Arabic in the present tense.

2.5   Motivating verb movement to tense

Given the analysis under which the verb undergoes movement in past tense sentences but does not have to move in present tense sentences, the question that can be raised at this point is about the property of the past tense that forces movement.

One long-held view is that processes that derive complex words from simple lexical items in the syntax, such as verb merger with tense and other functional categories, verb or noun incorporation, and perhaps also cliticization, are all driven by the need to provide morphological hosts for phonologically deficient elements.[21] The problem is that, since both the past tense and present tense are abstract morphemes, it is not obvious how phonological dependency can distinguish between the two.

Recent developments within the Minimalist Program, particularly Chomsky (1995), provide a possible solution that doesn't depend on phonological deficiency. According to Chomsky (1995), tense is specified for the categorical features [+D] (for nominal) and [+V] (for verbal). In English and French, for example, this accounts for the dependency between tense and the subject (EPP), on one hand, and tense and the verb, on the other. The dependency between tense and the subject explains subject movement to TP, and the dependency between tense and the verb explains V movement to T.

This analysis may be a viable alternative to account for the contrast between the past tense and the present tense in Arabic. Thus, suppose that in Arabic present tense is specified for the [+D] feature only while the past tense is specified for both the [+D] and [+V] features, as illustrated in (49) and (50) respectively:[22]

---

[21] The idea is that a phonologically dependent element must have a lexical host to be realized in the morphology. This idea has driven analyses of head movement and cliticization but has also been questioned given its reliance on an essentially phonological condition to drive a presumably syntactic process.

[22] Though under Chomsky's (1995) analysis, the categorical feature specifications are presumably assumed to be universal, there is no reason why that should be the case.

(49)

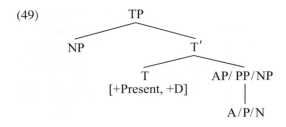

(50)

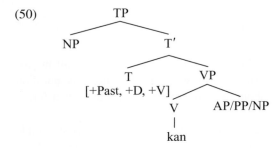

Restricting our attention to the verbal feature, since the past tense is specified for this feature, it follows within Chomsky's minimalist approach, that [+V] will attract the verb, which moves to T as a result. The present tense, by contrast, is not specified for [+V] and therefore no dependency is established between T and the verb. This accurately captures the various facts that suggest that the verb must move to T in the past tense but not in the present tense. Moreover, it explains why there is no verbal copula in the present tense but there must be one in the past. The copula is needed in order for the past tense to establish a dependency with the verb.

Interestingly, grounding the dependency between the verb and the past in a verbal feature captures one fact that a phonologically based analysis cannot capture, namely that the verbal copula must be present even when tense is hosted by negation (51). This fact, pointed out by Moutaouakil (1987), clearly shows that the presence of the verbal copula is not required to realize the past tense, since it is the negative particle in Standard Arabic that realizes it, as in (51b).

(51)   *Standard Arabic*
    a. *lam   mariiDun
       Neg.past ill

    b. lam   ya-kun mariiDan
       Neg.past 3-be   ill
       'He wasn't ill.'

Thus, the dependency between tense and the verb does not seem to be grounded morpho-phonologically. Rather, the distribution of the verbal copula suggests that the dependency is grounded in a requirement that past tense be paired with a verbal element.

2.6   The syntax of verbless sentences

As has already been observed, Arabic is a language (family) that allows sentences to have verbless predicates. An independent sentence in the present tense in Arabic may have only a subject and a non-verbal predicate.[23] The predicate can be a noun phrase, an adjective phrase, or a prepositional phrase, as illustrated by the sentences in (52) from Moroccan Arabic, the sentences in (53) from Standard Arabic, and (54) from Lebanese Arabic.

(52)   *Moroccan Arabic*
      a. ʕomar muʕəllim
         Omar   teacher
         'Omar is a teacher.'

      b. d-dar   kbira
         the-house big
         'The house is big.'

      c. lə-ktab   fuq l-məktəb
         the-book on   the-desk
         'The book is on the desk.'

(53)   *Standard Arabic*
      a. ʕomar muʕallim-un
         Omar   teacher-Nom
         'Omar is a teacher.'

      b. al-bayt-u   kabir-un
         the-house-Nom big-Nom
         'The house is big.'

---

[23] See Berman and Grosu (1976), Ayoub (1981), Bakir (1980), Jelinek (1981), Doron (1986), Moutaouakil (1987), Rapoport (1987), Heggie (1988), Eid (1991, 1993), Fassi Fehri (1993), Shlonsky (1997), Benmamoun (2000), and Greenberg (2002), among others.

c. al-kitab-u   ʕala l-maktab-i
  the-book-Nom on the-desk-Gen
  'The book is on the desk.'

(54)   *Lebanese Arabic*
a. ʕomar ʔisteez
  Omar teacher
  'Omar is a teacher.'

b. l-beet   kbir
  the-house big
  'The house is big.'

c. l-kteeb   ʕala l-maktab
  the-book on   the-desk
  'The book is on the desk.'

Despite the richness of the literature on this topic, there is still no consensus on the clause structure of the sentences such as the ones we have in (52–54). The debate generally centers around the issue of whether they are full clauses with the same set of functional and lexical categories as the copular constructions containing verbal copulas in the past tense (55a–57a), or the future tense (55b–57b), or whether they are small clauses consisting of a projection of the main predicates with no verbal or functional projections above it.

(55)   *Standard Arabic*
a. ʕomar kana   muʕallim-an
  Omar was.3ms teacher-Acc
  'Omar was a teacher.'

b. ʕomar sawfa ya-kunu fi-l-bayt-i
  Omar will 3-be   in-the-house-Gen
  'Omar will be in the house.'

(56)   *Moroccan Arabic*
a. ʕomar kan muʕəllim
  Omar was teacher
  'Omar was a teacher.'

b. ʕomar ɣadi y-kun f-d-dar
  Omar will 3-be in-the-house
  'Omar will be in the house.'

(57)   *Lebanese Arabic*
   a. ʕomar keen ʔisteez
      Omar was teacher
      'Omar was a teacher.'

   b. ʕomar raħ y-kun b-l-beet
      Omar will 3-be in-the-house
      'Omar will be in the house.'

We will show that neither approach is entirely correct. Let us start with the analysis that the sentences in (55–57) contain a verbal copula that is null, i.e. the equivalent of *kan* 'was' in present tense sentences.

(58)

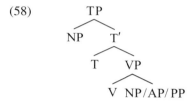

The representation in (58) preserves the assumption that clauses have a universal schema consisting of a TP layer that dominates a VP layer. It is also consistent with the idea that TP (and CP) may be an extended projection of the VP (Grimshaw 1991). However, there is no evidence that there is a verbal element in the sentences where no verbal copula appears, in (55–57). There are several arguments based on Case assignment, selection, and minimality effects, which are problematic for the null verbal copula analysis.

As is well known, the overt copulas in Standard Arabic assign Accusative Case to the nominal and adjectival predicate(s), as illustrated in (59) and (60).

(59)   a. kaana   r-ražul-u   muʕallim-an
           was.3ms the-man.Nom teacher-Acc
           'The man was a teacher.'

        b. *kaana   r-ražul-u   muʕallim-un
           was.3ms the-man.Nom teacher-Nom

(60)   a. sa-ya-kuunu r-ražul-u   muʕallim-an
           fut-3-be   the-man.Nom teacher-Acc
           'The man will be a teacher.'

        b. *sa-ya-kuunu r-ražul-u   muʕallim-un
           fut-3-be   the-man.Nom teacher-Nom

In (59–60) the verbal copula *kaana/yakuunu* 'be' assigns Accusative Case to the predicate *muʕallim* 'teacher,' which, in each sentence, carries the Accusative Case marker *-a(n)*. By contrast, in the present tense sentence in (61), the predicate is not marked for Accusative Case but for Nominative Case. The latter Case is usually the default Case in Arabic carried by elements that are not structurally Case marked, such as (clitic-)left dislocated noun phrases, and nouns in isolation.

(61)   a. r-ražul-u   muʕallim-un
           the-man-Nom teacher-Nom
           'The man is a teacher.'

        b. *r-ražul-u   muʕallim-an
           the-man-Nom teacher-Acc

If the sentence in (61a) has a verbal copula, it is not clear why it cannot assign Accusative Case, yielding the opposite acceptability judgments. It is also important to point out that the Case on the predicate does not depend on the tense of the clause; there are in fact present tense sentences involving negative heads (62) and aspectual heads (63) that can assign Accusative Case to the predicate.

(62)   *Standard Arabic*
        a. laysa r-ražul-u   muʕallim-an
           Neg   the-man-Nom teacher-Acc
           'The man is not a teacher.'

        b. *laysa r-ražul-u   muʕallim-un
           Neg   the-man-Nom teacher-Nom

(63)   *Standard Arabic*
        a. laazaala r-ražul-u   muʕallim-an
           still   the-man-Nom teacher-Acc
           'The man is still a teacher.'

        b. *laazaala r-ražul-u   muʕallim-un
           still   the-man-Nom teacher-Nom

Turning to selection, it is probably a cross-linguistic fact that modal heads select verbal complements. In Arabic dialects, this is clearly the case, as the following sentences from various Arabic dialects show.

(64)   a. yə-qdər yə-mši   *Moroccan Arabic*
           3m-may 3m-go
           'He may/can go.'

b. lazəm   yə-mši   *Moroccan Arabic*
necessary 3-go
'He must go.'

c. byiʔdir   yəmše   *Lebanese Arabic*
3m-may 3m-walk
'He may/can walk.'

d. leezəm   yə-mše   *Lebanese Arabic*
necessary 3-walk
'He must walk.'

If the present tense verbless sentences in (52–54) do contain a null copula, they should, all else being equal, allow for the occurrence of a modal head. This prediction does not obtain, as shown by the ungrammaticality of the examples in (65) and (66).

(65)   a. *ʕomar yə-qdər muʕəllim   *Moroccan Arabic*
         Omar   3-may   teacher

    b. *d-dar   tə-qdər kbira   *Moroccan Arabic*
         the-house 3f-may big

    c. *lə-ktab yə-qdər fuq l-məktəb   *Moroccan Arabic*
         the-book 3-may   on the-desk

    d. *ʕomar byi-ʔdir ʔisteez   *Lebanese Arabic*
         Omar   3-may   teacher

    e. *l-beet   byi-ʔdir kbir   *Lebanese Arabic*
         the-house 3-may   big

    f. *l-kteeb byi-ʔdir ʕala l-maktab   *Lebanese Arabic*
         the-book 3-may   on   the-desk

(66)   a. *ʕomar lazəm muʕəllim   *Moroccan Arabic*
         Omar   must   teacher

    b. *d-dar   lazəm kbira   *Moroccan Arabic*
         the-house must big

    c. *lə-ktab lazəm fuq l-məktəb   *Moroccan Arabic*
          the-book must   on the-desk

    d. *ʕomar leezim ʔisteez   *Lebanese Arabic*
         Omar   must   teacher

    e. *l-beet   leezim kbir   *Lebanese Arabic*
         the-house must   big

f. *l-kteeb leezim ʕala l-maktab   *Lebanese Arabic*
   the-book must   on   the-desk

The only conclusion that can be drawn from the above examples is that there is no null copula. In fact, if we insert the imperfective form of the copula in the sentences in (65) and (66), they become acceptable.

(67) a. ʕomar yə-qdər y-kun muʕəllim   *Moroccan Arabic*
          Omar 3-may 3m-be teacher
          'Omar may be a teacher.'

      b. d-dar   tə-qdər t-kun kbira   *Moroccan Arabic*
          the-house 3f-may 3f-be big
          'The house may be big.'

      c. lə-ktab   yə-qdər y-kun fuq l-məktəb   *Moroccan Arabic*
          the-book 3-may   3-be on the-desk
          'The book may be on the desk.'

      d. ʕomar byi-ʔdir y-kuun ʔisteez   *Lebanese Arabic*
          Omar 3-may   3m-be teacher
          'Omar may be a teacher.'

      e. l-beet   byi-ʔdir y-kuun kbir   *Lebanese Arabic*
          the-house 3-may   3m-be big
          'The house may be big.'

      f. l-kteeb   byi-ʔdir y-kuun ʕala l-maktab   *Lebanese Arabic*
          the-book 3m-may 3m-be on   the-desk
          'The book may be on the desk.'

(68) a. ʕomar lazəm y-kun muʕəllim   *Moroccan Arabic*
          Omar must 3-be teacher
          'Omar must be a teacher.'

      b. d-dar   lazəm t-kun kbira   *Moroccan Arabic*
          the-house must 3-be big
          'The house must be big.'

      c. lə-ktab   lazəm y-kun fuq l-məktəb   *Moroccan Arabic*
          the-book must 3-be on the-desk
          'The book must be on the desk.'

      d. ʕomar leezim y-kuun ʔisteez   *Lebanese Arabic*
          Omar must   3-be   teacher
          'Omar must be a teacher.'

e. l-beet   leezim y-kuun kbir   *Lebanese Arabic*
    the-house must   3-be   big
    'The house must be big.'

f. l-kteeb   leezim y-kuun ʕala l-maktab   *Lebanese Arabic*
    the-book   must   3-be   on   the-desk
    'The book must be on the desk.'

Recall that the imperfective form of the verb is the form that occurs in the present tense in Arabic dialects, thus the observed contrast between (65–66) and (67–68) casts serious doubt on the null copula analysis of present tense verbless sentences. Therefore, the question that remains is why the imperfective form of the copula cannot occur in the sentences in (55–57).

Let us turn next to minimality. Here, too, there is no evidence for a null verbal copula. Simplifying somewhat, minimality effects arise when an element moves or establishes a dependency across another element of the same category (level). We can appeal to minimality effects to explain why the adjective in (69a) cannot merge with negation (69b). The reason is that the merger of the adjective with negation must take place across the verbal copula. The movement would violate minimality because the copula is a closer head to negation.

(69)   *Moroccan Arabic*
       a. ʕomar ma-kan-š   mRiD
           Omar Neg-was.3ms-Neg ill
           'Omar was not ill.'

       b. *ʕomar ma-mRiD-š kan
           Omar   Neg-ill-Neg was.3ms

However, in Moroccan Arabic the adjective can optionally merge with negation as long as no other element intervenes, i.e., as long as the movement does not violate minimality. Thus (69b) becomes acceptable in the absence of the copula *kan* 'was,' as illustrated in (70b).

(70)   a. ʕomar ma-ši   mRiD
           Omar Neg-Neg ill
           'Omar is not ill.'

       b. ʕomar ma-mRiD-š
           Omar Neg-ill-Neg
           'Omar is not ill.'

However, under the approach that assumes the existence of a null copula in verbless sentences, the movement of the adjective to merge with negation to derive (70b) would still violate minimality. We expect (70b) to be on a par with (69b). This is contrary to fact. The reasonable conclusion then is that there is no null copula in present tense verbless sentences.

In short, the sentences in (55–57) do not display a null copula and consequently do not have a VP. The question then is whether such sentences are just small clauses containing the minimal structure that is the result of the merger of the predicate and its subject or whether they contain additional functional structure, particularly the category T.

It was argued here that there is a tense projection in sentences with verbal predicates. Present tense sentences lack verb movement to tense, and as such they contrast with past tense sentences. This idea provides a straightforward analysis for the distribution of the copula: there is a copula in the past tense sentences because tense attracts the verb and if there is no verb in the sentence, one must be inserted, hence the obligatory presence of the verbal copula in past tense sentences. In the present tense sentences, however, tense does not attract the verb, hence there is no need for a verbal copula in present tense sentences.[24]

One may argue that the sentences in (55–57) consist of the lexical layer only, with a default present tense interpretation. That is, one could argue for the absence of all functional structure above the lexical layer. However, there are reasons not to accept this proposal. The so-called verbless sentences display the syntax of full tensed clauses.

It can be shown that verbless sentences pattern with finite clauses with respect to the licensing of negative polarity items (NPIs) in Moroccan Arabic. Embedded verbless sentences with no overt complementizer are islands for NPI licensing (71a). In this respect, they pattern with embedded verbless sentences headed by an overt complementizer (71b).

(71)   *Moroccan Arabic*
      a. *ma-tanDən   ħətta waħəd f-d-dar
         Neg-believe.1s any   one   in-the-house

      b. *ma-tanDən   bəlli ħətta waħəd f-d-dar
         Neg-believe.1s that   any one   in-the-house

Thus, embedded verbless sentences behave like finite clauses rather than embedded non-finite clauses, which allow for licensing of an embedded NPI by the negative in the higher clause, as illustrated in (72).

(72)   ma-bɣit   ħətta waħəd yə-mši
      Neg-want.1s any   one   3-go
      'I don't want anyone to leave.'

---

[24] The future may have a modal feature that requires a verbal copula.

This parallelism between verbless sentences and finite clauses with respect to NPI licensing supports the analysis that verbless sentences have a full clause structure with the relevant projections that define the locality domain for long-distance dependencies, namely finite T and perhaps even C.

Another argument for projecting a TP in verbless sentences comes from Case assignment. The subject of verbless sentences appears in the Nominative Case in Standard Arabic (73), which is arguably a Case assigned to subjects by tense.

(73)   a. ʕaliy-un   muʕallim-un
           Ali-Nom teacher-Nom
           'Ali is a teacher.'

       b. al-ɣurfat-u   kabiirat-un
           the-room-Nom big-Nom
           'The room is big.'

       c. l-kitaab-u   ʕalaa l-maktab-i
           the-book-Nom on   the-desk-Gen
           'The book is on the desk.'

It is clear that the Nominative Case on the subject in (73) is structural and not the default nominative that appears on elements that are (clitic-)left dislocated.[25] Therefore, the subject in those sentences must have structural Case, which can only come from tense in those contexts. Moreover, the fact that an expletive can occur in verbless sentences (74) demonstrates that such sentences contain functional categories. This is so because expletives are not required and are not licensed by lexical categories but rather by functional categories, particularly T.

(74)   hunaaka Taalib-un   fii l-bayt-i   *Standard Arabic*
         there   student-Nom in the-house-Gen
         'There is a student in the house.'

Movement of the subject across negation also argues, albeit indirectly, for a functional projection headed by tense to dominate the lexical predicate in verbless sentences. Consider the contrast between the sentences in (75) and those in (76) from Moroccan Arabic.

---

[25] Left dislocation in Arabic is generally accompanied by resumption (see chapter 8). That is, the dislocated phrase is generally related to a pronominal element within the sentence. Since the predicates in the sentences in (73) do not show full agreement that would identify/license a null pronominal, and in the absence of a related pronoun, the left peripheral NP in those sentences cannot be considered a dislocated element.

(75)   a. ʕomar maši muʕəllim
            Omar not   teacher
            'Omar is not a teacher.'

       b. d-dar   maši kbira
           the-house not big
           'The house is not big.'

       c. lə-ktab   maši fuq l-məktəb
           the-book not on the-desk
           'The book is not on the desk.'

(76)   a. *maši ʕomar muʕəllim
            not   Omar teacher

       b. *maši d-dar   kbira
           not   the-house big

       c. *maši lə-ktab   fuq l-məktəb
           not   the-book on the-desk

The main difference between those paradigms is that in (75) the subject precedes sentential negation while it follows it in (76). One plausible reason for this difference is that the subject must move to TP to satisfy some property of T, such as the EPP.[26] On the other hand, if there are no functional categories in verbless sentences it is not clear why the movement of the subject is forced and why the sentences in (76) are all unacceptable.[27]

---

[26] The EPP (Extended Projection Principle), in its original incarnation (see Chomsky 1981), refers to the requirement that sentences must have subjects, which can be fulfilled by base-generation (of NPs or expletives) or movement of NPs (as in passives and subject-to-subject raising constructions) (see also footnote 10). Recently, it has been argued that this movement of the subject may not be necessary when there is a verb in the sentence inflected for agreement. It is plausible that agreement on the verb can fulfill the EPP, thus obviating the movement of the verb (Alexiadou and Anagnostopoulou 1999; Benmamoun 2000). Within recent versions of the Minimalist Program, the EPP essentially reduces to a requirement that an overt expression be in the specifier position of a phrase with the appropriate EPP feature (Chomsky 2004).

[27] Other facts are consistent with the analysis that argues for a TP in the clause structure of verbless sentences in Arabic. For instance, verbless sentences allow temporal adverbs, as illustrated in (i) from Moroccan Arabic:

(i)   ʕomar f-d-dar   daba
          Omar at-the-home now
          'Omar is at home now.'

If temporal adverbs must be syntactically anchored by tense, then there must be a tense projection in verbless sentences. See Mughazy (2004) for a detailed discussion about

In sum, we conclude that there are strong reasons to support the structure of verbless sentences given in (77) (see Jelinek 1981).[28]

(77)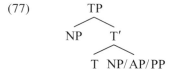

2.7   Conclusion

In this chapter, we discussed two core functional categories in the Arabic clause. Starting with the complementizer layer, we isolated two types of complementizers, a complementizer that occurs in the context of finite complement clauses and a complementizer that occurs in the context of non-finite complement clauses. With respect to the former, one intriguing property that has important syntactic implications concerns its ability to assign (Accusative) Case to the embedded subject. This fact raises important questions about the status of the embedded preverbal "subject" and its Case properties. We then discussed tense in various Arabic dialects, with a special focus on the syntactic differences between the past tense and the present tense. After establishing that both tenses are not realized morphologically but are rather abstract features that head syntactic (TP) projections, we provided arguments to show that the two tenses are very different syntactically. The past tense seems to require movement of the verb to tense while the present tense does not. This property seems to explain different empirical generalizations regarding the position of the person agreement morpheme in the verbal paradigm, word order in idiomatic expressions, the ability to merge with sentential negation, and the presence or absence of the copula in the context of non-verbal predicates. Finally, we discussed verbless sentences, which are constructions that do not display a copula in the present tense. We have shown that they project a TP but no VP.

the distribution of Egyptian Arabic temporal adverbs and its relevance to the issue of tense and aspectual classes in the language.

[28] See also Doron (1986) for Hebrew, and Carnie (1995) for Irish.

3

The syntax of subjects

3.1   Introduction

One of the most controversial issues in Arabic syntax concerns the position of the subject. As far as we know, in all dialects the subject can occur: before the verb and the object, displaying as such the Subject Verb Object (SVO) sequence (1); between the verb and the object, displaying the familiar Verb Subject Object (VSO) sequence (2); or after the verb and the object, displaying the Verb Object Subject (VOS) sequence (3).

(1)   a. ʕomar kla   t-təffaħa   *Moroccan Arabic*
           Omar   ate.3ms the-apple
           'Omar ate the apple.'

       b. ʔeħmad gaabal   mona   *Palestinian Arabic*
           Ahmed   met.3ms Mona
           'Ahmed met Mona.'

       c. maya beesit   mona   *Lebanese Arabic*
           Maya kissed.3fs Mona
           'Maya kissed Mona.'

(2)   a. kla   ʕomar t-təffaħa   *Moroccan Arabic*
           ate.3ms Omar   the-apple
           'Omar ate the apple.'

       b. gaabal   ʔeħmad mona   *Palestinian Arabic*
           met.3ms Ahmed   Mona
           'Ahmed met Mona.'

       c. beesit   maya ɣalil   *Lebanese Arabic*
           kissed.3fs Maya Khalil
           'Maya kissed Khalil.'

(3)   a. kla   t-təffaħa ʕomar   *Moroccan Arabic*
           ate.3ms the-apple Omar
           'Omar ate the apple.'

46

b. gaabal   mona ʔeḥmad   *Palestinian Arabic*
   met.3ms Mona Ahmed
   'Ahmed met Mona.'

c. beesit   khalil maya   *Lebanese Arabic*
   kissed.3fs Khalil Maya
   'Maya kissed Khalil.'

On the other hand, the orders illustrated in (4–6) are not allowed in many Arabic dialects. Mohammad (2000) has shown this on the basis of the data from Palestinian Arabic reproduced here. The same facts can be shown to obtain in Moroccan Arabic and Lebanese Arabic.

(4)   a. *t-təffaḥa kla   ʕomar   *Moroccan Arabic*
          the-apple ate.3ms Omar

       b. *mona gaabal   ʔeḥmad   *Palestinian Arabic*
          Mona met.3ms Ahmed

       c. *khalil beesit   maya   *Lebanese Arabic*
          Khalil kissed.3fs Maya

(5)   a. *t-təffaḥa ʕomar kla   *Moroccan Arabic*
          the-apple Omar ate.3ms

       b. *mona ʔeḥmad gaabal   *Palestinian Arabic*
          Mona Ahmed met.3ms

       c. *khalil maya beesit   *Lebanese Arabic*
          Khalil Maya kissed.3fs

(6)   a. *ʕomar t-təffaḥa kla   *Moroccan Arabic*
          Omar   the-apple ate.3ms

       b. *ʔeḥmad mona gaabal   *Palestinian Arabic*
          Ahmed   Mona met.3ms

       c. *maya khalil beesit   *Lebanese Arabic*
          Maya Khalil kissed.3fs

In (4) the object precedes the V-S sequence while in (5) it precedes the S-V sequence. In (6), the object occurs between the subject and the verb. All these orders are not acceptable in Moroccan Arabic, Lebanese Arabic and, as Mohammad (2000) also shows, Palestinian Arabic.

However, the OVS, OSV, and SOV orders are possible if the object is resumed by a pronominal clitic on the verb, which initially suggests that the object (and in the SOV order the subject) is not within the A-domain but is rather in the A′-domain of the clause, as a (clitic-)left dislocated NP.[1]

(7)   a. t-təffaħa kla-ha   ʕomar   *Moroccan Arabic*
            the-apple ate.3ms-it Omar
            'The apple, Omar ate it.'

       b. mona gaabal-ha   ʔeħmad   *Palestinian Arabic*
            Mona met.3ms-her Ahmad
            'Mona, Ahmad met her.'

       c. khalil beesit-o   maya   *Lebanese Arabic*
            Khalil kissed.3fs-him Maya
            'Khalil, Maya kissed him.'

(8)   a. t-təffaħa ʕomar kla-ha   *Moroccan Arabic*
            the-apple Omar ate.3ms-it
            'The apple, Omar ate it.'

       b. mona ʔeħmad gaabal-ha   *Palestinian Arabic*
            Mona Ahmad met.3ms-her
            'Mona, Ahmad met her.'

       c. khalil maya beesit-o   *Lebanese Arabic*
            Khalil Maya kissed.3fs-him
            'Khalil, Maya kissed him.'

(9)   a. ʕomar t-təffaħa kla-ha   *Moroccan Arabic*
            Omar the-apple ate.3ms-it
            'Omar, the apple, he ate it.'

       b. ʔeħmad mona gaabal-ha   *Palestinian Arabic*
            Ahmad Mona met.3ms-her
            'Ahmad, Mona, he met her.'

       c. maya khalil beesit-o   *Lebanese Arabic*
            Maya Khalil kissed.3fs-him
            'Maya, Khalil, she kissed him.'

---

[1] The OVS, OSV, and SOV orders illustrated in (4–6) also become acceptable if the object is contrastively focused. In such contexts, the object receives focal stress and is not related to a pronominal clitic on the verb. However, it can be said that in those constructions, as in clitic-left dislocation constructions, the object is not in the A-domain but in the A′-domain of the main clause. We discuss (clitic-)left dislocation and focus constructions in full detail in chapters 8 and 9.

In this chapter, we limit our attention to the syntactic distribution of subjects, and in particular to the SVO and VSO orders, which have received most of the attention in the relevant literature.

3.2   Subject position(s)

Given the number of positions that the subject can occupy in a sentence, the question that arises is whether all those positions are genuine subject positions. Genuine subject positions are designated as such in the sense that they are reserved for the subject within the A-domain of a clause.

3.2.1   Two subject positions

There is a general consensus within the Principles and Parameters framework that there are at least two positions within the clause that genuine subjects occupy (Koopman and Sportiche 1991; McCloskey 1996, 1997). One position is reserved for thematic subjects (those that can receive a thematic role from the predicate) and is within the thematic shell. For verbal predicates, the thematic shell can be identified with the VP, and the corresponding structure is illustrated in (10).[2]

(10)

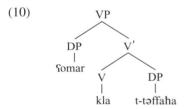

The other position that may host the subject is the specifier of TP, the functional projection that dominates the VP.

(11)

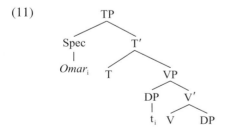

----

[2] There are variations on this proposal. For some, the subject is actually within a predicate phrase or a functional category that dominates the VP.

Three competing proposals have been put forth to account for the distribution of subjects in Arabic. According to one proposal, the subject in the VSO order is within the thematic shell (i.e. the VP) while the Spec of TP is left empty or potentially occupied by a null expletive.

(12)

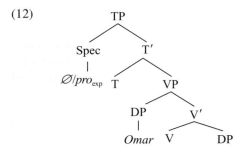

In this respect Arabic would be unlike other languages such as English or French, where it is claimed that the subject must overtly move from the Spec of VP to the Spec of TP (Koopman and Sportiche 1991). By contrast, the subject in the SVO order is in the Spec of TP and is related to a trace in the Spec of VP.[3]

(13)

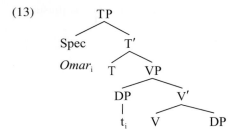

Thus, unlike in languages like English or French, movement of the subject in Arabic from the specifier of VP to the specifier of TP seems optional. But, as far as the status of the preverbal subject is concerned, there is no difference between Arabic and English/French. In all cases, the element occupying the specifier of TP is a genuine subject that occupies an A-position and displays the properties of subjects with respect to agreement, case, and binding.

3.2.2   One subject position

A second proposal that has been advanced to account for the distribution of subjects in Arabic claims that the only genuine overt subject occurs in the VSO

---

[3] The crucial assumption here is that the subject must be merged within the thematic shell so that it can receive its thematic role.

order and that it is located in the Spec of VP. The preverbal subject is thus not within the A-domain, but rather a topic or a clitic-left dislocated element that relates to or binds a resumptive pronominal clitic within the A-domain of the clause, as illustrated in (14).[4]

(14)

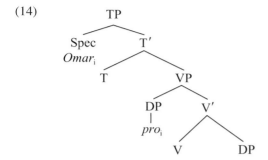

According to this proposal, Arabic and English or French are radically different as far as the syntax of subjects is concerned. In Arabic, the genuine subject is a (possibly null) pronoun that is merged in the Spec of VP and related to a lexical NP in the Spec of TP (or possibly a higher projection).

Another variation on the proposal that Arabic has one subject position is the claim that the subject in both the VSO and SVO orders is outside the VP domain. In the VSO order the subject is (at least) in the specifier of TP with the verb in a higher projection below CP (XP in (15)).

(15)

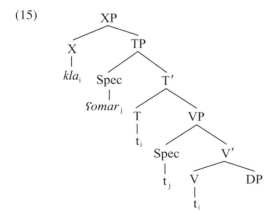

---

[4] Under such an analysis, whether the preverbal subject is located in the specifier of TP or the specifier of a functional projection dominating TP, that position is characterized as an A′-position.

In the SVO order both the verb and the subject could be in TP or in a higher projection or the subject could be in a higher projection and the verb in TP. This analysis avails itself of additional functional projections below CP that can host the verb and the subject. What is significant about this analysis is that it assumes that there is one genuine subject position in the A-domain, [Spec, TP], which is always filled by the overt subject. Thus, the difference between Arabic on one hand, and English or French on the other, is that the verb as well as the subject in Arabic may undergo further movement beyond TP.

There are expectedly other possible analyses that could be explored but the ones briefly mentioned here are representative of the current debate on the syntax of subjects and the verb in Arabic and other languages. Regardless of the diversity of the analyses, the main issues at stake remain the same, namely whether language variation has to do with the syntax of subjects, verbs, or both, and how many positions are available to the external argument.

3.3   Clausal structure and the status of the VP

Before going into the arguments presented for the analyses outlined above, we discuss and dismiss one option that has also been advanced for the syntax of VP in Arabic, namely the flat structure, whereby the verb, subject, and object are all sisters and immediate daughters of TP.[5]

(16)

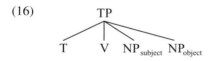

This is a traditional analysis for Arabic (Bakir 1980). The critical claim here is that there is no VP constituent in Arabic. This in turn implies that there should be no processes or constructions that refer to the VP constituent. Moreover, this analysis predicts that both the subject and the object are in a symmetric relation, which should have implications for the syntactic relations that are sensitive to symmetry in the structural relations between arguments.

3.3.1   Idioms

With respect to the VP constituent, Mohammad (2000) has argued that the fact that the verb and the object can form an idiomatic expression, as in the Palestinian Arabic sentence in (17), supports the claim that there is a VP.

---

[5] In the text and in (16) we use TP and CP anachronistically but for the purpose of uniformity. This analysis is more appropriately cast in terms of S and S'.

(17) ʔeħmad Dayyaʕ ʕagl-u   *Palestinian Arabic*
      Ahmed lost.3ms mind-his
      'Ahmad went crazy.'

Another piece of evidence that supports Mohammad's argument comes from other
Arabic dialects, namely Moroccan Arabic and Lebanese Arabic. On a par with
English, where the semantic interpretation of the subject seems to depend on both
the verb and its complement (Marantz 1984), in the Moroccan sentences in (18)
we see that the semantic interpretation of the subject varies greatly depending on
how the verb and its complement are interpreted.

(18) *Moroccan Arabic*
      a. Drəb   ʕomar r-ražəl
         hit.3ms Omar the-man
         'Omar hit the man.'

      b. Drəb   ʕomar T-Tər   b-nadia
         hit.3ms Omar the-tambourine with-Nadia
         'Omar told everybody about Nadia.'

      c. Drəb   ʕomar S-Sdaq
         hit.3ms Omar the-marriage contract
         'Omar concluded the marriage contract.'

      d. Drəb   ʕomar lə-ħsab
         hit.3ms Omar the-calculation
         'Omar was prepared.'

      e. Drəb   ʕomar f-x-xut-u
         hit.3ms Omar in-the-siblings-his
         'Omar ignored his siblings.'

(19) *Lebanese Arabic*
      a. mona Darabit saami
         Mona hit.3fs   Sami
         'Mona hit Sami.'

      b. mona Darabit ha-l-ħseeb
         Mona hit.3fs   this-the-calculation
         'Mona was prepared.'

In the Moroccan Arabic examples in (18a) and (18d) and their Lebanese Arabic
equivalents in (19), the asymmetry between subjects and objects is apparent: the
semantic interpretation of the subject in those sentences becomes clear only after

the object is interpreted with respect to the verb. This is what accounts for the difference in interpretation between (18a) and (19a) on one hand, and (18d) and (19b), on the other.

3.3.2   VP coordination

In addition to idiomatic expressions, there are other arguments for a VP constituent in Arabic. For example, in Lebanese Arabic as well as in Moroccan Arabic, VPs can be conjoined, as illustrated in (20).

(20)   a. *Lebanese Arabic*
  keen ʕomar ʕam yiʔra l-kteeb w yħarrik T-Tabxa
  was.3ms Omar Asp. reading the-book and stirring the-cooking
  'Omar was reading the book and stirring the cooking.'

  b. *Moroccan Arabic*
  kan ʕomar tayqra lə-ktab w yTəyyəb lə-ʕša
  was.3ms Omar reading the-book and cooking   the-dinner
  'Omar was reading the book and cooking dinner.'

In (20), there is a coordination of two constituents each containing both the verb and the object, excluding the subject. That this is indeed a coordination of VPs and not TPs is evident from the fact that both VPs are under the scope of the aspectual particle that is cliticized to the verb of the first conjunct. This indicates that the verb together with the object can form a constituent excluding the subject.

In short, the facts based on idioms and coordination clearly show that there is a VP constituent in Arabic, by showing the asymmetry between subjects and objects in their relation to the verb.

3.3.3   Wh-asymmetries

Mohammad (2000) also shows that, on a par with languages where there is clear evidence for an asymmetric relation between the subject and the object with respect to extractability, similar asymmetries seem to obtain in Arabic. For example, it is easier to extract an object than to extract a subject which is reflected by the form of the embedded complementizer. This generalization can be illustrated for both Standard Arabic (21) and Palestinian Arabic (22).[6]

---

[6] See also Kenstowicz (1989) for preverbal and postverbal asymmetries with respect to the extraction of the subject in two Arabic dialects of Jordan.

(21)   a. man qaala   ʔaħmad ʔanna mona raʔat
           who said.3ms Ahmed that   Mona saw.3fs
           'Who did Ahmed say that Mona saw?'

        b. *ʔayy-u   bint-in   qaala   ʔaħmad ʔanna raʔat   ʕali
           which-Nom girl-Gen said.3ms Ahmed that   saw.3fs Ali
           'Which girl did Ahmed say that saw Ali?'

        c. ʔayy-u bint-in qaala   ʔaħmad ʔanna-ha raʔat   ʕali
           which girl   said.3ms Ahmed that-she saw.3fs Ali
           'Which girl did Ahmed say that she saw Ali?'

(22)   a. min gaal   ʔeħmad ʔennu mona šafat
           who said.3ms Ahmed that   Mona saw.3fs
           'Who did Ahmed say that Mona saw?'

        b. *ʔanu bent gaal   ʔeħmad ʔennu šafat   ʕali
           which girl said.3ms Ahmed that   saw.3fs Ali
           'Which girl did Ahmed say that saw Ali?'

        c. ʔanu bent gaal   ʔeħmad ʔenn-ha šafat   ʕali
           which girl said.3ms Ahmed that-she saw.3fs Ali
           'Which girl did Ahmed say that she saw Ali?'

In (21a) and (22a) the wh-phrase *min/man* 'who' is moved from the object position of the embedded clause. The embedded complementizer shows up in its default form as *ʔennu* in Palestinian Arabic and *ʔanna* in Standard Arabic. By contrast, in (21b) and (22b) the wh-phrase *ʔanu bent/ʔayyu bintin* 'which girl' is extracted from the embedded subject position. The sentences are, however, unacceptable.[7] The sentences improve if the embedded complementizer is followed by an accusative clitic that resumes the wh-phrase in the matrix CP (21c) and (22c). The contrast observed then is that the extraction of the object does not force the resumption strategy but the extraction of the subject does. This asymmetry parallels more familiar asymmetries about the extraction of subject and objects in English and other languages. For example, in English it is easier to extract an object across the complementizer *that* (23a) than a subject (23b).

(23)   a. Who do you think that Mary met?
        b. *Who do you think that met Mary?

    The standard account in the Principles and Parameters theory attributes the contrast between the extraction of the object in (23a) and the extraction of the

---

[7] The equivalent of (21b) and (22b) in Lebanese Arabic is acceptable.

subject in (23b) to the ability of the verb to govern the object in (23a) and the absence of such government in (23b). Given that government is defined in terms of c-command or M-command, it is clear that such relation obtains between the verb and objects, which are within the VP, but not with the subject, which is in the specifier of TP. In short, the asymmetry between subjects and objects with respect to their extractability is configurational in that it is sensitive to the structural relation between the relevant argument and the verb.

Under the assumption that subject and object asymmetries are to be captured in configurational terms, assuming the configuration in (16) where both the subject and the object are governed by the verb, the prediction is that, all else being equal, there should be no contrast between extraction of subjects and objects, contrary to what the facts in (21–22) show.

3.3.4   Binding asymmetries

Similar contrasts obtain in contexts of anaphor binding (Mohammad 2000). The assumption in the Principles and Parameters framework is that the antecedent and the anaphor it binds must stand in an asymmetric relation, which, in configurational terms, is stated in terms of c-command.

(24)   a. The student praised herself
        b. *Herself praised the student

The unacceptability of (24b) is accounted for by the assumption that the antecedent contained within the VP projection does not c-command the anaphor in the specifier of TP. By contrast, in (24a) the asymmetric c-command relation obtains. Putting the irrelevant details aside, it can be said that the object and the subject in (24a) are in an asymmetric relation, with the subject c-commanding the object. This follows from the assumption that in addition to the major sentence constituent TP, there is also a constituent containing the verb and the object, namely the VP.

With respect to anaphors in Arabic the facts can be easily tested in Standard Arabic where Case is realized morphologically on the noun and where the verb and the subject agree.[8]

(25)   *Standard Arabic*
        a. madaħa   T-Taalib-u   nafs-a-hu
            praised.3ms the-student-Nom self.f-Acc-his
            'The student praised himself.'

---

[8] The anaphor *nafs* 'self' in Standard Arabic is feminine.

    b. *madaħat   nafs-u-hu   T-Taalib-a
       praised.3fs self.f-Nom-his the-student-Acc

As illustrated in (25), the only context where binding between the subject and the object can properly obtain is when the antecedent is in the subject position and the anaphor is in the object position (25a).[9] These facts can be straightforwardly accounted for if the subject in Arabic is in an asymmetric relation with the object, contrary to what is given in the configuration in (16).

    Summing up, there is strong evidence for a structure where the subject and object are in an asymmetric relation and therefore for a VP constituent in Arabic. The issue that we will deal with next concerns the position of the subject in the clause structure.

3.4   The status of preverbal subjects

    Several arguments have been advanced to argue that the preverbal subject is not a genuine subject but rather a dislocated NP related to/binding a (resumptive) pronominal. One argument is based on agreement asymmetries in Standard Arabic. Another is based on the distribution of non-specific indefinite subjects. We will take up these arguments in turn and examine the evidence provided for them.

3.4.1   Agreement asymmetries and the position of the subject

    In Standard Arabic, the verb and the subject agree, as shown in (26):

(26)   Ɂakala   l-muʕallim-u   *Standard Arabic*
        ate.3ms the-teacher.ms-Nom
        'The teacher ate.'

(27)   l-muʕallim-u   Ɂakala   *Standard Arabic*
        the-teacher.ms-Nom ate.3ms
        'The teacher ate.'

In (26) and (27) the same form of the verb is used regardless of whether the subject is preverbal or postverbal, which at first blush suggests that the verb always fully

---

[9] The Moroccan Arabic equivalent of (25b) is also ungrammatical.

(i)   *mədħat   rasha   l-bənt
        praised.3fs herself the-student.fs

agrees with the subject in Standard Arabic. However, the situation becomes more complex when we include plural subjects.

(28)   l-muʕallimuun   ʔakal-uu   *Standard Arabic*
        the-teacher.mp.Nom ate-3mp
        'The teachers ate.'

(29)   *l-muʕallimuun   ʔakala   *Standard Arabic*
        the-teacher.mp.Nom ate.3ms

As the examples in (28) and (29) illustrate, there is an agreement asymmetry that is sensitive to the relative ordering of the subject and the verb in Standard Arabic. When the subject precedes the verb, agreement is in number, person, and gender. When the subject follows the verb, agreement is in person and gender only. In particular, there is no morphological realization of number agreement. This asymmetry becomes even more striking when we consider the morphology of the imperfective, which differs from the perfective verb in being realized via both prefixation and suffixation, as the paradigms in (30a–b) show.

(30)   **a. Agreement System of the Standard Arabic Perfective**

Person	Number	Gender	Affix	Verb+Affix
1	Singular	F/M	-tu	daras-tu
2	S	M	-ta	daras-ta
2	S	F	-ti	daras-ti
3	S	M	-a	daras-a
3	S	F	-at	daras-at
2	Dual	M/F	-tumaa	daras-tumaa
3	D	M	-aa	daras-aa
3	D	F	-ataa	daras-ataa
1	Plural	M/F	-naa	daras-naa
2	P	M	-tum	daras-tum
2	P	F	-tunna	daras-tunna
3	P	M	-uu	daras-uu
3	P	F	-na	daras-na

b. Agreement System of the Standard Arabic Imperfective

Person	Number	Gender	Affix	Affix+Verb
1	Singular	M/F	ʔa-	ʔa-drus(a)
2	S	M	ta-	ta-drus(u)
2	S	F	ta—iin(a)	ta-drus-iin(a)
3	S	M	ya-	ya-drus(u)
3	S	F	ta-	ta-drus(u)

Person	Number	Gender	Affix	Affix+Verb
2	Dual	M/F	ta—aan(i)	ta-drus-aan(i)
3	D	M	ya—aan(i)	ya-drus-aan(i)
3	D	F	ta-aa	ta-drus-saan(i)
1	Plural	M/F	na-	na-drus(u)
2	P	M	ta—uun(a)	ta-drus-uun(a)
2	P	F	ta—na	ta-drus-na
3	P	M	ya—uun(a)	ya-drus-uun(a)
3	P	F	ya—na	ya-drus-na

As is clear from the paradigm in (30b), agreement on the imperfective is realized discontinuously. In most forms, the prefix carries person in addition to gender and the suffix carries number in addition to gender. What is striking is that when the subject follows the verb the suffix is absent, as shown in (31), but it is obligatorily present if the subject precedes the verb (32).[10]

(31)   a. ta-drusu   T-Taalibaat-u
           3f-study   the-students.fp-Nom
           'The students study.'

       b. ya-drusu   T-Tullaab-u
           3-study   the-students.mp-Nom
           'The students study.'

(32)   a. T-Taalibaat-u   ya-drus-na
           the-students.fp-Nom 3-study-fp
           'The students study.'

       b. T-Tullaab-u   ya-drus-uun
           The-students.mp-Nom 3-study-mp
           'The students study.'

Arabic is also a null-subject language (family). Hence, in Standard Arabic and the other dialects, the subject does not have to be overt:

(33)   a. ya-drus-uun
           3-study-mp
           'They study.'

       b. ya-drus-na
           3-study-fp
           'They study.'

---

[10] Note in (32a) that when the suffix carries gender the prefix tends not to do so (see Noyer 1992).

However, a null subject is only available in the context of full agreement. In the context of partial agreement, i.e. when the number marker is absent, null plural subjects are not possible. Hence the only viable interpretation in (34) is that where the pronominal is singular.

(34)   a. ya-drusu
            3-study
            'He studies.'
            *'They study.'

        b. ta-drusu
            3f-study
            'She studies.'
            *'They study.'

Building on the facts that there is an agreement asymmetry and that only full agreement can license null pronominal subjects, it has been argued that the only genuine agreement in Arabic is partial agreement and that full agreement indicates the presence of a pronominal subject. This in turn implies that the preverbal subject that co-occurs with agreement cannot be a subject, otherwise there would be two subjects in the sentence, the lexical subject and the pronominal subject.

This analysis is problematic whether one assumes only one subject position in the sentence (e.g. [Spec, TP]) or two subject positions ([Spec, VP] and [Spec, TP]). Under the former assumption there is only one subject position available and therefore either the preverbal NP or the pronominal related to it cannot be a genuine subject. Since dislocated NPs in Arabic occur in the left periphery and can bind resumptive pronouns, by analogy the preverbal subject can be treated as a left dislocated element. Under the second assumption, positing two genuine subject positions, one in [Spec, TP] and one in [Spec, VP], is equally problematic, and for various reasons. First, there is only one thematic role for the external argument, yet there are now two such arguments. Second, getting around the Thematic Criterion problem by coindexing two subjects and assigning the thematic role to the chain (Chomsky 1986) would yield a Principle B violation since the pronominal in [Spec, VP] would be locally A-bound by the argument in [Spec, TP].[11] Third, we have to ensure that both subjects are Case licensed, which is problematic as well because tense can usually Case license one subject only.

---

[11] Principle B of the Binding Theory (Chomsky 1981) regulates the distribution of pronouns. It mandates that they be free (unbound) in their local domain (governing category), which usually coincides with the sentence or noun phrase particularly when the latter has a subject.

However, it is not sufficient to deny the status of a genuine subject to the preverbal NP on the basis of the agreement asymmetries. There are cases where full agreement can be observed, though it is difficult to argue that the NP is clitic-left dislocated. Such a situation arises in the context of auxiliary verbs:

(35)   a. kaanat   T-Taalibaat-u   ya-drus-na
           be.past.3fs the-students.fp-Nom 3-study-fp
           'The students were studying.'

       b. T-Taalibaat-u   kunna   ya-drus-na
          the-students.fp-Nom be.past.3fp 3-study-fp
          'The students were studying.'

Under standard analyses both the auxiliary verb and the main verb are in the same clause. Thus, the NP between the auxiliary verb and the main verb in (35a) must be a subject rather than a clitic-left dislocated NP (see chapter 8 for further discussion on clitic-left dislocation in Arabic). Yet the verb that follows it carries full agreement and the verb that precedes it carries partial agreement, as the contrast between (35) and (36) illustrates.

(36)   a. *kunna   T-Taalibaat-u   ya-drus-na
           be.past.3fp the-student.fp-Nom 3-study-fp
           'The students were studying.'

       b. *T-Taalibaat-u   kaanat   ya-drus-na
          the-student.fp-Nom be.past-3fs 3-study-fp
          'The students were studying.'

In addition, if the subject is not lexical both the auxiliary verb and the main verb must have full agreement, as illustrated in (37).

(37)   a. kunna   ya-drus-na
           be.past.3fp 3-study-fp
           'They were studying.'

       b. *kaanat   ya-drus-na
          be.past.3fs 3-study-fp

If (37a) is given a monoclausal analysis and if full agreement indicates the presence of null pronouns as arguments of the verb, then we are forced to posit two arguments for the sentence in (37a), which leads into the problems mentioned earlier with the Thematic Criterion, Binding Principle B, and Case assignment.

In sum, full agreement does not seem to provide conclusive evidence against treating the preverbal NP as a genuine subject.

3.4.2   Indefinite subjects

While definite NP subjects in most Arabic dialects, including Standard Arabic, can occur in both preverbal and postverbal position, indefinite subjects have a more restricted distribution. As is the case in other languages, indefinite NP subjects in Arabic are not allowed in the preverbal position. This seems to be the case in Standard Arabic (Ayoub 1981), as well as other Arabic dialects like Palestinian Arabic (Mohammad 2000), Moroccan Arabic, and Lebanese Arabic.

(38)   *Standard Arabic*
    a. žaʔa   walad-un
       came.past.3ms boy-Nom.indef
       'A boy came.'

    b. *walad-un   žaʔa
       boy-Nom.indef came.past.3ms

(39)   *Palestinian Arabic*
    a. ʔadža   walad
       came.past.3ms boy
       'A boy came.'

    b. *walad ʔadža
       boy   came.past.3ms

(40)   *Moroccan Arabic*
    a. ža   wəld
       came.past.3ms boy
       'A boy came.'

    b. *wəld ža
       boy   came.past.3ms

(41)   *Lebanese Arabic*
    a. ʔəža   walad
       came.past.3ms child
       'A child came.'

    b. *walad ʔəža
       child   came.past.3ms

In some Arabic dialects, a modified indefinite NP subject seems to be allowed in the preverbal position, as shown by the acceptability of the following sentences from Palestinian Arabic (Mohammad 2000).

(42)   a. walad Tawiil ʔadža
           boy   tall   came.past.3ms
           'A tall boy came.'

        b. zalame dactoor ʔadža
           man   doctor came.past.3ms
           'A man (who is) a physician came.'

Similarly, if the indefinite NP subject in Palestinian Arabic is in the Construct State, it can occur in the preverbal position.

(43)   ʔiben dactoor ʔadža
        son   doctor came.past.3ms
        'A son of a doctor came.'

Those facts seem to indicate that the more specific the subject is the more freedom it has to occur in either the preverbal or postverbal position. It is not clear what to make of these data as far as the status of the preverbal position is concerned. Clearly, not all the "specific" indefinites function as topics in the sentences above, and therefore it cannot be said that the preverbal position is a topic position rather than a subject position. Moreover, there are NPs that do not seem to be specific and can still occur in the preverbal position. This is the case with negative polarity items (NPIs) in the various Arabic dialects. Benmamoun (1996) discusses the contrast between two types of negative polarity subjects in Moroccan Arabic: NPs headed by the particle ħətta and the bare NPI ħədd.[12]

(44)   a. ma-ža   ħətta waħəd
           Neg-came.past.3ms even one
           'No one came.'

        b. ma-ža   ħədd
           Neg-came.past.3ms no one
           'No one came.'

Interestingly, only NPIs headed by ħətta can occur in the preverbal position (45a); NPIs headed by ħədd are restricted to the postverbal position.

---

[12] We leave open the question of whether it is accurate to characterize both elements as NPIs. It may turn out that one is an NPI and the other is a negative quantifier. For the present purposes, the main relevant characterization is that they are both indefinite.

(45)   a. ħətta waħəd ma-ža
            even one   Neg-came.past.3ms
            'No one came.'

        b. *ħədd ma-ža
            no one Neg-came.past.3ms

Benmamoun (1996) argues that the reason why (45a) is grammatical is because the NPI *ħətta* is a presuppositional particle which can occur in the preverbal position. Moreover, NPIs headed by *ħətta* can be clitic-left dislocated, as evidenced by the presence of the pronominal clitic within the sentence in (46).

(46)   ħətta ktab ma-qrit-u
        even book Neg-read.past.3ms-it
        'I didn't read any book.'

These data indicate that the preverbal position has a more restricted distribution than the postverbal subject position. However, it does not seem to always function as a clitic-left dislocated element either, which casts doubt on the analysis of the preverbal subject as a dislocated element.

3.4.3   Broad vs. narrow subjects

The question that can be raised at this point is whether the preverbal NP can still accurately be called a subject. Doron and Heycock (1999) provide a compromise answer to this question. They argue that many languages, including Arabic, have multiple subjects or NPs in the Nominative Case (hence pattern with subjects) that bind resumptive pronouns. This is illustrated by the sentences in (47) from Standard Arabic:

(47)   a. hind-un   yuqaabilu-ha T-Tullaab-u
            Hind-Nom meet.3ms-her the-students-Nom
            'The students are meeting Hind.'
            Literally: 'Hind, the students are meeting her.'

        b. ʔal-bayt-u   ʔalwaan-u-hu zaahiyat-un
            the-house-Nom colors-Nom-its bright-Nom
            'The house has bright colors.'
            Literally: 'The house, its colors are bright.'

Doron and Heycock argue that the preverbal NP in (47a) and the two nominative noun phrases that precede the predicate adjective in (47b) are subjects rather than dislocated noun phrases, with the whole clause, which may also contain a subject, as predicate. They further distinguish between broad subjects and narrow subjects. In (47a) *hindun* is a broad subject while *ʔalwaan-u-hu* 'its colors' in (47b) is a narrow subject. Narrow subjects can precede or follow the predicate but broad subjects always precede the predicate. In fact, broad subjects precede narrow subjects when those occur before the predicate. One argument Doron and Heycock provide for treating some NPs as broad subjects is based on the so-called exceptional Case marking. In Arabic, the so-called broad subject can be marked with Accusative Case by a matrix verb, which is presumably not allowed for genuine left dislocated NPs.

(48) ðanan-tu   l-bayt-a   ʔalwaan-u-hu   zaahiyat-un
      thought-1s the-house-Acc colors-Nom-its bright-Nom
      'I believe the house to be of bright colors.'

Moreover, the broad subject can follow the auxiliary verb *kaan*, as illustrated in (49).

(49) kaana   l-bayt-u   ʔalwaan-u-hu   zaahiyat-un
      was.3ms the-house-Nom colors-its-Nom bright-Nom
      'The house was of bright colors.'

It is partly for these reasons that Doron and Heycock stress that elements like *l-bayt-a* 'the house' in (48) and *l-baytu* 'the house' in (49) are subjects. Syntactically, the broad subject occupies the same position as the narrow subject occurring before the predicate, namely [Spec, TP].[13] The crucial difference between narrow and broad subjects is that the latter are directly merged (base-generated) in [Spec, TP] while narrow subjects move to [Spec, TP] to derive the SV order.[14] However, as we will discuss in the next section, even the status of the postverbal subject is not clear.[15]

---

[13] Thus Doron and Heycock cast their analysis in a theory that allows multiple specifiers to be projected for a given head.

[14] Doron and Heycock assume that postverbal narrow subjects occur in [Spec, VP] and that partial agreement in the VS order is weak while full agreement is strong and thus forces subject movement from the VP to TP.

[15] It is not clear how the broad subject, if indeed a subject, gets its Case given that it is base-generated in its surface position, namely Spec TP. The only solution would be to allow tense or whatever functional element involved in Nominative Case assignment to enter into more than one Case relation. This is not a straightforward assumption, however.

3.5   The status of postverbal subjects

The idea that the thematic subject is generated in [Spec, VP] has provided a straightforward way to derive the VSO order in Standard Arabic and the modern dialects (Koopman and Sportiche 1991). According to Mohammad (1989, 2000), Benmamoun (1992a), and Fassi Fehri (1993), if we assume that the subject in (50) is in [Spec, VP], the VSO order can be derived by moving the verb to T, leaving the subject in its base position as illustrated in (51):

(50)   naama   T-Tiflu   *Standard Arabic*
        slept.3ms the-child
        'The child slept.'

(51)

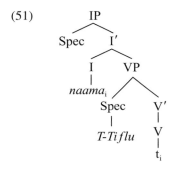

This seems to be an improvement over an analysis that takes the VSO order to involve verb movement to C, since the complementizer can co-occur with the VSO order, as shown in the following sentences:

(52)   a. tanDənn bəlli ža   ʕomar   *Moroccan Arabic*
            think.1s that came.3ms Omar
            'I think that Omar came.'

        b. biftikir ʔənno ʔiža   saami   *Lebanese Arabic*
            think.1s that   came.3ms Sami
            'I think that Sami came.'

However, there are reasons to maintain that the postverbal subject is not within the VP. Two pieces of evidence can be adduced to support the analysis that the VSO order does not necessarily entail that the subject is in the Spec of VP.[16]

---

[16] This is a weaker stance than saying that the postverbal subject is always outside the lexical projection.

3.5.1   Copular sentences in Moroccan Arabic

The first argument comes from the distribution of sentential negation in the context of copular constructions. Sentential negation in Moroccan Arabic consists of two morphemes, the pro-clitic *ma* and the enclitic *š*. If they attach to a verb, *ma* occurs as a prefix and *š* as a suffix (53):

(53)   ʕomar ma-qra-š   lə-ktab
        Omar   Neg-read.3ms-Neg the-book
        'Omar did not read the book.'

In Benmamoun (1992a), *ma* is posited as head of the negative projection located between TP and VP while *š* is analyzed as an adjunct to the VP, which accounts for the distribution of the negative elements with respect to the verbal head. Verb movement to T in Moroccan Arabic proceeds through the negative projection.

(54)

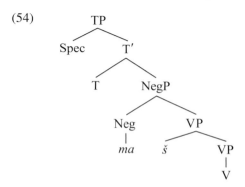

In copular sentences with present tense interpretation, the so-called verbless sentences, *ma* merges with *š:*

(55)   a. ʕomar ma-ši   f-d-dar
           Omar   Neg-Neg in-the-house
           'Omar is not in the house.'

        b. ʕomar ma-ši   kaddab
           Omar   Neg-Neg liar
           'Omar is not a liar.'

        c. ʕomar ma-ši   mriD
           Omar   Neg-Neg sick
           'Omar is not sick.'

This merger is not possible when there is a verb in the sentence:

(56)   a. *ʕomar ma-ši   qra   lə-ktab
             Omar   Neg-Neg read.3ms the-book

         b. *ʕomar qra   ma-ši   lə-ktab
             Omar   read.3ms Neg-Neg the-book

Example (56a) is ruled out because obligatory verb movement to T has not taken place. On the other hand, (56b) is ill-formed because the movement of the verb to T violates Relativized Minimality or the Head Movement Constraint (HMC): on its way to T, V has "skipped" the negative head. By contrast, in (55) the two negative elements merge since there is no verb in the sentence and therefore no head that would occur between them.[17]

With this brief background in mind, let us consider the distribution of the sentential subject. In sentences with a verbal head, the subject can either follow or precede the verb:

(57)   a. ʕomar ma-qra-š   lə-ktab
             Omar   Neg-read.3ms-Neg the-book
             'Omar did not read the book.'

         b. ma-qra-š   ʕomar lə-ktab
             Neg-read.3ms-Neg Omar   the-book
             'Omar did not read the book.'

Example (57a) follows straightforwardly if the subject is in [Spec, TP] and the verb, together with sentential negation, is in T. Turning to (57b), if the verb is in T then the natural assumption is that the subject must be in [Spec, VP], which is the analysis that has been provided for these constructions.[18] However, this analysis of the VSO order makes one prediction, namely that in copular constructions where there is no overt verbal head (such as in (55)), the subject can either precede or follow sentential negation. This prediction is not borne out. The subject must always precede sentential negation:

(58)   a. ʕomar ma-ši   mriD
             Omar   Neg-Neg sick
             'Omar is not sick.'

         b. *ma-ši   ʕomar mriD
             Neg-Neg Omar   sick

---

[17] In chapter 5 we discuss the syntax of sentential negation in greater detail, so we will confine our attention in this section to the aspects of the constructions that are relevant to the issue of the syntactic position of the postverbal subject.

[18] This raises the thorny issue of "optional" movement which we will put aside.

Consider the derivation of (58a). The underlying representation is as in (59):

(59)

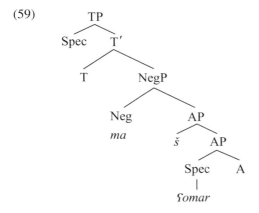

The NP ʕomar is generated in [Spec, AP] where it gets its thematic role. Assuming that movement to [Spec, TP] is optional, the subject can remain in [Spec, AP]. Since there is no head movement, *ma* merges with *š*. However, this analysis wrongly predicts (58b) to be well-formed, given that the movement of the subject to [Spec, TP] does not take place. This problem disappears if we give up the assumption that the VSO order always implies that the subject is in the specifier of the lexical projection where it gets its thematic role. Suppose that the subject must move to [Spec, TP] overtly. In standard minimalist analyses, this is due to the EPP. Then, (58b) is ruled out because the subject has not moved overtly to [Spec, TP]. If this is correct, the VSO order would still involve overt subject movement to [Spec, TP] with additional overt verb movement beyond TP (Aoun, Benmamoun, and Sportiche 1994).[19] This conclusion gains further support from word order in the context of existential constructions discussed in the next section.

3.5.2   Existential constructions

The second piece of evidence that the VSO order does not always entail that the subject is in the specifier of the lexical projection where it is assigned a semantic role comes from existential constructions in Standard Arabic.

---

[19] This means that it is not the movement of the subject that is optional but rather that of the verb. It is not clear what forces this movement. It is plausible that verb movement to the projection above IP is always obligatory. What is optional is the movement of the subject to the Spec of that projection.

As in English, the Arabic existential construction involves the locative pro-form *hunaaka* 'there' and an indefinite NP marked with Nominative Case, as illustrated in (60):

(60)   hunaaka Taalib-un   fii l-ħadiiqati
        there   student-Nom in the-garden
        'There is a student in the garden.'

Most analyses of the equivalent construction in English assume that the indefinite NP is in the specifier of the lexical projection, i.e. PP in (60), and the expletive is in [Spec, TP]:[20]

(61)

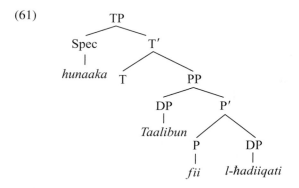

Now consider the sentence in (60) with an overt auxiliary:

(62)   kaana   hunaaka Taalib-un   fii l-ħadiiqati
        was.3ms there   student-Nom in the-garden
        'There was a student in the garden.'

In (62) the expletive follows the auxiliary verb. That sentence receives a straight-forward analysis if we assume that the expletive is in [Spec, TP] and the lexical NP is in [Spec, PP]. This shows clearly that the VSO order does not entail that the subject is within the thematic projection. It does, however, show that in the VSO order the verb is in a position higher than TP, a projection we neutrally call FP in (63):

---

[20] We will ignore the important problem of how the indefinite subject checks its case features. Obviously if the thematic subject is in [Spec, PP], obligatory movement to [Spec, TP] must be due to the EPP, a requirement that is satisfied by the expletive.

(63)

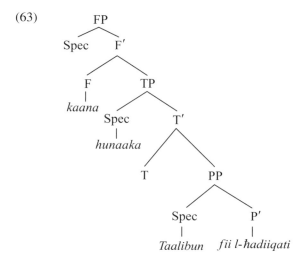

However, FP is not the familiar CP projection because the sentence in (62) can be embedded under a complementizer, as illustrated in (64):

(64) samiʕtu ʔanna-hu kaana   hunaaka Taalib-un   fii l-ħadiiqati
      heard.1s that-it   was.3ms there   student-Nom in the-garden
      'I heard that there was a student in the garden.'

While it is not clear at this point what the nature of FP is, the word order facts from existential constructions lead to the reasonable conclusion that the postverbal subject is not necessarily in the specifier of the projection of the thematic predicate. Since the expletive can also occur in the postverbal position, the postverbal subject position must be within a functional projection above the lexical thematic projection.

The conclusion that emerges from the above discussion is that the postverbal subject position is not within the lexical projection of the main predicate but rather in a functional projection that can be identified as TP. This leaves us with a puzzle: if the postverbal subject is likely to be in [Spec, TP], then what explains the SV order?

3.6   Conclusion

There is a consensus that the so-called postverbal subject is a genuine subject in Arabic dialects. It is not clear, however, whether it is overtly within the projection of the thematic predicate or whether it is within the functional projection of tense, i.e. TP. The fact that expletive subjects can occur in the postverbal position seems to support the latter view. With respect to the so-called preverbal subject, there is no consensus as to whether it should be treated as a subject. The fact that it is restricted semantically to definite and modified indefinite NPs and that they co-occur with full agreement seems to support the view that they are left dislocated or topicalized elements that bind resumptive pronouns. However, there are also arguments that indicate that this is not the case because they do not, according to Doron and Heycock (1999), always display properties of clitic-left dislocated NPs (see also chapter 8). The issue remains unresolved partly because the notion of subject itself is not conceptually well defined given that the traditional configurational notion of subject has become increasingly vague due to the assumptions that more than one position in the sentence can host the element usually labeled as subject.

4

Sentential agreement

4.1   Introduction

Arabic dialects have a rich system of subject–verb agreement.[1] A verb may agree with the subject in person, number, and gender. Standard Arabic (1) has the richest subject agreement paradigms. Thus, unlike in the modern dialects, the verb may display dual agreement in addition to singular and plural agreement. The modern dialects paradigms also differ from each other. Some, like Moroccan Arabic (2), do not display gender distinctions in the second person singular forms, while others, like Lebanese Arabic (3), display such distinctions.

(1)   **Agreement System of the Standard Arabic Perfective**

Person	Number	Gender	Affix	Verb+Affix
1	Singular	F/M	-tu	daras-tu
2	S	M	-ta	daras-ta
2	S	F	-ti	daras-ti
3	S	M	-a	daras-a
3	S	F	-at	daras-at
2	Dual	M/F	-tumaa	daras-tumaa
3	D	M	-aa	daras-aa
3	D	F	-ataa	daras-ataa
1	Plural	M/F	-naa	daras-naa
2	P	M	-tum	daras-tum
2	P	F	-tunna	daras-tunna
3	P	M	-uu	daras-uu
3	P	F	-na	daras-na

---

[1] In this chapter we deal only with subject–verb agreement. Arabic also displays agreement within the noun phrase. For detailed discussions of this issue in Arabic, the reader is referred to Aoun (1978), Benmamoun (2000, 2003), Borer (1996), Fassi Fehri (1999), Mohammad (1999b), Ritter (1988), Shlonsky (2004), and Siloni (1997), among others.

(2)   **Agreement System of the Moroccan Arabic Perfective**

Person	Number	Gender	Affix	Verb+Affix
1	Singular	F/M	-t	ktəbt
2	S	F/M	-ti	ktəbti
3	S	M	-Ø	ktəb
3	S	F	-at	kətbat
1	Plural	M/F	-na	ktəbna
2	P	M/F	-tu	ktəbtu
3	P	M/F	-u	kətbu

(3)   **Agreement System of the Lebanese Arabic Perfective**

Person	Number	Gender	Affix	Verb+Affix
1	Singular	F/M	-t	katabt
2	S	M	-t	katabt
2	S	F	-te	katabte
3	S	M	-Ø	katab
3	S	F	-it	katabit
1	Plural	M/F	-na	katabna
2	P	M/F	-to	katabto
3	P	M/F	-o	katabo

The agreement paradigms in (1–3) occur on the so-called perfective verb. As mentioned in chapters 1 and 2, in the perfective, subject agreement is realized as a suffix on the verb. In the imperfective, by contrast, the realization of agreement is radically different. It is realized by both prefixes and suffixes, as illustrated from Standard Arabic (4), Moroccan Arabic (5), and Lebanese Arabic (6).

(4)   **Agreement System of the Standard Arabic Imperfective**

Person	Number	Gender	Affix	Affix+Verb
1	Singular	M/F	ʔa-	ʔa-drus(u)
2	S	M	ta-	ta-drus(u)
2	S	F	ta—iin(a)	ta-drus-iin(a)
3	S	M	ya-	ya-drus(u)
3	S	F	ta-	ta-drus(u)
2	Dual	M/F	ta—aan(i)	ta-drus-aan(i)
3	D	M	ya—aan(i)	ya-drus-aan(i)
3	D	F	ta—aa	ta-drus-aan(i)
1	Plural	M/F	na-	na-drus(a)
2	P	M	ta—uun(a)	ta-drus-uun(a)
2	P	F	ta—na	ta-drus-na
3	P	M	ya—uun(a)	ya-drus-uun(a)
3	P	F	ya—na	ta-drus-na

(5)   **Agreement System of the Moroccan Arabic Imperfective**

Person	Number	Gender	Affix	Affix+Verb
1	Singular	M/F	n-	nəktəb
2	S	M	t-	təktəb
2	S	F	t—i	tkətbi
3	S	M	y-	yəktəb
3	S	F	t-	təktəb
1	Plural	M/F	n—u	nkətbu
2	P	M/F	t—u	tkətbu
3	P	M/F	y—u	ykətbu

(6)   **Agreement System of the Lebanese Arabic Imperfective**

Person	Number	Gender	Affix	Affix+Verb
1	Singular	M/F	?i-	?i-drus
2	S	M	ti-	ti-drus
2	S	F	ti—e	ti-dirs-e
3	S	M	yi-	yi-drus
3	S	F	ti-	ti-drus
1	Plural	M/F	ni-	ni-drus
2	P	M/F	ti—o	ti-dirs-o
3	P	M/F	yi—o	yi-dirs-o

In addition to the status of the subject in the SVO order no other issue has seen as much extensive debate as the issue of subject–verb agreement. Some of the main issues that have dominated the debate have revolved around the agreement asymmetry that Standard Arabic displays, which in turn relates to the issues of the status of the agreement morpheme, the structural conditions on agreement, and the status of the so-called preverbal subject. Another issue that gained a lot of attention in the last decade or so concerns another agreement asymmetry, namely the phenomenon of first conjunct agreement. We will start with the agreement asymmetry in Standard Arabic and then turn to first conjunct agreement. We will also briefly discuss agreement in the context of existential constructions at the end of the chapter.

4.2   Subject–verb agreement asymmetry in Standard Arabic

As is well known there is an agreement asymmetry in Standard Arabic that is sensitive to word order: in the VS order, with the subject following the verb, agreement between the verb and the subject is in gender, and perhaps person, only.[2]

(7)   *Standard Arabic*
    a. Ɂakala   l-muʕallim-uun
       ate.3ms the-teacher-mp.Nom
       'The teachers ate.'

    b. *Ɂakal-uu l-muʕallim-uun
       ate-3mp   the-teacher-mp.Nom

On the other hand, in the SV order, with the subject preceding the verb, the verb fully agrees with the subject, as shown by the presence of number in addition to gender, and perhaps person.

(8)   *Standard Arabic*
    a. l-muʕallim-uun   Ɂakal-uu
       the-teacher-mp.Nom ate-3mp
       'The teachers ate.'

    b. *l-muʕallim-uun   Ɂakala
       the-teacher-mp-Nom ate.3ms

There are at least three possible candidates for what is responsible for the agreement asymmetry in Standard Arabic: (i) in the VSO order there is a null expletive subject that is forcing agreement with the verb, hence there is actually no agreement asymmetry; (ii) full agreement on the verb is an incorporated pronominal, hence there is no agreement asymmetry because there is no subject–verb agreement, particularly in number; (iii) there is always full agreement between the verb and the subject but agreement features may be spelled-out/realized differently (in the post-syntactic morphological component which is referred to in the Principles and Parameters framework as PF), by a morpheme or by merger with the lexical subject. We will take up these analyses in order.

4.2.1   *Expletive subject and poor agreement*

Suppose that we assume that the structure of sentences such as (7a) is as in (9), with the subject in a lower projection, say the VP (Fassi Fehri 1993; Mohammad 2000).

---

[2] There is no consensus as to whether there is agreement in person in addition to gender under the VS order; see Fassi Fehri (1993) and Mohammad (2000) for discussion.

(9)

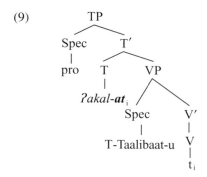

The verb raises from the VP to T while the subject remains lower. The Spec of TP is occupied by an expletive subject, which is null in (7a) but can be overt as in (10a, b) from Mohammad (2000:92–93).[3]

(10) a. ʔa-huwa mustaħiil-un   ʔan nattafiq-a   yawm-an
         Q-he/it   impossible-Nom that agree.1p-subj day-Acc
         'Is it impossible for us to ever agree?'

      b. zaʕamtu   ʔanna-hu mustaħiil-un   ʔan nattafiq-a   yawm-an
         claimed.1s that-he/it impossible-Nom that agree.1p-subj day-Acc
         'I claimed that it is impossible for us to ever agree.'

Note that the expletive is nominative, *huwa* 'he/it' in (10a), but accusative, *-hu* in (10b). This is as expected given that it is preceded by the complementizer *ʔanna*, which assigns Accusative Case to the NP that follows it (see chapter 2). Mohammad (2000) takes sentences such as (10b) as strong evidence for locating the expletive subject in Spec TP. Putting aside the issue of what forces the presence of the expletive in such contexts, the question is whether the expletive enters into an agreement relation with the verb which in turn could help account for the agreement asymmetry.

The main challenge for this account is partial agreement. It is not clear how in (7a) the verb agrees with the subject in gender if agreement is indeed with an expletive. The only alternative would be to find a way to allow number agreement with the putative expletive and gender (and probably person) agreement with the lexical postverbal subject. One option is that partial agreement does not reflect a syntactically grounded agreement relation but may be accidental. Ouhalla (1994a) attributes it to the fact that the subject is linearly adjacent to the verb at PF. This

---

[3] See also Fassi Fehri (1993) for detailed discussion of the expletive in Arabic.

last option should not be automatically discounted, but it needs to explain why this cannot also be the case when the subject precedes the verb.

4.2.2   Full agreement as an incorporated pronoun

It is tempting to take the complementary distribution between full agreement and the postverbal subject to indicate that full agreement is a realization of a pronominal that gets incorporated into the verb (Fassi Fehri 1993, 2000). This analysis explains why a postverbal subject cannot co-occur with full agreement. Under this analysis, full agreement, which is an incorporated subject pronoun, and the postverbal lexical subject compete for the same syntactic position and the semantic role associated with it.

There are at least three sets of facts that challenge the incorporation account. The first set of facts comes from preverbal lexical subjects, which co-occur with full agreement on the verb (8a). Under the incorporation account of full agreement, the preverbal NP cannot be a subject but rather a left dislocated element with the full agreement morpheme playing the role of the resumptive pronoun. This is a reasonable alternative that has been adopted by a number of students of Arabic (see chapter 3). However, there are contexts where it is not clear that the preverbal NP can be analyzed as a left dislocated element. These are cases where the subject is located between the main verb and an auxiliary verb (11a).

(11)   a. kaanat   T-Taalibaat-u   ya-drus-na
            be.past.3fs the-student.fp-Nom 3-study-fp
            'The students were studying.'

        b. T-Taalibaat-u   kunna   ya-drus-na
            the-student.fp-Nom   be.past.3fp   3-study-fp
            'The students were studying.'

As illustrated in (11a) the NP *T-Taalibaat-u* 'the students' precedes the main verb *ya-drus-na* 'study' and follows the auxiliary verb *kaanat* 'was.' The lexical verb is in the plural and the auxiliary is in the singular. The position of the NP *T-Taalibaat-u* 'the students' is not a position that has generally been associated with left dislocated elements (see chapter 8). It is rather a position that has been associated with regular NP subjects. Moreover, the fact that the auxiliary verb displays partial agreement clearly indicates that the NP *T-Taalibaat-u* 'the students' is a subject with respect to that verb. However, the main verb *ya-drus-na* 'study' displays full agreement, which under the incorporation account means that the subject is actually an incorporated pronominal. Thus, we end up with two subjects in the same sentence, exactly the situation that the incorporation account is set up to rule out.

The second set of facts comes from wh-movement contexts, particularly relative clauses. In Standard Arabic, a relativized object can leave a gap within the sentence:

(12)   ʔištaraytu l-kitaaba llaδii katabta
        bought.1s the-book that   wrote.2ms
        'I bought the book that you wrote.'

Interestingly, when the subject is relativized, full agreement on the verb is obligatory, as illustrated in (13).

(13)   raʔaytu l-kuttaaba llaδiina zaar-uu   l-žaamiʕata
        saw.1s the-authors who.mp visited-3mp the-university
        'I saw the authors who visited the university.'

Under the incorporation account, the full agreement on the verb within the relative clause indicates the presence of a pronominal subject. This in turn implies that relativization of the subject obligatorily deploys the resumptive pronoun strategy. However, it is not clear why this should be the case only in the context of subject relativization, particularly if the relativized object, as seen in (12) is extracted from the postverbal position, which is also the canonical position of the subject under the incorporation account. Postverbal positions are usually considered privileged positions as launching sites for displacement. Barring an independent explanation for why the putative resumptive strategy is only obligatory in the context of subject relativization, the facts in (13) remain a challenge for the incorporation account of full agreement.

The third set of facts that challenge the incorporation account of full agreement comes from the nature of the subject agreement morpheme. As shown above, in the perfective all the features of subject agreement are realized by a suffix on the verb. However, in the context of the imperfective verb, agreement is realized discontinuously, with person as prefix and number as suffix. It is not at all clear how this situation could be handled under an incorporation account since in most such cases all the features are spelled-out by one continuous phonological unit, since this is how pronouns are usually realized. In the present context, we would need to find a way to split the incorporated pronoun so that one part is realized as a prefix and one part as a suffix. While this is not implausible, and such analyses have been proposed, the question is whether such a complex analysis is warranted.

In addition to the empirical problems raised against the incorporation account of full agreement, there is also a conceptual problem that arises. Under this account, there are two agreement paradigms in Arabic. One agreement paradigm realizes partial agreement and another agreement paradigm realizes a full incorporated pronoun. Now, consider agreement in the context of a singular subject in both the VS and SV order.

(14)   a. naama   l-walad-u
            slept.3ms the-boy-Nom
            'The boy slept.'

        b. l-walad-u   naama
            the-boy-Nom slept.3ms
            'The boy slept.'

        c. naam-at l-bint-u
            slept-3fs the-girl-Nom
            'The girl slept.'

        d. l-bint-u   naam-at
            the-girl-Nom slept-3fs
            'The girl slept.'

(15)   a. ya-naamu l-walad-u
            3-sleep   the-boy-Nom
            'The boy is sleeping.'

        b. l-walad-u   ya-naamu
            the-boy-Nom 3-sleep
            'The boy is sleeping.'

        c. ta-naamu l-bint-u
            3f-sleep   the-girl-Nom
            'The girl is sleeping.'

        d. l-bint-u   ta-naamu
            the-girl-Nom 3f-sleep
            'The girl is sleeping.'

Notice that in both the perfective and imperfective verbs, the agreement morpheme is the same in both VS and SV order. According to the incorporation account, agreement is a pronominal in SV but a genuine agreement morpheme in VS since there is already a subject in the postverbal position. Under such an account, the fact that the two paradigms are identical is accidental.

4.2.3   Syntactic analyses of agreement asymmetry

There have been various syntactic approaches to account for the asymmetry in the context of subject–verb agreement in Standard Arabic. Though the approaches differ from each other, their main assumption is that the asymmetry can be explained in syntactic terms. We will discuss two approaches and their challenges. The first approach, first proposed in Benmamoun (1992a, b) and also explored by Bahloul and Harbert (1993), tries to capitalize on the surface configurational relation between the verb and the subject in the VS and SV orders.

Let's start with the VS order. Assuming the configuration in (16) for that order, notice that the verb governs the subject in [Spec, VP].

(16)

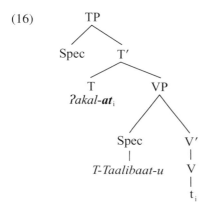

Turning to the SV order and assuming the configuration in (17), the verb and the subject in TP are both in a Spec-Head relation.

(17)

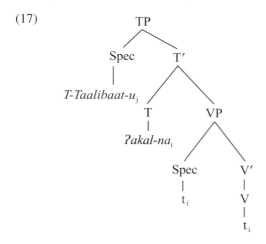

Given the configurations in (16) and (17), the agreement asymmetry seems to be sensitive to the configurational relation between the verb and the subject: the verb is in a government relation with the subject in (16) and in a Spec-Head relation with the subject in (17). Partial agreement seems to obtain under government and full agreement under Spec-Head agreement.

However, this account has its shortcomings. Notice that the verb and the subject are underlyingly in a Spec-Head relation (within the VP, as indicated in (16)) before verb movement occurs. Moreover, we saw in chapter 2 that in the VS order the subject may not actually be in the VP but in a higher projection, probably TP. Therefore, the subject and the verb are in a Spec-Head configuration at several points in the derivation regardless of the final surface order (Aoun, Benmamoun and Sportiche 1994). They are also in a government relation. Consequently, one would expect either partial or full agreement throughout. Conceptually, this analysis is suspect because it needs to rely on a disjunction using two separate configurations, the Spec-Head configuration, which is generally grounded in the X'-schema, and the government configuration which is not so grounded.

The second syntactic approach to asymmetric agreement overcomes this conceptual problem by assuming that only one configuration is relevant to agreement, namely the Spec-Head configuration. This relation can obtain overtly or covertly (in the component that deals with the interface between form and meaning, which is referred to in the Principles and Parameters framework as Logical Form or LF). If it obtains overtly, as it does in the SV order, full agreement takes place and is realized overtly. On the other hand, if the Spec-Head relation obtains covertly, for example due to covert raising of the subject, only partial agreement takes place. One version of such an analysis is provided by van Gelderen (1996). She suggests a syntactic solution to account for the difference between number and gender. She makes a number of assumptions that are crucial to her analysis. First, she assumes, following earlier work of Mohammad (1989), that there is an expletive subject in the VSO order that could possibly be null. Second, the expletive is specified for number but crucially not gender. Third, she assumes that number is a verbal feature that is strong and gender is a verbal feature that is weak. Fourth, she follows the earlier minimalist assumptions of Chomsky (1995), by maintaining that weak features do not require overt movement but strong features do. Fifth, the verb is also specified for nominal [+N] features that are always strong and hence require overt verb movement. Given these five assumptions, van Gelderen explains the presence of gender agreement under the VS order as follows: the verb always moves, presumably to T, where the (null) expletive is located. The verbal number feature is strong and the expletive checks it first before the putative LF movement of the subject takes place. With respect to gender, van Gelderen claims that since the feature is weak it does not need to be checked overtly but rather covertly, subsequent to the LF movement of the subject. By the end of the derivation, the verb has been through two agreement relations, with the expletive subject (number agreement) and the lexical subject (gender agreement).

Notice, however, that under this analysis a weak feature, such as gender, does not need to be overtly checked to be spelled-out in the morphology. This may not be a serious problem but it comes at a cost, namely that the subject does raise covertly, an assumption that does not seem to be independently motivated. In addition, it is not at all obvious why gender agreement on the verb, a non-interpretable feature in the sense of Chomsky (1995), should be present at LF and relevant to LF computations. Moreover, van Gelderen's analysis relies crucially on the assumption that the lexical subject remains within the VP, which conflicts with recent analyses that show that the subject is higher than VP in a position where it can itself play a role in number agreement overtly (see chapter 3).

In short, all the accounts discussed so far fall short of accounting for all the agreement facts in Arabic while remaining empirically and conceptually consistent. In the next section we will look at the latest alternative, where the main argument is that the asymmetry is inherently morphological rather than syntactic.

4.2.4   *Morphological analysis of the agreement asymmetry*

Rather than maintaining the core assumption that the asymmetry is fundamentally syntactic, Benmamoun (2000) argues that the asymmetry is morphological and is due to how the number feature is spelled-out in the morphology. This analysis builds on the analysis of Aoun, Benmamoun and Sportiche (1994). Those authors argue that there is only one agreement relation, the Spec-Head relation, between the verb and the subject, which obtains overtly. However, due to the placement of the verb higher than the subject (due to movement perhaps), the verb may lose its number feature. Benmamoun (2000) argues that the reason why the number morpheme does not surface in the VS order is because, in the morphology, the verb and the postverbal subject form a prosodic unit, which in turn makes the lexical subject an exponent of the number feature on the verb. Consequently, the presence of the number affix becomes redundant. The merger between the verb and the subject to form a prosodic unit obtains, post-syntactically, in the component that spells-out the terminal elements of the syntactic phrase marker and their features.

Benmamoun (2000) provides several arguments for this analysis. First, it explains the agreement situation that arises in the context where the subject is located between the auxiliary verb and the main verb: since the subject merges with the auxiliary verb to form a prosodic unit, the prediction is that it is this verb that will not display the number morpheme. The main verb, by contrast, will. Second, since the absence of number is contingent on merger with a postverbal lexical subject, the analysis makes the correct prediction that in the context of relativization, and whenever the postverbal subject is empty, the verb will display the number affix. Third, this analysis makes the VS order parallel to the Construct State in the context of noun phrases, where the argument for a prosodic merger between the Construct State members is better grounded.[4]

However, despite the fact that it does avoid the pitfalls of the purely syntactic accounts, the morphological analysis has its shortcomings. First, it must stipulate that the merger between the subject and the verb can only obtain in the VS order. This issue is discussed in Ackema and Neeleman (2003) and Benmamoun and Lorimor (2006) and seems to be part of a general tendency, particularly in head initial languages, but at this point it remains a stipulation. Second, unlike the Construct State, where the members cannot be so easily separated, the verb and the subject can be separated by NP objects and other constituents, as illustrated in (18).

(18)   kataba   r-risaalat-a   l-ʔawlaad-u
         wrote.3ms the-letter-Acc the-children
         'The children wrote the letter.'

A possible account for such facts is that both the subject and the object form a prosodic unit with the verb. This is not implausible but additional work needs to be done to determine whether they do form such a unit (see footnote 4).

Third, as is well known, in the modern Arabic dialects full agreement obtains regardless of word order.

(19)   *Moroccan Arabic*
         a. naʕs-u   l-əwlad
            slept-3p the-children
            'The children slept.'

         b. l-əwlad   naʕs-u
            the-children slept-3p
            'The children slept.'

(20)   *Lebanese Arabic*
         a. neem-o l-wleed
            slept-3p the-children
            'The children slept.'

---

[4] Benmamoun (2003) provides a historical explanation for the parallelism between sentences and Construct State noun phrases and for its correlation with the absence of number on the verb and (in-)definiteness marker on all but the last members of the Construct State. He then argues the VS order has gradually lost its Construct State status, leading up to the situation in the modern dialects where agreement is full regardless of word order. Under such a scenario the asymmetry in Standard Arabic survives from a stage where the verb and the postverbal subject were strictly adjacent.

> b. l-wleed   neem-o
>   the-children slept-3p
>   'The children slept.'

All the above analyses, whether syntactic or morphological, need to make additional assumptions to deal with agreement in the modern dialects. Under the morphological account, the claim is straightforward, namely that there is no merger between the verb and the subject. But that raises the question of whether there is independent evidence for such merger and why such merger is absent in all the modern dialects.

4.3   First conjunct agreement in the Modern Arabic dialects

Another intriguing agreement phenomenon that has been prominently debated is the phenomenon of first conjunct agreement (FCA). FCA, illustrated in (21a) and (22a), from Moroccan Arabic and Lebanese Arabic respectively, involves a coordinated subject whose lefthand member agrees with the verb. Full agreement with the postverbal coordinated subject is also an option, as illustrated in (21d) and (22d). On the other hand, a preverbal coordinated subject does not display FCA, as shown in (21c) and (22c) (in contrast with (21b) and (22b) respectively)

(21)   *Moroccan Arabic*
>   a. ža   ʕomar w   karim
>   came.3ms Omar and Karim
>   'Omar and Karim came.'

>   b. ʕomar w   karim žaw
>   Omar and Karim came.3p
>   'Omar and Karim came.'

>   c. *ʕomar w   karim ža
>   Omar   and Karim came.3ms

>   d. žaw   ʕomar w   kariim
>   came.3p Omar and Karim
>   'Omar and Karim came.'

(22)   *Lebanese Arabic*
>   a. raaħ   kariim w   marwaan
>   left.3ms Karim and Marwan
>   'Karim and Marwan left.'

b. kariim w   marwaan raaħo
   Karim and Marwan left.3p
   'Karim and Marwan left.'

c. *kariim w   marwaan raaħ
   Karim and Marwan left.3ms

d. raaħo kariim w   marwaan
   left.3p Karim and Marwan
   'Karim and Marwan left.'

All the main patterns of agreement illustrated above are schematized in (23).

(23)   a. V_{sg} NP_{sg}+NP_{sg} (Obj)   b. NP_{sg}+NP_{sg} V_{pl} (Obj)
         c. *NP_{sg}+NP_{sg} V_{sg} (Obj)   d. V_{pl} NP_{sg}+NP_{sg} (Obj)

   The main topic of contention has been whether FCA agreement, which arises under the VS order, is due to a biclausal structure of the conjunction or to some syntactic property that allows the verb to target the lefthand member of a conjoined NP. Aoun, Benmamoun and Sportiche (1994, 1999), and Aoun and Benmamoun (1999) take up this issue in detail and argue for a biclausal analysis. The main evidence comes from the fact that FCA is not compatible with verbs that require plural subjects, as illustrated in (24–29).

         Meet
(24)   *Moroccan Arabic*
         a. *tlaqa   ʕomar w   karim
            met.3ms Omar and Karim

         b. tlaqaw ʕomar w   karim
            met.3p Omar and Karim
            'Omar and Karim met.'

         c. ʕomar w   karim tlaqaw
            Omar and Karim met.3p
            'Omar and Karim met.'

(25)   *Lebanese Arabic*
         a. *ltaʔa   kariim w   marwaan
            met.3ms Karim and Marwan

         b. ltaʔo   kariim w   marwaan
            met.3p Karim and Marwan
            'Karim and Marwan met.'

c. kariim w   marwaan lta?o
   Karim and Marwan   met.3p
   'Karim and Marwan met.'

Share

(26) *Moroccan Arabic*

a. *tqasəm   ʕomar w   karim l-ɣəlla
   divided.3ms Omar and Karim the-harvest

b. tqasmu   ʕomar w   karim l-ɣəlla
   divided.3p Omar and Karim the-harvest
   'Omar and Karim divided the harvest.'

c. ʕomar w   kariim tqasmu   l-ɣəlla
   Omar and Karim divided.3p the-harvest
   'Omar and Karim divided the harvest.'

(27) *Lebanese Arabic*

a. *t?asam   ʕomar w   kariim l-ɣalle
   divided.3ms Omar and Karim the-harvest

b. t?asamo   ʕomar w   kariim l-ɣalle
   divided.3p Omar and Karim the-harvest
   'Omar and Karim divided the harvest.'

c. ʕomar w   kariim t?asamo   l-ɣalle
   Omar and Karim divided.3p the-harvest
   'Omar and Karim divided the harvest.'

Embrace

(28) *Moroccan Arabic*

a. *tʕanəq   ʕomar w   nadia
   embraced.3ms Omar and Nadia

b. tʕanqu   ʕomar w   nadia
   embraced.3p Omar and Nadia
   'Omar and Nadia embraced.'

c. ʕomar w   nadia tʕanqu
   Omar and Nadia embraced.3p
   'Omar and Nadia embraced.'

(29) *Lebanese Arabic*

a. *tʕana?   ʕomar w   naadia
   embraced.3ms Omar and Nadia

b. tʕanaʔo   ʕomar w   naadia
embraced.3p Omar and Nadia
'Omar and Nadia embraced.'

c. ʕomar w   naadia tʕanaʔo
Omar and Nadia embraced.3p
'Omar and Nadia embraced.'

Similar facts obtain in the context of particles that require a plural subject within the same clause. These particles can be quantifiers (30–33) that modify the verb or the subject, or reciprocals (34–35) and reflexives (36), which require a local binder within the same clausal domain.

Together/Both

(30) *Moroccan Arabic*

a. *lʕəb   ʕomar w   karim bžužhum
play.3ms Omar   and Karim together

b. ləʕbu   ʕomar w   karim bžužhum
play.3p Omar   and Karim together
'Omar and Karim played together.'

c. ʕomar w   karim ləʕbu   bžužhum
Omar   and Karim play.3p together
'Omar and Karim played together.'

(31) *Lebanese Arabic*

a. *raaħ   kariim w   marwaan sawa
left.3ms Karim and Marwan together

b. raaħo kariim w   marwaan sawa
left.3p Karim and Marwan together
'Karim and Marwan left together.'

c. kariim w   marwaan raaħo sawa
Karim and Marwan left.3p together
'Karim and Marwan left together.'

Each

(32) *Moroccan Arabic*

a. *χda   ʕomar w   karim təffaaħa l-waħəd
took.3ms Omar   and Karim apple   to-each

b. χdaw   ʕomar w   karim təffaaħa l-waħəd
took.3p Omar   and Karim apple   to-each
'Omar and Karim took one apple each.'

c. ʕomar w   karim χdaw   təffaaħa l-waħəd
Omar and Karim took.3p apple   to-each
'Omar and Karim took one apple each.'

(33) *Lebanese Arabic*

a. *ʔakal kariim w   marwaan təffaaħa kill   waaħad
ate.3ms Karim and Marwan apple   each one

b. ʔakalo kariim w   marwaan təffaaħa kill   waaħad
ate.3p Karim and Marwan apple   each one
'Karim and Marwan each ate an apple.'

c. kariim w   marwaan ʔakalo təffaaħa kill   waaħad
Karim and Marwan ate.3p apple   each one
'Karim and Marwan each ate an apple.'

Reciprocals

(34) *Moroccan Arabic*

a. *gləs   ʕomar w   karim ħda bəʕDhum
sat.3ms Omar and Karim near each other

b. gəlsu ʕomar w   karim ħda bəʕDhum
sat.3p Omar and Karim near each other
'Omar and Karim sat near each other.'

c. ʕomar w   karim gəlsu ħda bəʕDhum
Omar and Karim sat.3p near each other
'Omar and Karim sat near each other.'

(35) *Lebanese Arabic*

a. *ʔaʕad ʕomar w   kariim ħad baʕDun
sat.3ms Omar and Karim near each other

b. ʔaʕado ʕomar w   kariim ħad baʕDun
sat.3p Omar and Karim near each other
'Omar and Karim sat near each other.'

c. ʕomar w   kariim ʔaʕado ħad baʕDun
Omar and Karim sat.3p near each other
'Omar and Karim sat near each other.'

Reflexives

(36) *Lebanese Arabic*

a. *biħibb kariim w   marwaan ħaalun
love.3ms Karim and Marwan themselves

    b. biħibbo kariim w   marwaan ħaalun
        love.3p Karim and Marwan themselves
        'Karim and Marwan love themselves.'

    c. kariim w   marwaan biħibbo ħaalun
        Karim and Marwan love.3p themselves
        'Karim and Marwan love themselves.'

Finally, control structures (37–38) also resist FCA. This is also because obligatory control requires an anaphoric-like relation between the controller and the controlled. In particular, split antecedents are usually not allowed, a situation that would arise under the biclausal analysis of FCA.

        Control
(37)   *Moroccan Arabic*
    a. *rfəD   ʕomar w   karim yəmšiw
        refused.3ms Omar and Karim go

    b. rəfDu   ʕomar w   karim yəmšiw
        refused.3p Omar and Karim go
        'Omar and Karim refused to go.'

(38)   *Lebanese Arabic*
    a. *rafaD   ʕomar w   kariim yfillo
        refused.3ms Omar and Karim go

    b. rafaDo   ʕomar w   kariim yfillo
        refused.3p Omar and Karim go
        'Omar and Karim refused to go.'

All the above facts are compatible with a clausal coordination account of FCA, i.e. each NP is the subject of its own clause while the second clausal conjunct contains a gapped verb.[5]

4.4   First conjunct agreement in Standard Arabic

At first blush, the facts from Standard Arabic present direct counter-arguments to the biclausal analysis of FCA in the modern Arabic dialects. It appears that, unlike in the other dialects of Arabic, in Standard Arabic, FCA can occur in the context of predicates and elements that require a plural subject in the

---

[5] The reader is referred to Aoun, Benmamoun and Sportiche (1994) for the details of the analysis.

same clause. For example, in (39) the sentence contains a reflexive bound by the conjoined subject, yet the verb is singular.

(39)   ʔiʕtamada kariim wa marwaan ʕalaa nafsayhimaa   *Standard Arabic*
        relied.3ms Karim and Marwan on   themselves
        'Karim and Marwan relied on themselves.'

The same facts obtain in the context of control, as in (40), and collective predicates, as in (41).

(40)   ħaawala   kariim w   marwaan ʔan yafuuzaa   *Standard Arabic*
        tried.3ms Karim and Marwan to win.3m.dual
        bi-l-žaaʔiza
        with-the-award
        'Karim and Marwan tried to win the award.'

(41)   ʔižtamaʕa l-raaʔiis-u   wa l-waziir-u   *Standard Arabic*
        met.3ms   the-president-Nom and the-minister-Nom
        'The president and the minister met.'

Harbert and Bahloul (2002:58–60) consider these facts challenging for the biclausal analysis of FCA. The main argument is that, in Standard Arabic, FCA can obtain in situations where a monoclausal/phrasal coordination analysis is forced, as in the data in (39–41). However, notice that Standard Arabic, as opposed to the modern Arabic dialects, displays partial agreement in the context of postverbal plural subjects. This in turn implies that what appears as FCA may in fact be a manifestation of partial agreement.

However, there are facts that remain difficult to reconcile with the biclausal analysis of FCA. In Standard Arabic it appears that there are cases of genuine FCA. Harbert and Bahloul (2002:59) provide the example in (42), where the verb agrees with the first subject pronoun on the right. The latter is in turn conjoined with an NP and both bind a reciprocal.

(42)   tuħibbu hiya wa ʔaxuu-haa baʕDahumaa
        love.3fs she and brother-her each.other
        'She and her brother love each other.'

In (42), the lefthand subject pronoun is feminine singular, thus agreeing clearly with the verb. The status of the sentence in (42) is not clear. Such sentences, however, may not provide a fatal challenge to the biclausal account of FCA. Gender agreement does behave differently from number in Arabic. After all, it is the agreement that may be preserved under the VS order. It may turn out that gender agreement with the first conjunct is due to the morphological merger that takes place between the subject and the verb and is more sensitive to the linear relation with the postverbal subject (Ouhalla 1994a). This hypothesis is plausible, given that in the Arabic dialects studied by Aoun, Benmamoun and Sportiche (1994), which do not have the option of merging the subject and the verb in the morphology, the equivalent of the sentence in (42) is ungrammatical.

(43)   *tatbɣi   hiya w   xu-ha   baʕDhum   *Moroccan Arabic*
        loves.3fs she   and brother-her each.other

(44)   *bitħibb   hiya w   xayy-a   baʕDun   *Lebanese Arabic*
        loves.3fs she   and brother-her each.other

Clearly more research is warranted on the distribution of the agreement features in Arabic. An in-depth analysis of the contrast between number and gender may help shed light on whether a biclausal analysis can be maintained for FCA.[6]

4.5   Impersonal agreement

The agreement asymmetries we have discussed so far mostly involve full or partial agreement between the verb and the subject. One type of agreement that has not received adequate attention is impersonal agreement. This is the type of agreement that arises in the context of existential constructions where the indefinite lexical subject co-occurs with an expletive. In this section, we will rely exclusively on the data and analyses discussed by Halila (1992) and Hoyt (2002).[7]

Hoyt deals with Rural Palestinian Arabic (RPA), where he discovered that existential constructions display an alternation between full agreement with the lexical subject or no (impersonal) agreement. The sentences in (45) from Hoyt (2002:111) clearly illustrate this alternation.

(45)   a. baKa/baKu   fiih   xams izlam fi-d-daar
           was.3ms/were.3mp there five   men   in-the-house
           'There were five men in the house.'

        b. baaKi/baaKye   hanaak ixtyaare waraa-ha Kowm Kawiyin
           be.part.ms/be.part.fs there   old.fs   behind-her clan strong
           'There was an old woman there who had a strong clan behind her.'

---

[6] See Soltan (2007) for a minimalist analysis of FCA.
[7] See also Eid (1993) and Mohammad (1999b) for further discussion of the syntax of inflected prepositions and existential constructions.

In (45a) the auxiliary verb alternates between no agreement (*baKa*) or full agreement (*baKu*). That this alternation is clearly one of presence vs. absence of agreement is confirmed by (45b). In (45b) the lexical subject is feminine, yet the auxiliary participle alternates between feminine agreement and the default third person masculine form. In other words, unlike the agreement asymmetry relative to word order that is attested in Standard Arabic, where gender agreement may obtain under both alternations, in existential constructions in RPA, no partial agreement with the lexical subject is attested. Rather, the subject either fully agrees or doesn't agree with the verb or participle.

Halila (1992:301–302) provides similar facts from Tunisian Arabic. In sentences containing the expletive particle *famma*, the auxiliary verb can optionally agree with the lexical subject.[8]

(46)   a. kaan   famma talvza   fuuq T-Taawla
           be.past.3ms there   television.fs on   the-table
           'There was a TV set on the table.'

        b. kaan   famma barša ktub   fuuq T-Taawla
           be.past.3ms there   many books on   the-table
           'There were many books on the table.'

(47)   a. kaanit   famma talvza   fuuq T-Taawla
           be.past.3fs there   television.fs on   the-table
           'There was a TV set on the table.'

        b. kaanuu   famma barša ktub   fuuq T-Taawla
           be.past.3p there   many books on   the-table
           'There were many books on the table.'

Notice that in (46a) the main lexical subject is feminine singular while the auxiliary verb carries (default) masculine singular agreement. Similarly, in (46b) the main lexical subject is plural while the auxiliary verb again carries (default) masculine singular agreement. By contrast, in (47) the auxiliary verb fully agrees with the lexical subject. The auxiliary verb in (47a) carries feminine singular agreement and thus agrees with the feminine singular lexical subject and in (47b) it carries plural agreement and therefore agrees with the plural lexical subject.

Hoyt advances strong arguments to show that the alternation in question is sensitive to the scope of the indefinite lexical subject. He provides the sentences in (48) to illustrate this interplay between agreement and scope.

---

[8] The original transcriptions and glosses have been slightly modified to be consistent with the conventions followed in this book.

(48)   a. čill   yowm b-iǐji   la-l-Saff   ulaad
         Every day   ind-come.3ms to-the-class boys.3p
         'Every day, boys (some or another) come to class.'

         b. čill   yowm b-iǐju   la-l-Saff   ulaad
         Every day   ind-come.3p to-the-class boys.3p
         'Every day, (some particular) boys come to class.'

In (48a) the universal quantifier takes scope over the existential quantifier. By contrast, in (48b) the existential quantifier takes scope over the universal quantifier. The latter interpretation strongly correlates with full agreement on the verb.

Hoyt discusses further instances of the alternation between full agreement and impersonal agreement. The alternation in general seems to be semantically grounded. Hoyt provides a syntactic account for the agreement alternation. The essence of the analysis is that the indefinite lexical subject may be an NP without a determiner or a DP with a determiner. The critical assumption that Hoyt makes is that Case is a property of the determiner (the DP layer of the nominal phrase). His main idea is that a nominal phrase endowed with a non-interpretable feature such as Case is forced to enter into agreement relations resulting in full agreement in the existential predicate. Nominal phrases that do not have the DP layer and therefore lack Case do not enter into such relations, which in turn results in impersonal agreement.

This analysis raises a number of questions. First, it is not at all evident that in the context of impersonal agreement, the indefinite lexical subject is not structurally Case marked. It is plausible that it is Case marked but with partitive lexical Case. However, the data provided by Hoyt do not provide any support one way or the other. Second, the two nominal projections, the putative NP and DP, are overtly identical and the question is whether there is any independent motivation for the claim that there is an additional functional projection, namely DP, in one but not the other.

These problems notwithstanding, the agreement alternation in existential contexts adds another layer of complexity to the overall problem of subject agreement in Arabic. It is clearly different from the well-known Standard Arabic agreement asymmetry. It is not sensitive to word order and the asymmetry at hand seems to involve absence vs. presence of agreement rather than partial vs. full agreement. This in turn suggests that a unified account may not be possible or even desirable. The two different asymmetries and alternations may require separate accounts.

4.6   Conclusion

Subject–verb agreement in Standard Arabic and the spoken modern dialects provide a rich array of agreement facts. The fact that in the imperfective paradigm person and number features occur on opposite sides of the verb (as prefixes and suffixes respectively) raises questions about whether they constitute a discontinuous morpheme or whether they are separate and independent morphemes. This is an important question for both morphology and syntax. With regard to the agreement asymmetries in Standard Arabic, we have provided arguments to support a non-syntactic morpho-phonological account whose main import is that the number feature in the VS order is present syntactically but spelled-out by the merged subject in PF. This option is not available to the modern dialects where the verb and the subject tend to fully agree regardless of the relative order of the verb and the subject. A question that remains is whether this difference between the two main Arabic varieties can be reduced to some independent property or parameter. Another related asymmetry we discussed arises in the context of coordinated subjects where only in the VS order may the verb agree with the closest (left hand) conjunct. The approach we discussed argues for a clausal coordination account for close conjunct agreement on the basis of the distribution of number sensitive items. If it turns out that the clausal analysis for first conjunct agreement is not warranted, a question then would arise as to whether the agreement asymmetry that Standard Arabic displays in the context of simple plural subjects and the agreement asymmetry that the spoken modern dialects display in the context of coordinated subjects can receive a unified analysis. It is not clear to us that such unified analysis is warranted, but the fact that both asymmetries arise in the same context (VS) is, to put it mildly, intriguing. One could add to this puzzle the agreement asymmetry that arises in the context of indefinite subjects in some Arabic dialects.[9] In short, agreement in Arabic varieties is a rich testing ground for issues related to morphology and syntax and the relation between them and also for issues related to language variation and change.

---

[9] For further discussion of the absence of agreement in Lebanese Arabic VS sentences the reader is referred to Hallman (2000).

5

The syntax of sentential negation

5.1 Introduction

Modern Standard Arabic and the modern Arabic dialects have different realizations of sentential negation, where the negative markers vary as to whether they are hosted by a head and whether they carry tense and agreement. In all dialects, however, the agreement paradigm of negative imperatives is richer than the agreement paradigm of positive imperatives. The negative markers also interact in intriguing ways with negative polarity items. We will take up each issue in order.

5.2 Sentential negation in the modern Arabic dialects

In most modern Arabic dialects, there may be at least two possible forms of sentential negation, depending on whether the negative is hosted by the verb or whether it is realized independently, a fact that will become significant as we proceed.

In Moroccan Arabic (1a), sentential negation, when it attaches to the verb, is realized by the "discontinuous" negative *ma-š*. In Lebanese Arabic (1b), the negative enclitic *š* is optional.

(1)   a. ma-qra-š   l-wəld
              Neg-read.past.3ms-Neg the-boy
              'The boy didn't read.'

        b. l-walad ma-ʔara-(š)   l-kteeb
              the-boy Neg-read.past.3ms-(Neg) the-book
              'The boy didn't read the book.'

In other dialects such as Syrian Arabic (2a; Cowell 1964:383[1]) and Kuwaiti (2b; Brustad 2000:285) only *ma* is used.

---

[1] The gloss is ours.

(2)　　a. ʔəl-li,　　baʕəd maa zərt　　　　　ʔasaaraat ləbnaan
　　　　　　tell-me, yet　　Neg visited.2ms ruins　　　Lebanon
　　　　　　'Tell me, haven't you visited the ruins of Lebanon yet?'

　　　　b. maa xallaw šay　　maa χaduu
　　　　　　Neg left.3p thing Neg took.3p
　　　　　　'They didn't leave anything they didn't take.'

In the context of some verbal predicates and non-verbal predicates, sentential negation may be realized differently. In Moroccan Arabic (3a), the negative proclitic *ma* and the negative enclitic *š* are realized as one single non-discontinuous element. In Egyptian Arabic (3b, Brustad 2000:283) and Lebanese Arabic, there is also a non-discontinuous element *mi-š* (3c). In yet other dialects, such as Syrian (3d, Cowell 1964:386), the negative *muu* is used (3d).

(3)　　　a. huwa maši hna
　　　　　　he　　Neg here
　　　　　　'He is not here.'

　　　　b. huwwa miš hina
　　　　　　he　　　Neg here
　　　　　　'He is not here.'

　　　　c. huwwe miš hon
　　　　　　he　　　Neg here
　　　　　　'He is not here.'

　　　　d. ʔana muu mabSuut əlyom
　　　　　　I　　Neg well　　　today
　　　　　　'I am not feeling well today.'

Brustad (2000) provides a detailed discussion of the two different negative forms and their syntactic and pragmatic properties in different dialects representing the different regions of the Arabic-speaking world. She provides the table given in (4), which gives the range of variation between dialects (see Brustad 2000:282). Brustad refers to the negative that is used in the context of non-verbal predicates and some verbal predicates as predicate negation, which she contrasts with what she calls verbal negation, which is used in the context of verbal predicates.

(4)　　**Particles of Negation**

	Verbal Negation	Predicate Negation
Moroccan	maa-š(i)	maaši
Egyptian	maa-š(i)	miš
Syrian	maa	muu
Kuwaiti	maa	muu

We will discuss a possible syntactic account for the bifurcation in the table above, but first we need to settle the issues of the syntactic status of sentential negation (as head, specifier, or adverbial) and whether it is generated directly on its host, when it has one, rather than merging with its host in the syntax (or even post-syntax).

5.2.1   The syntactic representation and derivation of sentential negation

There are good reasons to treat the negative *ma* as the head of its own syntactic projection. First, *ma* and its variant *ma-š* can host subject clitics, which is a property of heads. This situation obtains in various dialects as shown by the paradigms below from Moroccan (Caubet 1996:3), Egyptian (Eid 1991:50), and Kuwaiti (Brustad 2000:296).

(5)

a. *Moroccan Arabic*	b. *Egyptian Arabic*	c. *Kuwaiti Arabic*	
ma-ni-š	ma-nii-š	maani	I + neg
ma-nta-š	ma-ntaa-š	mint/mant	you.ms + Neg
ma-nti-š	ma-ntii-š	minti	you.fs + Neg
ma-huwa-š	ma-huwwaa-š	muhu	he + Neg
ma-hiya-š	ma-hiyyaa-š	mihi	she + Neg
ma-ħna-š	ma-ħnaa-š	miħna	we + Neg
ma-ntuma-š	ma-ntuu-š	mintu/mantu	you.p + Neg
ma-huma-š	ma-hummaa-š	muhum	they + Neg

Second, in some dialects, the negative element carries agreement, again a property of heads, as illustrated in (6) from a Gulf dialect (Matar 1976).

(6)   haadhi mi zoojti
       this   not wife-my
       'This is not my wife.'

Therefore, it is reasonable to conclude that the negative is a head element.

The next issue is whether the negative element heads its own syntactic projection. For the independent (Brustad's predicate) negation, if it is a head, then it most likely heads its own syntactic projection. For the dependent (Brustad's verbal) negation, there are arguments from recent analyses of sentential negation in various languages that it also heads its own projection (see e.g. Ouhalla 1991; Benmamoun 1992a, 2000; Shlonsky 1997). By allowing the negative to host its own syntactic projection, we won't have to posit two types of negatives. Suppose that the difference between verbal and predicate negation has to do with whether negation has merged with a host. Notice that the element that always merges with negation is the verb in past tense sentences. As far as we know there are no dialects of Arabic where this is not the case. How can this be explained? Recall from chapter 2 that in past tense sentences in Arabic dialects the verb must move to tense. Now, if we generate sentential negation between TP and VP (7), the fact that in the past tense only the verbal negation form is allowed follows.

(7)

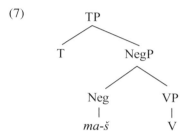

The verb must move to tense but because of minimality it cannot cross over the negative head. The only way to circumvent minimality is for the verb to move to negation, merge with it and then move to tense, as illustrated in (8).

(8)

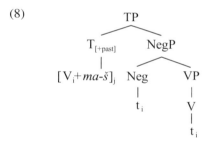

Let us turn now to the so-called predicate negation. Here the negative is independent in that it is not supported phonologically by another head. Elaborate data on both negatives is given in Brustad (2000). The contexts where this negative occurs in these sources are given below.[2]

(9)   Participles and Adjectives
    a. maši šarfa bəzzaf   *Moroccan Arabic*
       Neg old   a-lot
       'She isn't very old.'

---

[2] The predicate negative is used in the context of NP and PP predicates but that is expected.

b. ?aana muu maakil   šay Tuul   *Kuwaiti Arabic*
   I   Neg having-eaten thing throughout

   id-duhər
   the–afternoon
   'I haven't eaten anything all afternoon.'

(10)   Verbs: Imperfectives
        a. miš bar?uS   *Egyptian Arabic*
           Neg indic.I.dance
           'I don't dance.'

        b. il-waaħid byimši   šwayy šwayy, muu byiži   *Syrian Arabic*
           the-one   he-moves a-little a-little, Neg he.comes
           Darbe waħde
           blow   one

           'One moves a little at a time, [it] isn't [the case that] it happens all at
           once.'

(11)   Verbs: Perfectives
        a. miš gibti   badla?   *Egyptian Arabic*
           Neg got.you suit
           'Didn't you get a suit?'

        b. maši kunti   f d-daar?   *Moroccan Arabic*
           Neg were.you in the-house
           'Weren't you in the house?'

        c. muu xallaS?   *Syrian Arabic*
           Neg finished.he
           'Didn't he finish?'

With respect to (9) and (10), where the negative occurs in the context of adjectives,
participles and the imperfective verb, the syntactic analysis captures the facts. In
those sentences, the main predicate, be it an adjective, participle, or a verb, does
not need to raise to T, there is no need to merge with negation.[3] Optional merger
with negation may have to do with focus and scope (see Brustad 2000).[4]

---

[3] Brustad glosses (9b) as a past tense sentence. Actually, it would be more accurate to
     gloss it as a present perfect sentence. See Mughazy (2004) for an insightful analysis of
     the so-called present perfect in Egyptian Arabic.
[4] This situation obtains with a wide range of non-verbal predicates in Moroccan. In (i–v)
     we give a more exhaustive list of contexts where merger is optional.

(12)

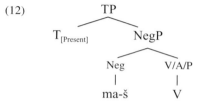

The potentially problematic cases are in (11), where predicate negation is used in the context of a past tense sentence. However, a closer look at the facts reveals that they are actually not problematic. Notice that in all dialects, the sentences in (11) are yes-no questions. While we cannot make judgments about the Egyptian and Syrian sentences, as far as the Moroccan sentence is concerned, it has the interpretation of *isn't it the case that you were in the house*, with the part of the statement *you were in the house* embedded within an interrogative sentence that consists of the negative only because expletive subjects are null in Arabic and so is the present tense. In addition, there is no verbal copula in the present tense, which basically leads to a sentence whose only overt element is the negative. Therefore, a more accurate analysis of, certainly (11b), and most probably (11a,c), is as in (13).

(i)   a. huwa ma-ši   Twil
        he   Neg-Neg tall
        'He is not tall.'

    b. huwa ma-Twil-š
        he   Neg-tall-Neg
        'He is not tall.'

(ii)   a. huwa ma-ši   fəllaḥ
        he   Neg-Neg farmer
        'He is not a farmer.'

    b. huwa ma-fəllaḥ-š
        he   Neg-farmer-Neg
        'He is not a farmer'.

(iii) a. huwa ma-ši   mʕa-ha
        he   Neg-Neg with-her
        'He is not with her.'

    b. huwa ma-mʕa-ha-š
        he   Neg-with-her-Neg
        'He is not with her.'

(iv) a. ma-ši   ʕənd-ii
        Neg-Neg at-me
        'I don't have [it].'

    b. ma-ʕənd-i-š
        Neg-at-me-Neg
        'I don't have [it].'

(13)

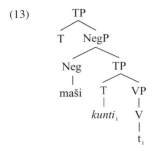

The past tense sentence is embedded within the matrix present tense negative sentence. Within the past tense sentence the verb must move to tense. The matrix negative sentence is a present tense sentence and since there is nothing that merges or that must merge with negation the independent form of negation (i.e. the predicate negation) is used.

This analysis immediately predicts that we should be able to get sentential negation in the embedded clauses, which in turn must merge with the verb since the sentence is in the past tense. This prediction is correct. Consider the example in (14):

(14)   maši ma-kunti-š   f   d-daar?   *Moroccan Arabic*
         Neg Neg-be.past.2sf-Neg in the-house
         'Isn't it the case that you were not in the house?'

By positing two sentences in (14), with a main clause and a subordinate clause, we accommodate two sentential negatives, one in the higher clause and one in the lower clause. The negative in the lower clause must merge with the verb because of the past tense of the sentence.

(15)

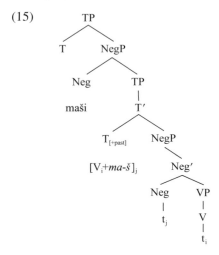

Moreover, since the embedded sentence is in the past tense (and not in the present tense as the matrix sentence), we predict the merger between the verb and negation. That is, we expect only verbal negation but not predicate negation, in the sense of Brustad. This prediction is also correct.

(16)   *maši maši kunti   f-d-dar?   *Moroccan Arabic*
        Neg   Neg be.past.2fs in-the-house

In short, it is safe to conclude that the distribution of the two negative forms can receive a syntactic analysis relying on the interaction between the tense, negation, and the predicate. The apparent problematic cases involving the use of the verbal negative in the context of the past tense can be explained after a careful analysis of the cases in question that reveals that they are complex sentences where the negative and the verb are located in independent clauses. Therefore, a simpler analysis would be to posit one single negative and spell it out as the so-called verbal negation when it merges with a head and a predicate negation when it does not merge with a head. Below we will show that the same analysis can be extended to Standard Arabic. However, before doing that we need to discuss one issue that arises if we consider the two surface negatives as the realization/spell-out of the same negative.

5.2.2   The status of the two negative morphemes ma and š

Recall that in some dialects, such as Egyptian and Moroccan, when negation merges with the predicate (be it verbal or nominal), *ma* is realized as enclitic and *š* as proclitic. The issue is to explain how the merged predicate ends up between the two elements of sentential negation. There are various possibilities but we will consider only two here. The first analysis that has been suggested is that *ma* is the head of negation and *š* is its specifier, as illustrated in (17).

(17)

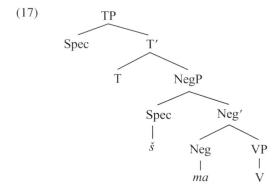

This analysis, which echoes similar analyses of Standard French where negation is realized by two elements that can sandwich the verb (Pollock 1989; Ouhalla 1990; Moritz and Valois 1994), derives the proclitic nature of *ma* by generating it in the head position and allowing the verb to merge with it. The enclitic nature of *š*, on the other hand, is derived simply by cliticizing it onto the complex verb+*ma* in T, as illustrated in (18).

(18)

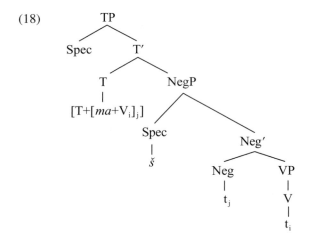

One major attractive feature of this analysis is that by generating both *ma* and *š* in NegP, the problem of the absence of a double negative reading that would have arisen if they were generated in different negative projections is avoided. There is no double negation because there is only negative projection. However, there are problems with the configuration in (17) and the analysis that is based on it.

First, notice that in the configuration in (17), the head of negation *ma* follows its specifier. Therefore, if nothing happens, i.e. if no head merges with *ma* and takes it higher, it is not clear how the two negatives are not spelled-out with *ma* as proclitic and *š* as enclitic. That is, it is not clear why we do not get the opposite order, whereby *š* precedes *ma*. Moreover, as shown above, not all predicates obligatorily merge with negation.

(19)   huwa maši hna
        he   Neg here
        'He is not here.'

In fact some of them, such as PPs and complex NP predicates, do not allow the extraction of the head and the stranding of the rest of the phrase (21), or the movement of the whole phrase to merge with *ma* (22) ((21–22) contrast with (20)).

(20)   a. hiya ma-ši   fə-l-mədrasa
           she Neg-Neg in-the-school
           'She is not at school.'

       b. hada ma-ši   ktab l-wəld
           this Neg-Neg book the-boy
           'This is not the boy's book.'

(21)   a. *hiya ma-f-ši   l-mədrasa
           she   Neg-in-Neg in-the-school

       b. *hada ma-ktab-ši   l-wəld
           this   Neg-book-Neg the-boy

(22)   a. *hiya ma-f-l-mədrasa-ši
           she   Neg-in the-school-Neg

       b. *hada ma-ktab   l-wəld-ši
           this   Neg-book the-boy-Neg

Of course, we can force the head of negation to move, probably in order to take scope over tense (as in Laka 1990). However, this solution would not extend to constituent negation, where clearly no movement of *ma* takes place to get the right order.

(23)   ma-ši   kull   wəld hna
        Neg-Neg every boy   here
        'Not every boy is here.'

In constituent negation, as in (23), the two negative particles occur in a fixed order with *ma* preceding *š(i)*.

Second, Watson (1993) provides examples where the negative *maaši* is used in negative answers to questions (p. 226) and in elliptical contexts (p. 121).

(24)   a. zawžiš   yi-safir al-yaman
           husband.your 3-travel the-Yemen
           'Will your husband go to Yemen?'

       b. maaši (maa y-saafur-š   al-yaman)
           no   Neg 3-travel-Neg the-Yemen
           'No, he will not go to Yemen.'

(25)   bih   naas   yi-šill-u   l-žild   u-naas   maaši
        there people 3-take-p off the-skin and-people no
        'There are people who take off the skin and some people who don't.'

The three contexts in (23–25) challenge the idea that *š* is in the specifier of a projection headed by *ma*.

Benmamoun (2000) provides an alternative account whereby both *ma* and *š* occupy the head position of negation, as illustrated in (26).

(26)

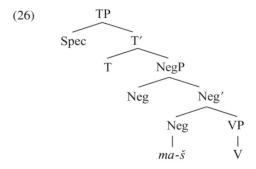

This analysis may not be elegant, but by treating both *ma* and *š* effectively as heads of NegP it allows for the variation we see in the realization of sentential negation across Arabic dialects, which is consistent with the historical evolution of sentential negation. As we mentioned above, in some dialects only *ma* is used while in other dialects both *ma* and *š* are used. Interestingly, there are other dialects that use *š* only. Abu-Haidar (1979:110) discusses this possibility in the Lebanese dialect of Baskinta (27a) and Palva (1972:42) reports the same phenomenon in a Jordanian dialect (27b):

(27)   a. bi-t-ḥib-š   šiʁl   il-bayt
           Asp-3f-likes-Neg work the-house
           'She does not like housework.'

        b. bədd-i-š
           want-my-Neg
           'I don't want.'

This shows that *š* can realize sentential negation on its own. Putting it in the head position of negation allows it to fulfill that function.

  ma is undoubtedly related to the Standard Arabic negative *maa* that we will discuss below. *š*, on the other hand, evolved from the word *šayʔ*, which means 'thing' (Ouhalla 2002).[5] Compared to *ma*, *š* seems to have evolved relatively lately to reinforce the negative *ma*, very much on a par with the situation in Romance

---

[5] While maintaining that -*š*(i) is probably generated in the Spec of the negative headed by *ma*, Ouhalla (2002), based on the distribution of this element in other contexts (mainly wh-phrases and existential quantifiers), argues for an insightful analysis whereby -*š(i)* is a variable.

(Zanuttini 1997). Therefore, it is reasonable to expect an element that has evolved to reinforce another element to be generated with it, i.e. in the same position, namely the head of NegP. We should point out that this is tentative and further investigation of the history of sentential negation in Arabic (and other grammatical markers) is critically needed.

5.2.3   A negative copula?

As pointed out above, negation seems to be able to merge with a nominative pronominal subject. As can be seen from the table in (28), the independent nominative pronoun is nearly completely identical to the pronoun incorporated into negation.

(28)   Moroccan Arabic

1	ʔana	ma-ni-ši
2ms	nta	ma-nta-š
2fs	nti	ma-nti-š
3ms	huwa	ma-huwa-š
3fs	hiya	ma-hiya-š
1p	ħna	ma-ħna-š
2p	ntuma	ma-ntuma-š
3p	huma	ma-huma-š

As is typical of such situations, at least two possibilities suggest themselves.[6] On the one hand, the incorporated pronoun could be treated as a realization of agreement features on negation that agrees with a subject, possibly null. On the other hand, the incorporated pronoun could be analyzed as a genuine pronominal subject generated in the canonical subject position, Spec of the projection where it gets its semantic role, and incorporated into negation by a syntactic or post-syntactic morphological process.

The proposal that the incorporated "pronoun" is a realization of agreement is not far-fetched because there are instances where negation clearly agrees with a subject. We saw one case above from a Gulf dialect. Standard Arabic offers a more dramatic example where the negative *laysa* displays the full array of subject agreement features displayed by verbs.

---

[6] The same issue arises in the context of accusative and genitive clitics, and, for some, even subject agreement, in Arabic. The issue is whether the clitics, and subject agreement, are incorporated pronouns generated in argument position or genuine agreement affixes (licensing a null pronoun under analyses that posit such an element).

(29)   las-naa fii l-bayt-i
        Neg-1p in the-house-Gen
        'We are not in the house.'

However, there are reasons not to accept the agreement account and opt rather
for the incorporation account. First, unlike genuine cases of subject agreement in
Moroccan Arabic, where a verb can fully agree with a postverbal subject (30),[7]
in the case of negation, a post-negative subject is not allowed. In other words, the
negative-plus-pronoun complex is in complementary distribution with a lexical
subject (31).[8]

(30)   qra-w   lə-wlad
        studied-3p the-children
        'The children studied.'

(31)   *ma-huwa-š l-wəld   f-d-dar
        Neg-he-Neg the-child in-the-house

The ungrammaticality of (31) follows under the incorporation account since the
pronoun would compete with the lexical subject for the subject position.

    Second, if this were a case of agreement we would expect it to be able to
co-occur with a verb, such as the past tense verb, but this prediction is not borne
out.

(32)   *ma-huwa-š qra
        Neg-he-Neg read.3ms

The negative-plus-pronoun variant seems to be found mostly in copular constructions. Since Arabic dialects allow the subject to agree with more than one head
(such as an auxiliary or aspectual verb and the main verb), it is not clear why the
negative that agrees with the subject should be restricted only to copular constructions. While it would require some additional assumptions to preempt movement
of the pronominal subject in the context of a verbal predicate, in the context of past
tense sentences this follows easily from the need of the verb to move to T. If the
subject moves to Neg, the verb would then need to cross over negation, in violation
of minimality. With respect to imperfective verbs the situation is somewhat more
complicated. In Moroccan Arabic, we saw in chapter 2 that the verb obligatorily
merges with negation. It would be interesting to see what the situation is like in
dialects where the imperfective verb does not need to merge with negation. All

---

[7] See chapter 4 for a detailed discussion of subject–verb agreement.
[8] (31) seems to improve with a pause between negation and the lexical "subject," in which
     case the latter could be treated as an appositive.

else being equal, both options should exist, i.e. either the verb or the pronoun could merge with negation.

Therefore, we can maintain the assumption that there is only one negative element that can be realized in different forms depending on merger with the verb and the subject or no merger at all.

There is a potentially more difficult challenge for the incorporation account. In some dialects, the incorporated pronoun is in the Accusative Case rather than Nominative. This is attested in Hassaniya (Iaach 1996:168) and in Lebanese Arabic.

(33)   maani   my+Neg   *Hassaniyya Arabic*
        maanaak your.s+Neg
        maahu   his+Neg
        maahi   her+Neg
        manna   our+Neg
        mankum   your.p+Neg
        maahum   their+Neg

(34)   manne   I+Neg   *Lebanese Arabic*
        mannak   you.s+Neg
        manno   he+Neg
        manna   she+Neg
        manna   we+Neg
        mannkun you.p+Neg
        mannun   they+Neg

As far as Lebanese Arabic is concerned, recall that the complementizer also assigns Accusative Case to the embedded "subject," as evidenced by the fact that the subject is realized as an accusative clitic on the complementizer (see chapter 2). Therefore, it is not far-fetched to assume that negation can also assign Accusative Case to the subject that merges with it. We have already seen a case of the negative *laysa* assigning Accusative Case to the predicate.

Moreover, in Moroccan Arabic the negative ʕammər 'never' assigns Genitive or Accusative Case to the embedded subject:

(35)   a. ʕammər-i ma-tlaqit-u
           never-my Neg-met.1s-him
           'I never met him.'

        b. ʕammər-ni ma-tlaqit-u
           never-me Neg-met.1s-him
           'I never met him.'

Therefore, it is plausible that the negative assigns Accusative Case to the pronominal subject that merges with it in Lebanese Arabic, in which case the incorporation account can be maintained.

5.3   Sentential negation in Standard Arabic

Standard Arabic has at least five distinct negative particles (Moutaouakil 1993). The negative particle *laa* occurs in sentences with verbal predicates with present tense interpretation (36).

(36)   a. T-Tullaab-u   ya-drus-uu-n
            the-students   3-study-mp-ind
            'The students study.'

        b. T-Tullab-u   laa   ya-drus–uu-n
            the-students Neg 3-study-mp-ind
            'The students do not study.'

The tensed variants of *laa* are *lam* and *lan*. The former, *lam*, occurs in past tense sentences (37) and the latter, *lan*, is used in future tense sentences (38). Notice that in the non-negative form the verb is in the perfective form in the past tense.

(37)   a. T-Tullaab-u   lam   ya-drus-uu
            the-students-Nom Neg.past 3-study-mp
            'The students did not study.'

        b. T-Tullaab-u   daras-uu
            the-students-Nom study.past-3mp
            'The students studied.'

(38)   a. T-Tullabu   lan   ya-drus-uu
            the-students Neg.fut 3-study-mp
            'The students will not study.'

        b. T-Tullabu   sa-ya-drus-uun
            the-students fut-3-study-mp
            'The students will study.'

In addition to these three negative particles, Standard Arabic has another variant of *laa*, *laysa*, that occurs in the context of non-verbal predicates (39a–c) and also in present tense sentences containing verbal predicates (39d) (Moutaouakil 1993:85–86; Fassi Fehri 1993:173).[9]

---

[9] (39d) is from Moutaouakil (1993:85).

(39) a. lays-at   muʕallimat-an
         Neg-3fs teacher-Acc
         'She is not a teacher.'

      b. las-ta   mariiD-an
         Neg-2ms ill-Acc
         'You are not ill.'

      c. las-naa   fii l-bayt-i
         Neg-1pl in the-house-Gen
         'We are not in the house.'

      d. laysa   xaalid-un   ya-ktubu š-šiʕr-a
         Neg.3ms Khalid-Nom 3-write   the-poetry-Acc
         'Khalid does not write poetry.'

laysa is also notable for the fact that it carries subject agreement and assigns Accusative Case to the predicate, as is clear from the examples in (39a,b). In (39a), for example, the negative carries third person feminine agreement and assigns Accusative Case to the predicate adjective.

The fifth negative is *maa*, which is undoubtedly related to the negative that occurs in the modern Arabic dialects. This negative occurs in a variety of contexts, as illustrated by the following examples from Moutaouakil (1993:80–81):

(40) a. maa saafarat   hindun
         Neg traveled.past.3fs Hind
         'Hind did not travel/go on a trip.'

      b. maa yu-saafiru ʕamrun ʔilla   fii S-Sayfi
         Neg 3-travel   Amr   except in the-summer
         'Amr travels only during the summer.'

      c. maa muħammadun kaatibun
         Neg Mohammad   writer
         'Mohammad is not a writer.'

      d. maa hindun ħaziinatun
         Neg Hind   sad
         'Hind is not sad.'

      e. maa xaalidun fii l-bayti
         Neg Khalid   in the-house'
         'Khalid is not in the house.'

In (40a) *maa* negates a past tense sentence. In (40b) it negates an habitual present tense sentence. In (40c–e) it negates a verbless sentence with a nominal, adjectival, and PP predicate respectively.

To sum up, there are five different negatives in Modern Standard Arabic, a situation that appears to differ radically from the one that obtains in the modern dialects. In the latter, there are at most three surface realizations of sentential negation (if we include the negative that incorporates the subject pronouns). However, we suggested above that it might be possible to posit one single negative form and syntactically derive the distribution of the three surface forms. Can the same approach be used to analyze negation in Standard Arabic, which displays even more surface forms than the modern dialects?

5.3.1   laa *and its tensed variants*

Let us start with *laa* and its tensed variants *lam* and *lan*. *laa* occurs in the present tense and we showed in chapter 2 that the present tense is not morpho-phonologically realized in all Arabic dialects. Since *laa* occurs in the present tense it is the only one among the trio of *laa*, *lam*, and *lan* that does not carry tense. This assumption has ample support but we will just list three contexts. First, unlike the truly tensed negatives *lam* and *lan*, *laa* is used as a constituent negative, as illustrated by (41) from Moutaouakil (1993:86).

(41)   laa   ražula fii d-dari
          Neg man   in the-house
          'No man is in the house.'

Second, it is the only negative used to negate imperative sentences (42), which are not tensed (Ouhalla 1993).

(42)   laa   ta-bkii
          Neg 2-cry
          'Do not cry.'

Third, it is the only negative that is used as the particle for denial in discourse (43).

(43)   laa, lam   ?a-ktub
          no, Neg.past 1s-write
          'No, I didn't write.' [as an answer to a question]

Turning to the tensed variants of *laa*, namely *lam* and *lan*, the analysis is rather straightforward. Suppose that *laa* heads a negation between TP and VP, as argued in Benmamoun (1992a, 2000) and Ouhalla (1993), as illustrated in (44).

(44)

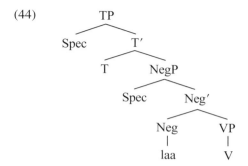

Since past tense and future tense features are located in T, the closest head to T is the negative. The negative is able to support tense in Standard Arabic, which in turn obviates the need for verb movement. If T contains past tense features, the negative is spelled-out as *lam*. On the other hand, if tense contains future tense features it is spelled-out as *lan*. If negation stays in situ and does not merge with any functional element, it is spelled-out as the default tenseless negative *laa*.

Notice that given minimality the verb cannot move to tense across the negative head to yield the ungrammatical forms in (45).

(45)   a. *T-Tullaab-u   daras-uu   laa
            the-students-Nom study.past-3mp Neg

        b. *T-Tullaab-u   sa-ya-drus-uu-n   laa
            the-students-Nom fut-3-study-mp-ind Neg

The sentences in (45) are ungrammatical because they violate minimality, as illustrated in (46).

(46)

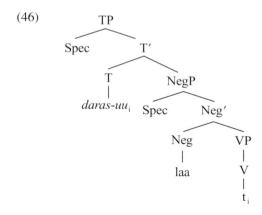

In this respect, the main difference between Standard Arabic and the modern dialects has to do with whether negation can carry tense. In Standard Arabic this possibility is available, resulting in different surface realizations of negation but the same verb form, namely the imperfective form. On the other hand, in the modern dialects negation is not a possible host for tense, which in turn forces verb movement through negation in the contexts of the tense that forces such movement, namely the past tense.[10]

5.3.2   laysa

Let us now turn to *laysa*. This negative has traditionally been analyzed as a verb. The main reason is because it carries the same subject agreement inflection as verbs. In (47) the full agreement paradigm of *laysa* is given.[11]

(47)   Agreement Paradigm of *laysa*

Person	Number	Gender	Affix	Neg+Affix
1	Singular	F/M	-tu	las-tu
2	S	M	-ta	las-ta
2	S	F	-ti	las-ti
3	S	M	-a	lays-a
3	S	F	-at	lays-at
2	Dual	M/F	-tumaa	las-tumaa
3	D	M	-aa	lays-aa
3	D	F	-ataa	lays-ataa
1	Plural	M/F	-naa	las-naa
2	P	M	-tum	las-tum
2	P	F	-tunna	las-tunna
3	P	M	-uu	lays-uu
3	P	F	-na	las-na

The agreement paradigm on *laysa* is the paradigm that is usually found on perfective verbs, which are mainly restricted to the past tense.[12] However, this by

---

[10] Recall, however, that the verb must be adjacent to the tensed negative, which suggests that morphological support is not the only motivation for the dependency between tense and the verb. See chapter 2 for a brief discussion and Benmamoun (2000) for a more detailed exploration of the dependency between these two elements.

[11] Ouhalla (1993:278) suggests that *laysa* is composed of three elements: the negative *laa*, a verbal copula *s*, and agreement.

[12] The perfective form is also found in conditionals; see Wright (1889) and Wise (1975).

itself does not settle the issue of the categorical status of *laysa* since it is very plausible that diachronically the reason that agreement morphology is exclusively suffixal is because in the present tense where tense does not need a verb, the subject may remain lower, opening up the option of a pronominal subject clitic encliticizing onto the negative.[13] Thus, the derivation of the suffixal agreement morphology on *laysa* in (48) could be represented as in (49).

(48)   las-naa fii l-bayti
           Neg-1p in the-house
           'We are not in the house.'

(49)

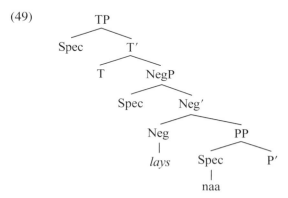

That the suffix can follow the negative *laysa* is attested synchronically, as is evident from the sentence in (50) from Moutaouakil (1993:85).

(50)   laysa xaalid-un   ya-ktubu š-šiʕr-a
           Neg.3s Khalid-Nom 3-write   the-poetry-Acc
           'Khalid does not write poetry.'

Therefore, the agreement on *laysa* may be just a historical relic of a cliticization process. This should not be surprising since the negative *laa* can carry tense, and also the modern Arabic dialects negative can incorporate subjects as discussed above.

    The main problem with the analysis that *laysa* is a verb is the fact that present tense sentences with non-verbal predicates do not have VPs, presumably because the present tense does not need to interact with a verb, as was discussed in chapter 2. Thus, if we were to posit a VP in the context of *laysa*, that would be the

---

[13] The other option is that the negative moves higher than the subject, which in turn yields an encliticization configuration.

only context where there is a VP in copular constructions.[14] The most reasonable assumption would be not to treat *laysa* as a verb but rather just as a variant of *laa* that is peculiar in that it can carry agreement.[15]

To sum up the discussion so far, we have discussed the distribution of *laa*, *lam*, *lan*, and *laysa*. We have explored the possibility that they are all realizations of a negative generated in a negative projection located between TP and VP. The two tensed negatives, *lam* and *lan*, carry tense because they move to T, preempting the movement of the verb in the process. *laa* and *laysa* do not carry tense, but the latter is a variant of *laa* that can carry agreement. *laa* is the simplest default negative that carries neither tense nor agreement. This leaves us with the negative *maa*, which is clearly different from *laa* and its variants, at least phonologically. The question is whether the differences go deeper in that they involve the semantics and syntax of the negative *maa*. We take up this issue in the next section.

5.3.3   *The negative* maa

As pointed out above, *maa* can occur in the context of both past (51a) and present tense sentences with verbal predicates (51b).

(51)   a. maa saafarat   hindun
           Neg traveled.past.3fs Hind
           'Hind did not travel/go on a trip.'

        b. maa yu-saafiru ʕamrun ʔilla   fii S-Sayfi
           Neg 3-travel   Amr   except in the-summer
           'Amr travels only during the summer.'

In addition, *maa* can negate the subject (52a–c).

(52)   a. maa muħammad-un   kaatib-un
           Neg Mohammad-Nom writer-Nom
           'Mohammad is not a writer.'

---

[14] A verbal copula can occur in generic present tense sentences. Benmamoun (2000) argues that there is a modal in those contexts that requires a verbal element.

[15] The reason why the other variants of *laa*, namely *lam* and *lan*, do not carry agreement is maybe because they need to be adjacent to the verb, which already carries agreement. A restriction not to realize agreement twice on a morphological complex may be at play. See Benmamoun (2000) for a discussion of such an analysis.

b. maa hind-un   ħaziinat-un
   Neg Hind-Nom sad-Nom
   'Hind is not sad.'

c. maa xaalid-un   fii l-bayt-i
   Neg Khalid-Nom in the-house-Gen
   'Khalid is not in the house.'

Equally crucial is the fact that *maa* can negate a preposed object NP (53a) and a preposed instrumental PP (53b), as illustrated by the examples in (53) from Moutaouakil (1993:81).

(53)   a. maa bakr-an   žaraħa   xaalid-un   bi-s-sikkin-i
           Neg Bakr-Acc wounded.3ms Khalid-Nom with-the-knife-Gen
           'It is not Bakr that Khalid wounded with the knife.'

        b. maa bi-s-sikkin-i   žaraħa   xaalid-un   bakr-an
           Neg with-the-knife-Gen wounded.3ms Khalid-Nom Bakr-Acc
           'It is not with the knife that Khalid wounded Bakr.'

To account for the facts that *maa* occurs in both present and past tense sentences without blocking verb movement to T in the latter, and that it can attach to the subject, Benmamoun (2000) proposed that while *maa* patterns with *laa* in being located in a negative projection between TP and the predicate, it occupies the specifier position of negation rather than the head. The configuration proposed by Benmamoun (2000:108) and the analysis of (52a) are given in (54) and (55) respectively.

(54)

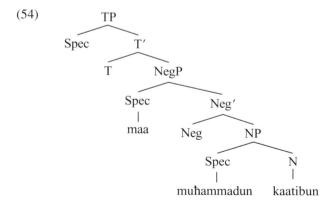

(55)

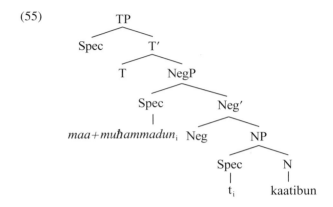

The main idea is that the subject moves through [Spec, NegP], where it picks up the negative *maa*.

This analysis maintains that negation has one fixed position in the Arabic clause. The differences between the negatives are then reduced to their structural position and their ability or inability to host inflection, such as agreement and tense.

However, this analysis does not actually account for all the facts listed above. To allow the negative to occur on the verb in the past tense, we must have the latter move from the head position of VP to the Spec of NegP and then to the head position of T, a pattern of movement that is theoretically problematic (it violates structure preservation) and is not independently motivated.

Ouhalla (1993) advances an alternative analysis that captures all the syntactic properties of *maa* mentioned above. Ouhalla starts off with the observation that *maa* not only negates the constituent it takes scope over but also contrastively focuses it (see also Moutaouakil 1993). Thus, the interpretation of (53a) is that it is not *Bakr* who was wounded with the knife but someone else. Similarly, in (53b) the interpretation is that it is not the knife that was the instrument of wounding but some other instrument. The examples in (53) illustrate cases of contrastive focus that impact one constituent, the object NP and instrumental PP respectively. Negative contrastive focus can also impact a whole proposition. As Ouhalla puts it, "negative contrastive focus is used to assert the falsity of a given prevailing piece of information, which can be encoded in a whole proposition (sentence) . . . or in just a constituent of the sentence."

Ouhalla advances more arguments to show that *maa* patterns with affirmative focus elements that occupy the left periphery of the clause in Standard Arabic. In particular, he draws a parallelism between *maa* and the focus/emphasis particles

ʔinna and *qad* that can also focus the whole proposition, as in (56), or a constituent, as in (57).[16,17]

(56)   a. ʔinna zaynab-a   laa   tu-ʔallifu   šiʕr-an
            FM   Zaynab-Acc Neg 3f-write   poetry-Acc
            '(I assert that) Zaynab (indeed) does not write poetry.'

       b. qad waSala   zayd-un
            FM   arrived.past.3ms Zayd-Nom
            '(I assert that) Zayd has arrived.'

(57)   ʔinna zaynab-a   (LA-) ŠAAʕIRAT-UN (laa riwaaʔiyyat-un)
        FM   Zaynab-Acc FM   poet-Nom   not novelist-Nom
        'Zaynab is a POET (not a novelist).'

Based on these facts, among others, Ouhalla argues that unlike *laa* and its variants, which head a negative projection between TP/IP and the predicate, *maa* occupies the head position of a focus projection located above TP/IP. The representation that Ouhalla (1993:288) suggests is given in (58).

(58)

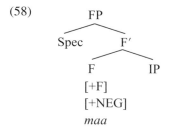

From its position in the head F of FP, *maa* can enter into dependency relations with elements that undergo negative contrastive focus. The relation can obtain at a distance and does not have to involve the displacement, which is the case with negative contrastive focus that impacts the whole proposition or a constituent within the sentence, as in (59), which Ouhalla uses to illustrate constituent focus at a distance.

(59)   maa ʔanaa ŠAAʕIR-UN (bal rasuul-un) . . .
         Neg   I   poet-Nom   (but messenger-Nom)
         'It is not a poet that I am (but a messenger . . .)'

---

[16] Note that the focus particle takes scope over the constituent at a distance. See Ouhalla for an analysis of how the dependencies between focus markers and the elements that are focused are captured.

[17] FM stands for focus marker. Ouhalla (1993:279) uses capitals to indicate focus.

With respect to cases where the constituent that is contrastively focused (52–53) is fronted and attaches to *maa*, Ouhalla suggests that in this situation FP is not overtly filled. Rather, the negative *maa* is generated within the phrase headed by the focused constituent inside the clause and the whole phrase moves to the Spec of FP.

(60)

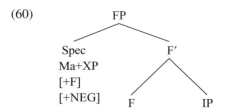

Ouhalla successfully captures the similarities between *maa* and focus markers. His analysis also avoids the problem of why *maa* does not block verb movement. Under his analysis, this simply follows from the fact that *maa* is not in the path of verb movement to tense, since it is either generated in a higher head, FP, or within a phrase. In fact, under Ouhalla's account, *maa* does not head a negative projection but only provides/spells-out the negative feature of the focus head.

5.4   Person agreement and positive imperatives versus negative imperatives

In all Arabic dialects, there is a major difference between negative imperatives and positive imperatives. The difference has to do with person agreement. In positive imperatives, person agreement is not realized while in negative imperatives it must be realized, as illustrated by the paradigms in (61a), (61b), and (61c) from Standard Arabic, Lebanese Arabic, and Moroccan Arabic respectively.

(61)   **Agreement on Imperative Verbs**
    a. Standard Arabic
       Positive Imperatives[18]

žlis	žlis-ii	žlis-aa	žlis-uu	žlis-na
sit.ms	sit-fs	sit.d	sit-mp	sit-fp
'Sit.'	'Sit.'	'Sit.'	'Sit.'	'Sit.'

---

[18] Note that Standard Arabic does not allow initial consonant clusters. When such a situation arises a glottal stop and a vowel are inserted. See Brame (1970).

*ta-žlis	*ta-žlis-ii	*ta-žlis-aa	*ta-žlis-uu	*ta-žlis-na
2-sit.ms	2-sit-fs	2-sit-d	2-sit-mp	2-sit-fp

Negative Imperatives

laa ta-žlis	laa ta-žlis-ii	laa ta-žlis-aa
Neg 2-sit.ms	Neg 2-sit-fs	Neg 2-sit-d
'Do not sit.'	'Do not sit.'	'Do not sit.'

laa ta-žlis-uu	laa ta-žlis-na
Neg 2-sit-mp	Neg 2-sit-fp
'Do not sit.'	'Do not sit.'

*laa žlis	*laa žlis-ii	*laa žlis-aa
Neg sit.ms	Neg sit-fs	Neg sit-d

*laa žlis-uu	laa žlis-na
Neg sit-mp	Neg sit-fp

b. Lebanese Arabic

Positive Imperatives

ktob	ktəb-e	ktəb-o
write.ms	write-fs	write-p
'Write.'	'Write.'	'Write.'
*tə-ktob	*tə-kətb-e	*tə-kətb-o
2-write.ms	2-write-fs	2-write-p

Negative Imperatives

ma-tə-ktob	ma-tə-kətb-e	ma-tə-kətb-o
Neg-2-write.ms	Neg-2-write-fs	Neg-2-write-p
'Do not write.'	'Do not write.'	'Do not write.'
*ma-ktob	*ma-ktəb-e	*ma-ktəb-o
Neg-write.ms	Neg-write-fs	Neg-write-p

c. Moroccan Arabic

Positive Imperatives

gləs	gəls-i	gəls-u
sit.ms	sit-fs	sit-p
'Sit.'	'Sit.'	'Sit.'
*tə-gləs	*t-gəls-i	*t-gəls-u
2-sit.ms	2-sit-fs	2-sit-p

Negative Imperatives

ma-tə-gləs-š	ma-t-gəls-i-š	ma-t-gəls-u-š
Neg-2-sit.ms-Neg	Neg-2-sit-fs-Neg	Neg-2-sit-p-Neg
'Do not sit.'	'Do not sit.'	'Do not sit.'
*ma-gləs-š	*ma-gəls-i-š	*ma-gəls-u-š
Neg-sit.ms-Neg	Neg-sit-fs-Neg	Neg-sit-p-Neg

In Standard Arabic, which marks mood morphologically, both positive and negative imperatives belong to the jussive paradigm. The jussive paradigm is characterized by the absence of the vowel and nasal ending that is found in indicative forms (Wright 1889).[19]

The only distinction between positive and negative imperatives seems to be in person agreement. The question then is: why is person obligatorily absent in positive imperatives and obligatorily present in negative imperatives? There are no clear answers to this question, which hasn't been dealt with extensively in the literature. For Benmamoun (2000), the reason for the difference is that negation has a nominal feature that needs to be paired with a nominal element. Since there is no nominal element in imperative sentences (there being no subject), person agreement, which is nominal in nature, is inserted to satisfy the nominal requirement of negation. Another possible analysis that could be promising is that on a par with other languages where different verbal paradigms are used in negative imperatives, the difference could be to do with some requirement of negation, for example, that it be licensed by a temporal head, which in turn comes with its complete set of agreement features. Clearly, this is an area that requires further exploration and where comparative research can be particularly valuable.

Finally, another notable fact about imperatives is that they require the negative *laa* in Standard Arabic (62) and merger with negation in the Modern dialects, as illustrated in the Moroccan Arabic sentences in (63).[20]

(62)   a. laa   ta-žlis-uu
           Neg 2-sit-mp
           'Do not sit.'

        b. *maa   ta-žlis-uu
           Neg   2-sit-mp

        c. *laysa ta-žlis-uu
           Neg   2-sit-mp

(63)   a. ma-t-gəls-u-š
           Neg-2-sit-p-Neg
           'Do not sit.'

        b. *ma-ši   t-gəls-u
           Neg-Neg 2-sit-p

---

[19] See Fassi Fehri (1993), Ouhalla (1993), and Benmamoun (2000) for a discussion of mood in Arabic.

[20] Some dialects of the Gulf area use *laa* in imperatives.

Those facts follow if there is a projection higher than negation to which the verb must move.[21]

5.5   Negative polarity items in Moroccan Arabic

Moroccan Arabic NPIs present a mixed picture. One class of NPIs cannot precede sentential negation, as shown by the ungrammaticality of (64d).[22]

(64)   a. ma-ža   ħədd
           Neg-came.3ms one
           'No one came.'

        b. ma-šəft   ħədd
           Neg-saw.1s one
           'I didn't see anyone.'

        c. ma-tlaqit   ħədd
           Neg-met.1s one
           'I didn't meet with anyone.'

        d. *ħədd ma-ža
           one   Neg-came.3ms

The NPI *ħədd* seems to require the negative licenser to c-command it.

However, another class of NPIs can precede the sentential negative. We can distinguish two major types of such NPIs. Nominal NPIs and what we will refer to as head NPIs, following Benmamoun (2006). Let us start with nominal NPIs. Consider the sentences in (65).

(65)   a. ma-qrit   ħətta ktab
           Neg-read.1s even book
           'I didn't read any book.'

        b. ma-ža   ħətta waħəd
           Neg-came.3ms even one
           'No one came.'

        c. ħətta waħəd ma-ža
           even one   Neg-came.3ms
           'No one came.'

---

[21] Benmamoun (2000) posits a projection headed by an imperative feature, following various analyses that have proposed similar projections for other languages.

[22] Moroccan Arabic NPIs are in complementary distribution with *š*. This is not the case in all dialects (see Benmamoun 1997, 2000). See Ouhalla (2002) for a possible analysis.

The NPI containing *ħətta* can both follow (65a,b) and precede (65d) sentential negation. Benmamoun (1997) takes such cases as evidence that the Spec-Head configuration whereby the NPI in the specifier of a projection containing the negative licenser should also be added to c-command as a licensing configuration. One strong argument for Spec-Head configuration as another licensing structure comes from left dislocated NPIs binding resumptive pronouns (Benmamoun 1997:281):

(66)   a. ħətta ktab ma-qrat-u   səlwa
            even book Neg-read-it Salwa
            'Salwa didn't read any book.'

         b. *ħətta ktab səlwa ma-qrat-u
            even   book Salwa Neg-read-it
            *'Any book, Salwa did not read it.'

If it turns out that in Moroccan Arabic left dislocated elements are not derived by movement but rather base-generated in their surface position, then the Spec-Head configuration is the only way to license the NPI in (66a). Notice that if the subject intervenes between the NPI and the negative licenser the sentence becomes ill-formed (66b). However, allowing the Spec-Head configuration as a licensing option raises the question of why the same configuration is not available to the Moroccan Arabic NPI in (64d).

This problem is taken up in Benmamoun (1996) where, building on the well-known generalization that Arabic dialects do not allow non-specific indefinites in the preverbal subject position (see chapter 3), he argues that the reason the NPI containing *ħətta* can occur in the preverbal negative position is because *ħətta* is a focus and presupposition particle. This usage of *ħətta* is illustrated in (67).

(67)   a. ħətta nadia žat
            even Nadia came.3fs
            'Even Nadia came.'

         b. ħətta nadia tlaqit-ha   lbarəħ
            even Nadia, met.1s-her yesterday
            'Even Nadia, I met her yesterday.'

The main idea then is that the NPI containing *ħətta* can occur in the preverbal pre-negative position thanks to the focus particle it contains. The focus particle allows it to be fronted to left peripheral positions where focused elements can occur (Ouhalla 1997).

In short, the distribution of Moroccan Arabic NPIs reduces to their lexical properties. In Moroccan Arabic, one type of NPI contains a focus particle which allows it to occur in positions not usually reserved for the other type, namely the NPI *ħədd*.

We turn now to the other class of Moroccan Arabic NPIs that have a different distribution from nominal NPIs. Consider the sentences in (68).

(68)   a. nadia ʕəmmər-ha ma-žat
            Nadia never-her   Neg-came
            'Nadia never came.'

        b. ʕomar baqi ma-ža
            Omar yet Neg-came
            'Omar hasn't come yet.'

The NPIs in (68) are clearly not in Spec-Head configuration with negation nor are they in its c-command domain. They are not in Spec-Head relation because they are heads displaying all properties of heads, such as the ability to agree (69a) and to host clitics (69b).

(69)   a. nadia baq-a ma-žat
            Nadia yet.fs Neg-came.3fs
            'Nadia hasn't come yet.'

        b. nadia ʕəmmər-ha ma-žat
            Nadia never-her   Neg-came
            'Nadia never came.'

Benmamoun (2006) capitalizes on the head status of the NPIs in (69) to argue that because the NPIs are heads they can be licensed by virtue of the fact that they merge with their complement, which contains the negative clause. Therefore, the only licensing condition they are subject to is c-command. Admittedly, this is highly tentative and would require a more exhaustive analysis of NPIs in Arabic dialects and their distribution.

5.6   Conclusion

In this chapter, we discussed the syntax of sentential negation in the spoken Arabic dialects and Standard Arabic. The main difference between the two main varieties relates to the fact that Standard Arabic has two negative markers, namely *lam* and *lan*, which occur in the context of past and future tenses respectively. We showed that positing a negative projection between TP and VP accounts for this fact. The verb cannot raise to tense across negation because of minimality.

Negation, in turn, can host tense in Standard Arabic while it cannot do so in the spoken dialects. In those dialects the same negative is used regardless of tense. However, the negative in question merges with the verb, which circumvents relativized minimality. By contrast, in the so-called verbless sentences the negative heads in the two main varieties of Arabic display similar syntactic distributions. We also discussed the distribution of negative sensitive items such as negative polarity items and negative quantifiers in Moroccan Arabic. These elements consist of two types, phrases and heads. The phrases, in turn, can be divided into one class that is restricted to the post-negative position and another class that freely occurs in the pre- and post-negative positions. The analysis we discussed requires both Spec-Head and c-command as configurational restrictions on the distribution of these elements. C-command seems to be also a condition on the licensing of head NPIs. The status of the latter elements is a topic that requires further investigation.

6

Modes of wh-interrogation

6.1   Introduction

One of the defining features of human language is displacement (from the "here" and "now"). In syntax, displacement is observed when some elements of sentence structure appear in positions different from those where they are interpreted. Typically, this is the case of wh-phrases in questions. One important goal of syntactic analysis is to adequately capture and explain long-distance dependencies between elements displaced to the periphery, e.g. wh-phrases, and the position within the sentence to which they are related, and which can be occupied either by a gap or by a pronominal resumptive element. An active area of research within this domain is the variation between the resumption strategy and the gap strategy.[1] Some of the questions that are raised in that regard are the following:

(1)   a. Are the grammars of the languages that use resumption instead of the more conventional gap strategy different? How so?
       b. What is the nature of the resumptive element?
       c. Is the resumption strategy a uniform strategy having the same properties cross-linguistically?
       d. Is the relation between a displaced element and its corresponding resumptive similar to the relation between a displaced element and its corresponding gap?

The various Arabic dialects provide a good empirical base for tackling these questions. The resumption strategy is used productively in those dialects alongside the gap strategy, allowing one to study the difference between these strategies within the same given language, as well as across the various Arabic dialects.

---

[1] For references within the study of Semitic languages, see Fassi Fehri (1982), Wahba (1984), Demirdache (1991), Aoun and Benmamoun (1998), Shlonsky (2002), Aoun and Choueiri (1996, 1999, 2000), Aoun and Li (2003), Sells (1984), and Aoun, Choueiri, and Hornstein (2001), among others.

In this chapter, we analyze and discuss the different strategies available in Arabic for forming wh-interrogatives. Because several strategies are available within a given dialect, we are able to examine the syntactic and interpretive differences between them. This will lead to the conclusion that chains involving gaps are different from resumptive chains, that is, the relation between a fronted wh-phrase and its corresponding gap is different in several respects from the relation between a fronted wh-phrase and its corresponding resumptive element. The chapter starts with a brief overview of wh-words and wh-interrogative forming strategies in Arabic and then goes on to discuss the gap strategy in comparison with the resumptive strategy. We then turn to two other strategies available in Arabic for forming questions and discuss their similarities and differences with the gap and resumptive strategies. To conclude, we provide the new generalizations that the study of Arabic wh-questions contributes to the study of wh-question formation and long-distance dependencies in general.

6.2   Wh-words and wh-interrogatives in Arabic

Four strategies are available to form wh-interrogatives in Arabic: three of them involve a fronted wh-constituent and the fourth is an in-situ strategy. The sentences in (2), from Lebanese Arabic, illustrate these four strategies.

(2)   a. ʔayya mmasil šəft   Ø b-l-maTʕam?   *Gap Strategy*
          which actor   saw.2ms   in-the-restaurant
          'Which actor did you see in the restaurant?'

       b. ʔayya mmasil šəft-o   b-l-maTʕam?   *Resumptive Strategy*
          which actor   saw.2ms-him in-the-restaurant
          'Which actor did you see in the restaurant?'

       c. miin (ya)lli šəft-o   b-l-maTʕam?   *Class II Resumptive*
          who that   saw.2ms-him in-the-restaurant   *Strategy*
          'Who is it that you saw in the restaurant?'

       d. šəft   ʔayya mmasil b-l-maTʕam?   *In-situ Strategy*
          saw.2ms which actor   in-the-restaurant
          'Which actor did you see in the restaurant?'

In (2a), the wh-constituent appears on the left edge of a clause and is related to a gap in the variable position, the sentence internal position of the wh-constituent (the gap strategy). In (2b), the wh-constituent appearing on the left edge of the clause is related to a resumptive pronominal element in the sentence internal position corresponding to the wh-constituent (the resumptive strategy). Example (2c) is a variation on the resumptive strategy whereby the clause initial wh-constituent, which is related to a resumptive pronominal element in the sentence internal position corresponding to the wh-constituent, immediately precedes the (definite) relative clause complementizer *(ya)lli* 'that' (Class II resumptive strategy). Finally, in (2d), the wh-constituent appears in a sentence internal position, which corresponds to the variable position in (2a).

On the other hand, wh-words in Arabic can be divided into two classes: nominal wh-words and adverbial wh-words.[2] The following tables list the wh-words in use in three different Arabic dialects.

(3)   *Wh*-words in Lebanese Arabic

Nominal		**Adverbial**	
a. miin	'who'	e. ween	'where'
b. šu	'what'	f. ʔeemta	'when'
c. ʔayya	'which'	g. kiif	'how'
d. kam	'how many'	h. lee(š)/lašu	'why'
		i. ʔaddee(š)	'how much'

---

[2] Wahba (1984) categorizes the various wh-words in Egyptian Arabic into two groups: nominal wh-words (i) and non-nominal wh-words (ii). Her classification can easily carry over to all wh-words in Arabic.

(i)   Nominal wh-phrases: *miin* 'who,' *ʔeh* 'what,' *ʔanhi NP* 'which NP'

(ii)   Non-nominal wh-phrases: a. Prepositional phrases: *maʕa miin* 'with whom,' *min ʔimta* 'how long,' *ʕala feen* 'where to'
b. Adverbial wh-phrases: *feen* 'where,' *ʔimta* 'when,' *ʔizzay* 'how,' *leeh* 'why'

It is not clear which criteria are used to classify the wh-words as they are in Wahba (1984). For instance, why is a wh-word like *ʔimta* 'when' classified as non-nominal, when it can clearly occur as the complement of a preposition, as illustrated in *min ʔimta* 'how long,' a position typically reserved for nominal elements. Similarly, in Lebanese Arabic, *ween* 'where' and *ʔeemta* 'when' can be classified as nominal since they can occur as complements of prepositions, as illustrated in (iii):

(iii)   a. ħadd-ween seekniin?
near-where live.p
'Near where do you/they/we live?'

b. la-ʔeemta bee?yiin
to-when   staying.p
'Until when are you/they/we staying?'

(4)   *Wh*-words in Modern Standard Arabic

Nominal		**Adverbial**	
a. man	'who'	e. Payn	'where'
b. maaðaa	'what'	f. mataa	'when'
c. Payy	'which'	g. kayfa	'how'
d. kam	'how many/much'	h. limaaðaa	'why'

(5)   *Wh*-words in Egyptian Arabic

Nominal		**Adverbial**	
a. miin	'who'	e. feen	'where'
b. Peh	'what'	f. Pimta	'when'
c. Pan(h)i	'which'	g. Pizzay	'how'
d. kam	'how many/much'	h. lee(h)	'why'

All the strategies illustrated in (2) are in use in various Arabic dialects; however, not all the Arabic dialects make use of all four strategies. Lebanese Arabic seems to have all four available and will therefore be used here to illustrate the various generalizations regarding wh-interrogatives. Modern Standard Arabic does not make use of the in-situ strategy, which is the default strategy for Egyptian Arabic. When a language makes use of more than one strategy for forming wh-interrogatives, the question is to characterize the differences between those strategies, in terms of their syntactic and interpretive properties. This is the task we set for ourselves in this chapter.

6.3   The gap strategy and the resumptive strategy

In dialects that make use of both the gap strategy and the resumptive strategy, one can detect a contrast between wh-words that can be related to a gap inside a wh-interrogative and those that can be related to a resumptive element inside a wh-interrogative. Wh-words in Arabic can thus be divided into two classes with respect to the possibility of being resumed by a pronominal: whereas all wh-words in Arabic can be used in wh-questions involving gaps, there are restrictions on which wh-elements can appear in wh-questions involving resumptives.

The sentences in (6) and (7) illustrate the gap strategy in Lebanese Arabic and Modern Standard Arabic respectively:[3]

---

[3] Arabic does not allow preposition stranding, therefore, when a wh-word occurs within a prepositional phrase, the whole PP is pied-piped to the sentence initial position, as indicated in (i):

(6)   a. miin/ʔayya mariiD zeerit   nada?
         who/which patient visited.3fs Nada
         'Who/which patient did Nada visit?'

       b. šu/ʔayya   Saħn Talabit   laila b-l-maTʕam?
         what/which dish ordered.3fs Laila in-the-restaurant
         'What/which dish did Laila order at the restaurant?'

       c. ween rəħto   baʕd l-ʁada?
         where went.2p after the-lunch
         'Where did you go after lunch?'

       d. ʔeemta rəħto   ʕa-l-maTʕam?
         when   went.2p to-the-restaurant
         'When did you go to the restaurant?'

       e. kiif/lee(š)/lašu Sallaħto r-radio?
         how/why   fixed.2p the-radio
         'How/why did you fix the radio?'

       f. kiif biruuħo ʕa-l-matħaf?
         how go.3p   to-the-museum
         'How does one go to the museum?'

       g. kam   kteeb ʔəryo t-tleemiz?
         how many book read.3p the-students
         'How many books did the students read?'

       h. ʔaddee(š) dafaʕto ʕa-s-siyyaara la-tSalħuw-a
         how much paid.2p on-the-car   to-fix.2p-her
         'How much did you pay for the car to fix it?'

  (i)   a. maʕa man takallamat zeina?
         with who talked.3fs Zeina
         'With whom did Zeina talk?'

       b. maʕ miin ħəkyit   zeina?
         with who talked.3fs Zeina
         'With whom did Zeina talk?'

  (ii)   a. *man takallamat zeina maʕa?
         who talked.3fs Zeina with
         'With whom did Zeina talk?'

       b. *miin ħəkyit   zeina maʕ?
         who talked.3fs Zeina with
         'With whom did Zeina talk?'

(7)   a. man/ʔayya mariiDin zaarat   naadia?
          who/which patient   visited.3fs Nadia
          'Who/which patient did Nadia visit?'

      b. maaðaa/ʔayya kitaabin ʔištarat   laila fi-l-maktabati?
          what/which   book   bought.3fs Laila in-the-bookstore
          'What/which book did Laila buy at the bookstore?'

      c. ʔayna ðahabtum baʕda l-ʁadaaʔi?
          where went.2p   after the-lunch
          'Where did you go after lunch?'

      d. mataa ħaDartum l-masraħiyyata?
          when saw.2p   the-play
          'When did you see the play?'

      e. kayfa/limaaðaa mazzaqta l-kitaaba?
          how/why   tore.2ms the-book
          'How/why did you tear the book?'

      f. kayfa naSilu   ʔilaa l-matħafi?
          how   arrive.1p to   the-museum
          'How do we get to the museum?'

      g. kam   kitaabin qaraʔa   t-talaamiiðu?
          how many book   read.3ms the-students
          'How many books did the students read?'

      h. kam   dafaʕtum li-taSliiħi s-sayyaarati
          how much paid.2p   to-fixing the-car
          'How much did you pay to fix the car?'

Whereas all *wh*-words in Standard Arabic and in Lebanese Arabic can be related to a gap inside the sentence, as illustrated in (6) and (7), only *miin/man* 'who' and *ʔayy(a) NP* 'which NP' can be related to a resumptive element inside a simple sentence. This fact is illustrated in (8).

(8)   a. miin/ʔayya mariiD zeerit-o   naadia?
          who/which patient visited.3fs-him Nadia
          'Who/which patient did Nadia visit?'

      b. man/ʔayya mariiDin zaarat-hu   naadia?
          Who/which patient   visited.3fs-him Nadia
          'Who/which patient did Nadia visit?'

The resumptive element which occurs within the sentence is equivalent to the weak pronominal element that appears in non-subject argument positions in Arabic.

In those positions, the pronominal element cliticizes onto the lexical head that precedes it, be it a V, N, or P, as illustrated in (9–12) for Lebanese Arabic and (13–16) for Standard Arabic.

(9)   *Weak pronominals in Lebanese Arabic*

	Singular		**Plural**
	Masculine	*Feminine*	
1st Person	-(n)e[4]		-na
2nd Person	-ak	-ik	-kun
3rd Person	-o/-e/-i/-u[5]	-a	-un

(10)   a. ħabbayt-ne/-na
           liked.2ms-me/-us
           'You liked me/us.'

       b. bayt-e/-na
           house-my/-our
           'My/Our house.'

       c. maʕ-e/-na
           with-me/-us
           'With me/us.'

(11)   a. ħabbayt-ak/-ik/-kun
           liked.1s-you.ms/-you.fs/-you.p
           'I liked you.'

       b. bayt-ak/-ik/-kun
           house-you.ms/-you.fs/-you.p
           'Your house.'

       c. maʕ-ak/-ik/-kun
           with-you.ms/-you.fs/-you.p
           'With you.'

(12)   a. ħabbayt-o/-a/-un
           liked.2ms-him/-her/-them
           'You liked it/him/her/them.'

---

[4] *-ne* occurs on verbal heads, whereas *-e* occurs on nouns and prepositions.
[5] The third person singular form of the weak pronominal element has four phonological variants. *-o* is the morpheme that attaches to stems that end with a consonant.

    b. bayt-o/-a/-un
       house-his/-her/-their
       'Its/His/Her/Their house.'

    c. maʕ-o/-a/-un
       with-him/-her/-them
       'With it/him/her/them.'

(13)   *Weak pronominals in Standard Arabic*

	Singular		**Plural**		**Dual**
	Masculine	*Feminine*	*Masculine*	*Feminine*	
1ˢᵗ Person	-(n)i[6]	-(n)i	-na	-na	-na
2ⁿᵈ Person	-ka	-ki	-kum	-kunna	-kumaa
3ʳᵈ Person	-hu	-ha	-hum	-hunna	-humaa

(14)   a. ʔaħbabta-ni/-na
       liked.2ms-me/-us
       'You liked me/us.'

    b. bayt-i/-(u/a/i)na
       house-my/-our
       'My/Our house.'

    c. maʕ-i/-na
       with-me/-us
       'With me/us.'

(15)   a. ʔaħbabtu-ka/-ki/-kumaa/-kum/-kunna
       liked.1s-you.ms/-you.fs/-you.dual/-you.mp/-you.fp
       'I liked you.'

    b. bayt(u/a/i)-ka/-ki/-kumaa/-kum/-kunna
       house-you.ms/-you.fs/-you.dual/-you.mp/-you.fp
       'Your house.'

    c. maʕa-ka/-ki/-kumaa/-kum/-kunna
       with-you.ms/-you.fs/-you.dual/-you.mp/-you.fp
       'With you.'

(16)   a. ʔaħbabta-hu/-ha/-humaa/-hum/-hunna
       liked.2ms-him/-her/-them.dual/-them.mp/-them.fp
       'You liked it/him/her/them.'

---

[6] *-ni* occurs on verbal heads, whereas *-i* occurs on nouns and prepositions.

b. bayt(u/a/i)-hu/-ha/-humaa/-hum/-hunna
house-its/his/-her/-their.dual/-their.mp/-their.fp
'Its/His/Her/Their house.'

c. maʕa-hu/-ha/-humaa/-hum/-hunna
with-him/-her/-them.dual/-them.mp/-them.fp
'With it/him/her/them.'

The resumptive element related to *miin/man* 'who' is always third person mascu-line and singular, whereas the features of the resumptive element related to *ʔayy(a) NP* 'which NP' vary with those of the NP complement of *ʔayy(a)* 'which,' as illus-trated in (17).

(17)   a. ʔayya muraDa zaarit-un   Nada?   *Lebanese Arabic*
          which patients visited.3fs-them Nada
          'Which patients did Nada visit?'

       b. ʔayya marDaa zaarat-hum   Nada?   *Standard Arabic*
          which patients visited.3fs-them Nada
          'Which patients did Nada visit?'

Other nominal wh-words like *šu/maaðaa* 'what,' *ʔaddee(š)* 'how much,' and *kam* 'how many' are excluded from wh-questions involving resumptives, as evi-denced by the unacceptability of the sentences in (18) from Lebanese Arabic and (19) from Standard Arabic.

(18)   a. *šu Talabit-o   laila b-l-maTʕam?
          what ordered.3fs-it Laila in-the-restaurant
          'What did Laila order at the restaurant?'

       b. *kam   kteeb ʔəryuw-un   t-tleemiz?
          how many book read.3p-them the-students
          'How many books did the students read?'

       c. *ʔaddee(š) dafaʕtu-u ʕa-s-siyyaara la-tSalħuw-a
          how much paid.2p-it on-the-car   to-fix.2p-her
          'How much did you pay for the car to fix it?'

(19)   a. *maaðaa ʔištarat-hu   laila min al-maktabati?
          what   bought.3fs-it Laila from the-bookstore
          'What did Laila buy from the bookstore?'

       b. *kam   kitaabin qaraʔa-hum   at-talaamiiðu?
          how-many book   read.3ms-them the-students
          'How many books did the students read?'

In particular, (18a) and (19a), which involve the wh-word *šu/maaðaa* 'what,' contrast minimally with those in (20), which involve *ʔayy(a)* NP 'which NP.' With the resumptive element occurring in the variable position, the sentences in (20) are acceptable.

(20)   a. ʔayya Saħn Talabit-o   laila b-l-maTʕam?
           which dish ordered.3fs-it Laila in-the-restaurant
           'Which dish did Laila order at the restaurant?'

        b. ʔayya kitaabin ʔištarat-hu   laila min al-maktabati?
           which book   bought.3fs-it Laila from the-bookstore
           'Which book did Laila buy from the bookstore?'

All adverbial wh-words are excluded from resumptive wh-questions. This can be clearly seen in contexts where the construction involving an adverbial wh-word has a counterpart with *ʔayya NP* 'which NP.' The following sentences from Lebanese Arabic illustrate this point.

(21)   a. ʔayya maTʕam rəħtuu-l-o?
           which restaurant went.2p-to-it
           'Which restaurant did you go to?'

        b. *ween rəħtuu-l-o?
           where went.2p-to-it
           'Where did you go to?'

(22)   a. ʔayya nhaar xləSto   fi-i š-šəʁəl?
           which day   finished.2p in-it the-work
           'Which day did you finish the work?'

        b. *ʔeemta xləSto   fi-i š-šəʁəl?
           when   finished.2p in-it the-work
           'When did you finish the work?'

When *ween* 'where' and *ʔeemta* 'when' are respectively replaced by *ʔayya maTʕam* 'which restaurant' and *ʔayya nhaar* 'which day,' the use of a resumptive element inside the sentence becomes perfectly acceptable.[7]

---

[7] The contrast between *ʔeemta* 'when' and *ʔayya nhaar* 'which day' with respect to their ability to occur in resumptive wh-interrogatives might be taken as an indication that *ʔeemta* 'when' (and *ween* 'where') are non-nominal. Since resumptive elements in Arabic only correspond to NPs, this would explain why these elements cannot be related to resumptives in those languages. However, this explanation cannot extend to *šu* 'what,' which is clearly a nominal wh-word, and is in contradiction with the fact that wh-words like *ʔeemta* 'when' and *ween* 'where' can occur as complements of prepositions (see footnote 2).

The pronominal clitics occur as resumptive elements in non-subject positions. In subject positions, however, there is generally no pronoun in the variable position, as evidenced by the following sentences from Lebanese Arabic (23) and Standard Arabic (24) respectively:

(23)   a. ʔayya wleed   ʔəlto   ʔənno/-un rəbħo   l-žeeyze
          which children said.2p that/-they won.3p the-prize
          'Which children did you say that (they) won the prize?'

       b. miin ʔəlto   ʔənn-o rəbiħ   l-žeeyze
          who said.2p that/-he won.3ms the-prize
          'Who did you say that (he) won the prize?'

(24)   a. ʔayy-u   fataat-in ʕalim-tum ʔanna-*(ha) qad rabiħat
          which-Nom girl-Gen learned-2p that-*(she) prt. won.3fs
          l-žaaʔizata
          the-prize-Acc
          'Which girl did you learn that she has won the prize?'

       b. man ʕalim-tum ʔanna-*(hu) qad rabiħa   l-žaaʔizata
          who learned-2p that-*(he) prt. won.3ms the-prize-Acc
          'Who did you learn that he has won the prize?'

Instead, we either find the accusative clitic on the complementizer, as illustrated by the examples from Lebanese Arabic and Standard Arabic in (23–24), or alternatively, as in Lebanese Arabic, there is no pronominal element marking the variable site. However, as can be noted in the Lebanese Arabic examples as well as in the Standard Arabic examples, the verb in all cases bears the agreement features that identify the wh-phrases as a subject. In fact, in verbless contexts, extraction from subject positions without a resumptive clitic on the complementizer is not acceptable:

(25)   a. ʔayya wleed   ʔəlto   ʔənn- *o/un b-l-beet
          which children said.2p that-they   in-the-house
          'Which children did you say that they were at home?'

       b. ʔayyu   ʔawlad-in   qult-um ʔanna- *Ø/hum fi-l-bayt-i
          which.Nom children-Gen said.2p that-they   in-the-house-Gen
          'Which children did you say that they were at home?'

In traditional analyses of subject–object asymmetries within the Principles and Parameters approach, the required resumptive clitic on the complementizer in (25) is due to a prohibition against having the complementizer be followed by a trace; a typical *that-t* effect.

Briefly, the gap and resumptive strategies in wh-question formation alternate for *miin/man* 'who' and *ʔayya NP* 'which NP' when they are in non-subject positions. The gap strategy is the only strategy available for adverbial wh-words as well as nominal *šu* 'what,' *kam NP* 'how many NP,' and *ʔadeeš* 'how much.' The resumptive strategy seems to be the only one available for questioning subjects in Standard Arabic and Lebanese Arabic, an observation that can be attributed to a *that-t* effect. This is evidenced in the sentences in (25). There is one noteworthy difference between Lebanese Arabic and Standard Arabic, illustrated in the contrast between (23) and (24), which might indicate that *that-t* effects are stronger in Standard Arabic than they are in Lebanese Arabic: Standard Arabic, unlike Lebanese Arabic, requires the resumptive clitic on the complementizer even though the verbs in (23) and (24) bear agreement features that identify the null resumptive pronominal. This difference between Standard Arabic and Lebanese Arabic can be reduced to a difference between the two complementizers *ʔanna* and *ʔinno*: the Standard Arabic complementizer *ʔanna* requires the specifier of the projection below it to be overtly realized. Thus, even in declarative sentences, where no extraction takes place, *ʔanna* must be followed by a clitic agreeing in person, gender, and number with the subject (26a) (see also chapter 2), but this requirement seems to be waived if a PP is preposed to a preverbal position (27).

(26)   a. samiʕtu ʔanna-*(hu) nažaħa   *Standard Arabic*
           heard.1s that-*(he)   passed.3ms
           'I heard that he passed.'

       b. smiʕt   ʔinno nižħit   *Lebanese Arabic*
           heard.1s that   passed.3fs
           'I heard that she passed.'

(27)   samiʕtu ʔanna fi-l-bayt-i   walad-un   *Standard Arabic*
       heard.1s that   in-the-house-Gen child-Nom
       'I heard that in the house, there is a child.'

As indicated by the acceptability of (26b) from Lebanese Arabic, the complementizer *ʔinno* does not require a pronominal clitic to follow it. Thus, the difference between (23) and (24) is attributed to the fact that the specifier of the projection immediately dominated by *ʔanna* in Standard Arabic cannot be empty, that is, it can be neither a trace of movement nor an empty pronominal element.

The table below summarizes the facts that we are trying to generalize over.

(28)   **Resumptive elements**

Yes	No
ʔayy(a) NP	*šu/maaδaa* 'what,' *kam NP* 'how many
'which	NP,' *ʔaddee(š)* 'how much,' *ween/ʔayna*
NP,' *miin/man*	'where,' *ʔeemta/mataa* 'when,'
'who'	*kiif/kayfa* 'how,' *lee(š)/limaaδaa* 'why'

6.3.1   Resumptive wh-interrogatives and d-linking

In the previous section, we surveyed the distribution of gaps and resumptives in wh-interrogatives and noted that there are constraints imposed on that distribution. One constraint that we have touched upon and which we take up now in detail is related to the nature of the A′-antecedent: we have already observed that whereas all wh-words can be related to gaps, only *ʔayy(a) NP* 'which NP' and *miin/man* 'who' are able to occur in resumptive wh-interrogatives. More specifically, even nominal wh-words like *šu* 'what,' or wh-phrases like *kam NP* 'how many NP,' cannot be resumed by a clitic.

The parallel behavior of adverbial wh-phrases, like *kiif* 'how' and *lee(š)* 'why,' and measure phrases, like *kam NP* 'how many NP' and *ʔaddee(š)* 'how much,' with respect to wh-extraction is not surprising. This observation has been made cross-linguistically (see Aoun 1986; Cinque 1990; Rizzi 1990). Thus, it is observed that measure phrases in English, like adjunct wh-words, cannot be extracted from a wh-island. The paradigm in (29–32) provides evidence for this generalization.

(29)   a. ?Which problem do you wonder how to solve it?
        b. *How do you wonder which problem to solve it?

Examples (29a–b) are an illustration of the classic argument-adjunct asymmetry: Whereas object extraction from a wh-island is marginally acceptable (29a), extraction of an adverbial wh-phrase from a wh-island gives rise to strong unacceptability in English. The same asymmetry is found in the context of selected measure phrases, like *200lbs* in (30b).

(30)   a. John weighed apples.
        b. John weighed 200lbs.

(31)   ?What did John wonder how to weigh?

(32)   What did John weigh?

An ambiguous verb like *weigh* can be agentive, taking a direct object complement, as in (30a), or stative, selecting a measure phrase complement, as in (30b). Whereas both types of complements can be questioned, as evidenced in the ambiguity of (32), when *what* is extracted from a wh-island, as illustrated in (31), only the agentive meaning survives and a question like (31) can only be felicitously answered with "apples" and not with "200lbs."

It is not clear, however, what brings adjuncts and measure phrases together with *šu* 'what' in not allowing resumption.[8]

One difference one can point out between *šu* 'what' and *ʔayya NP* 'which NP' has been captured by the notion of membership in a presupposed set (see Kuroda 1968). In a discourse context, as in (33), where the speaker presents the hearer with a choice between two books, the follow-up question must be one that involves *ʔayya NP* 'which NP,' as indicated by the contrast between (34a) and (34b).

(33)   S: fii   kaliila wa dimna   w   fii   n-nabi
             in-it *Kalila and Dimna* and in-it *The-Prophet*
             'There is *Kalila and Dimna* and there is *The Prophet*.'

(34)   a. šu   baddak   təʔra   b-l-ʔawwal?
             what want.2ms read.2ms in-the-first
             'What do you want to read first?'

         b. ʔayya kteeb baddak   təʔra   b-l-ʔawwal?
             which book want.2ms read.2ms in-the-first
             'Which book do you want to read first?'

šu 'what' is unable to pick up a discourse referent as antecedent and therefore (34a) is infelicitous in the context of the discourse in (33).

Thus, *šu* 'what' cannot refer to a member of a presupposed set, whereas *ʔayya NP* 'which NP' does. The notion of membership in a presupposed set is what underlies the concept of referential noun phrase, developed in Cinque (1990) and which is itself related to the notion of d-linking (Pesetsky 1987). Cinque (1990) understands referential noun phrases to be noun phrases that are associated with a presupposition of existence. A characteristic property of referential noun phrases is that they can easily enter into coreference relations with pronouns in discourse:

(35)   a. ʔarrit   l-mʕallme   **l-kteeb** la-t-tleemiiz   w   ʔana
             read.caus.3fs the-teacher.fs the-book to-the-students and I
             kameen ʔriit-**o**
             too   read-it
             'The teacher made the students read the book. And I too read it.'

---

[8] The contrast between *šu/maaðaa* 'what' and *ʔayy(a) NP* 'which NP' is reminiscent of what can be observed in English long extraction (Kroch 1989):

(i)   a.? What were you wondering how to fix e?
         b. Which car were you wondering how to fix e?

Whereas the extraction of *what* out of a wh-island is relatively unacceptable, the extraction of a *which*-phrase is perfectly acceptable, as indicated in the contrast between (ia) and (ib) above.

b. saami ʕam bi-fattiš ʕala **seeʕa** dahab w laila ʕam
Sami Asp. look.3ms on   watch gold   and Laila Asp.

bi-tfattiš **ʔalay-a** kameen
look.3fs on-it   too
'Sami is looking for a gold watch and Laila is looking for it too.'

c. A: **ʔayya kteeb** ʔiryo   t-tleemiiz?
Which book read.3p the-students
'Which book did the students read?'

B: ma baʕrif,   bas l-mʕallme   ʔaalit   ʔənno ma ħabbu-**u**
Neg. know.1s, but the-teacher.fs said.3fs that   Neg. like.3p-it
'I don't know, but the teacher said that they didn't like it.'

A definite noun phrase, an indefinite noun phrase interpreted referentially, and a *which* phrase can all be coreferent with a pronoun in discourse. Given this definition, *šu* 'what' is not a referential noun phrase, because it cannot enter into coreference relations with a pronoun, as illustrated in (36).

(36)   *A: **šu**   ʔiryo   t-tleemiiz?
What   read.3p the-students
'What did the students read?'

B: ma baʕrif,   bas l-mʔallme   ʔaalit   ʔənno ma ħabbu-**u**
Neg. know.1s, but the-teacher.fs said.3fs that   Neg. like.3p-it
'I don't know, but the teacher said that they didn't like it.'

A second and related difference between *šu* 'what' and *ʔayya NP* 'which NP' is that, unlike *ʔayya NP* 'which NP,' *šu* 'what' cannot participate in partitive expressions:

(37)   a. *šu   mn ha-l-kətub
what of this-the-books

b. ʔayya waaħad/kteeb mn ha-l-kətub
which one/book   of this-the-books
'Which one of these books.'

Partitivity is closely related to referentiality as defined in Cinque (1990), as it clearly signals membership in a presupposed set. Thus, an initial generalization can be put forth to account for which wh-words can be related to resumptive elements:

(38)   wh-phrases related to resumptive elements must be referential.

Despite the fact that the notion of referentiality characterizes accurately the difference between *šu* 'what,' *ween* 'where,' *ʔeemta* 'when,' and *ʔayya NP* 'which NP,' it does not carry over to *kam NP* 'how many NP.'

The possibility of a referential interpretation for *kam NP* 'how many NP' phrases is documented in the literature (see among others, Heycock (1995), Fox (1999), and references therein) and is clear in that those phrases, like *ʔayya NP* 'which NP' phrases, can pick out a discourse referent (39):[9]

(39)　　a. fii　　ħakiim ʔalb, ħakiim sneen, ħakiim məʕde, ħakiim
　　　　　　　in-it doctor heart doctor teeth　doctor stomach doctor

　　　　　　　nəfseene.
　　　　　　　spiritual
　　　　　　　'There is a cardiologist, a dentist, an internal medicine specialist, and
　　　　　　　a psychiatrist.'

　　　　b. kam　　　　ħakiim/waaħad baddak　　tšuuf?
　　　　　　how many doctor/one　　　　want.2ms see.2ms
　　　　　　How many doctors/ones do you want to see?'

---

[9] The referential reading of *kam NP* 'how many NP' can be identified with what the literature has termed the *presuppositional* reading. Heycock (1995) clearly shows that questions involving *kam NP* 'how many NP' are ambiguous between two readings: a presuppositional reading and an amount reading. This ambiguity shows up when the wh-phrase *kam NP* 'how many NP' co-occurs with other scope sensitive elements in the sentence, as explained in Fox (1999). Consider the following sentence:

(i)　　　kam　　　　Təbbax badda　tšaɣɣil　　　Nada b-l-maTʕam?
　　　　　how many cook　　want.3fs employ.3fs Nada in-the-restaurant
　　　　　'How many cooks does Nada want to hire for the restaurant?'

To distinguish between the two readings, Fox (1999) suggests interpreting the question given the scenario in (ii). In such a context, the two different readings of (i) give rise to two different answers.

(ii)　　　*S1*
　　　　　Nada is opening a new restaurant in a few weeks and she wants to hire three
　　　　　cooks to man the kitchen. After a long day of interviews she decides that she
　　　　　wants to hire two of the cooks she has interviewed, leaving the task to hire the
　　　　　third one for later.

The reading where *kam Təbbax* 'how many cooks' takes its scope below the verb *badda* 'she wants' – the non-referential reading – corresponds to the answer "three" in S1. Under the interpretation where *kam Təbbax* 'how many cooks' takes its scope higher than the verb *badda* 'she wants' – the referential reading – the answer to the question in (i) is "two." This reading corresponds to a presuppositional interpretation of the wh-noun phrase. That is, what is being asked is how many of the cooks (that she has interviewed) Nada wants to hire for the restaurant.

In the context of the discourse presented in (39a), when the addressee hears the question in (39b), he or she is expected to respond by picking out a number of doctors from those listed by the speaker in the discourse in (39a), as evidenced by the ability to use the pronominal form *waaħad* 'one.' Thus, *kam NP* 'how many NP' in (39b) is able to pick up its referent from the preceding discourse.

Similarly, *kam NP* 'how many NP' can participate in partitive constructions (40):

(40)   kam   kteeb mn hal-kətub   ʔriito?
         how many book of   this-the-books read.2p
         'How many of these books did you read?'

Interestingly however, *kam NP* 'how many NP' phrases, unlike *ʔayya NP* 'which NP' phrases, cannot be related to resumptive elements in wh-questions, as was observed earlier. Thus, while all wh-phrases which can be related to resumptives must be referential, i.e. *miin* 'who' and *ʔayya NP* 'which NP,' not all referential wh-phrases can be related to a resumptive element. Thus, the notion of referentiality is not sufficient to pick out all the wh-phrases that participate in wh-questions involving resumptives.[10]

6.3.2   The syntax of wh-constituents

The question can be raised now as to what *šu/maaðaa* 'what' and *kam NP* 'how many NP' have in common that distinguishes them from both *ʔayy(a) NP* 'which NP' and *miin/man* 'who.' The proposal we would like to put forth is summarized in (41).

(41)   a. Wh-phrases can be decomposed into two parts: (i) a wh-element,
            which bears the question feature, and (ii) a noun phrase, which can
            either be a full DP, or not.
         b. Only those wh-phrases which are composed of a wh-element
            co-occuring with a full DP can be related to a resumptive element.

Under this proposal, *ʔayya NP* 'which NP' and *miin* 'who' have the representation in (42), whereas *šu* 'what' and *kam NP* 'how many NP' have the representation in (43).

---

[10] We take up this issue again in chapters 7 and 8, where this generalization will be revised in light of the distribution of resumption in restrictive relatives and in clitic-left dislocation constructions.

(42)   *miin/man/ ʔayy(a)*

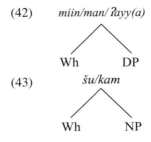

Wh   DP

(43)   *šu/kam*

Wh   NP

Independent evidence suggests that this proposal is on the right track to distinguish between *ʔayya* 'which' and *kam* 'how many.' *ʔayya* 'which' can be separated from the following noun phrase by a numerical element, whereas *kam* 'how many' cannot (44). This indicates that the complement of *ʔayya* 'which' is more complex than that of *kam* 'how many.'

(44)   a.   ʔayya (tleet) wleed ʔižo?
              which (three) boys   came
              'Which three boys came?'

        b.   *kam   (tleet) wleed ʔižo?
              how many (three) boys   came
              'How many three boys came?'

In fact, the complement of *kam* 'how many' cannot be plural, as indicated by the unacceptability of (44b), even when it doesn't involve the numerical *tleet*(e) 'three.' The complement of *kam* can only be a singular count noun, indicating that it is structurally simpler than the complement of *ʔayya* (44a), which can be a quantified noun phrase or a plural noun phrase. Thus the generalization is that:

(45)   Resumptive elements correspond to the full DP complement of *wh*.

6.3.3   *Long-distance wh-dependencies and island sensitivity*

Sentence initial wh-phrases can be related to a gap or a resumptive element – when the latter is available – across clause boundaries. Sentences (46–50) from Lebanese Arabic illustrate this generalization.

(46)   a.   miin/ʔayya mariiD ʔəlto   ʔənno zeerit   Nada?
              who/which patient said.2p that   visited.3fs Nada
              'Who/which patient did you say that Nada visited?'

b. miin/ʔayya mariiD ʔəlto   ʔənno zeerit-o   Nada?
   who/which patient said.2p that   visited.3fs-him Nada
   'Who/which patient did you say that Nada visited?'

(47) a. šu/ʔayya   Saħn ʔəlto   ʔənno Talabit   laila b-l-maTʕam?
      what/which dish said.2p that   ordered.3fs Laila in-the-restaurant
      'What/Which dish did you say that Laila ordered at the restaurant?'

   b. ʔayya Saħn ʔəlto   ʔənno Talabit-o   laila b-l-maTʕam?
      which dish said.2p that   ordered.3fs-it Laila in-the-restaurant
      'What/Which dish did you say that Laila ordered at the restaurant?'

(48) a. ween ʔəlto   ʔənno raħ truuħo baʕd l-ʁada?
      where said.2p that   fut. go.2p after the-lunch
      'Where did you say you are going after lunch?'

   b. ʔayya maTʕam ʔəlto   ʔənno raħ truuħuu-l-o ʕa-l-ʁada?
      which restaurant said.2p that   fut. go.2p-to-it on-the-lunch
      'Which restaurant did you say you are going there for lunch?'

(49) a. ʔeemta ʔəlto   ʔənno raħ truuħo ʕa-l-maTʕam?
      when said.2p that   fut. go.2p to-the-restaurant
      'When did you say you are going to the restaurant?'

   b. ʔayya nhaar ʔəlto   ʔənno raħ truuħo fi-i ʕa-l-maTʕam?
      which day said.2p that   fut. go.2p in-it to-the-restaurant
      'Which day did you say you are going then to the restaurant?'

(50) a. kam   kteeb ʔəlto   ʔənno ʔəryo t-tleemiz?
      how many book said.2p that   read.3p the-students
      'How many books did you say that the students read?'

   b. ʔaddee(š) ʔəlto   ʔənno dafaʕto ʕa-s-siyyaara la-tSalħuw-a
      how much said.2p that   paid.2p on-the-car   to-fix.2p-her
      'How much did you say you paid for the car to fix it?'

As observed in (48–50), adverbial wh-phrases like *ween* 'where' and *ʔeemta* 'when' can be related to a gap across clause boundaries. These have been termed *referential* adjuncts in the relevant literature, due to the fact that, in some languages, there are pronouns that correspond to these wh-words. Thus, in English, *then* and *there* correspond to *when* and *where* respectively. However, non-referential adjunct wh-phrases like *kiif* 'how' or *lee(š)/lašu* 'why' cannot be related to a gap across clause boundaries, as evidenced by the unacceptability of the sentences in (51).

(51)   a. *kiif/lee(š)/lašu ʔəlto   ʔənno Sallaħto r-radio?
        how/why   said.2p that   fixed.2p the-radio
        'How/why did you say that you fixed the radio?'

        b. *kiif ʔəlto   ʔənno biruuħo ʕa-l-matħaf?
        how said.2p that   go.3p   to-the-museum
        'How did you say that one goes to the museum?'

In both (51a) and (51b) the sentence initial wh-word cannot be interpreted with respect to the embedded verb. It is that interpretation that is starred in those sentences.

As has been known since Ross (1967), wh-questions which involve gaps, unlike those involving resumptive elements, obey island conditions. Thus, we have a systematic contrast between wh-words related to gaps and wh-words related to resumptives, when the gap or the resumptive occurs inside an island. We have chosen to illustrate this observation in Lebanese Arabic, using relative clause islands (52), wh-islands (53), and adjunct clauses (54).

(52)   *Relative clauses*
        a. *miin/ʔayya mariiD btaʕrfo l-mara   yalli zeerit?
        who/which   patient know.2p the-woman that visited.3fs
        'Who/which patient do you know the woman that visited?'

        b. miin/ʔayya mariiD btaʕrfo l-mara   yalli zeerit-**o**?
        who/which   patient know.2p the-woman that visited.3fs-him
        'Who/which patient do you know the woman that visited him?'

(53)   *Wh-islands*
        a. *šu/ʔayya Saħn baddkun taʕrfo   ʔəza Talabit   laila
        what/which dish want.2p know.2p whether ordered.3fs Laila

        b-l-maTʕam?
        in-the-restaurant
        'What/Which dish do you want to know whether Laila ordered at the restaurant?'

        b. ʔayya Saħn baddkun taʕrfo   ʔəza   Talabit-**o**
        which dish want.2p know.2p whether ordered.3fs-it

        laila b-l-maTʕam?
        Laila in-the-restaurant
        'Which dish do you want to know whether Laila ordered at the restaurant?'

(54)   *Adjunct clauses*
   a. *ween seefarto   ?ablma truuħo ʕa-l-ʁada?
      where travel.2p before go.2p on-the-lunch
      'Where did you travel before you went after lunch?'
   b. ?ayya maTʕam   seefarto   ?ablma truuħuu-**l-o** ʕa-l-ʁada?
      which restaurant travelled.2p before go.2p-to-it on-the-lunch
      'Which restaurant did you travel before going there for lunch?'

Whereas a wh-element in sentence initial position can be related to a resumptive element inside a relative clause (52b), a wh-island (53b), or an adjunct clause (54b), it cannot be related to a gap inside any of those islands.

6.3.4   Summary

This section has shed light on two systematic differences between gapped wh-interrogatives and resumptive wh-interrogatives in Arabic: (1) the occurrence of a resumptive pronominal inside a wh-interrogative is restricted to those constructions involving a wh-word that consists of a wh-feature with a full DP complement; (2) resumptive wh-interrogatives, but not gapped wh-interrogatives, violate various island conditions. This fact has been taken as evidence that resumptive wh-interrogatives, unlike gapped wh-interrogatives are not generated by movement of the wh-phrase to the clause initial position. Thus resumptive wh-interrogatives and gapped wh-interrogatives have been given the respective representations in (55a) and (55b) to account for this difference.

(55)   a. wh-element$_i$ . . . . trace$_i$ *Gapped wh-interrogatives*
        b. wh-element$_i$ . . . . pro$_i$ – clitic   *Resumptive wh-interrogatives*

6.4   Class II resumptive interrogatives

In addition to the conventional resumptive strategy for forming wh-interrogatives, which requires the presence of a pronominal clitic in the variable position to which the sentence initial wh-phrase is related, various Arabic dialects make use of another resumptive strategy in forming wh-questions, which Shlonsky (2002) terms Class II interrogatives. The following sentences from Palestinian Arabic (56a), Egyptian Arabic (56b), and Standard Arabic (56c) illustrate the Class II resumptive strategy:[11]

[11] Unless otherwise indicated, the Palestinian Arabic examples are from Shlonsky (2002) and the Egyptian Arabic sentences are from Wahba (1984).

(56)   a.   šu   ʔilli ʔinti katabti-i   mbaariħ?   *Palestinian Arabic*
                what that you wrote.2fs-it yesterday
                'What did you write yesterday?'

        b.   ʔeh lli   mona ʔarit-uh?   *Egyptian Arabic*
                what that Mona read.3fs-it
                'What did Mona read?'

        c.   man llaði   raʔat-hu   mona?   *Standard Arabic*
                who that.ms saw.3fs-him Mona
                'Who did Mona see?'

These sentences parallel the one in Lebanese Arabic given in (2c) and repeated below:

(57)   miin (ya)lli šəft-**o**   b-l-maTʕam?   *Lebanese Arabic*
        who that   saw.2ms-him in-the-restaurant
        'Who is it that you saw in the restaurant?'

As noted at the outset of this chapter, Arabic makes use of two types of wh-interrogatives involving resumption, and thus in Lebanese Arabic (57) contrasts with (58).

(58)   miin šəft-**o**   b-l-maTʕam?   *Lebanese Arabic*
        who saw.2ms-him in-the-restaurant
        'Who did you see in the restaurant?'

The two types of resumptive interrogative constructions share several properties. First, both strategies can express an unbounded dependency between the wh-element and the resumptive pronominal, as illustrated in (59) from Lebanese Arabic, and (60) from Palestinian Arabic.

(59)   a.   miin ʔəlte   ʔənno raħ yiʕzmu-u   ʕa-l-ħafle?
                who said.2fs that   fut. invite.3p-him to-the-party
                'Who did you say that they will invite to the party?'

        b.   miin lli   ʔəlte   ʔənno raħ yiʕzmu-u   ʕa-l-ħafle?
                who that said.2fs that   fut. invite.3p-him to-the-party
                'Who is it that you said that they will invite to the party?'

(60)   ʔayy maktuub ʔilli mona qaalat   ʔinnu mary fakkarat
        which letter   that Mona said.3fs that   Mary thought.3fs

        ʔinnu faatme baʕθat-o la-mħemmad?
        that   Faatme sent.3fs-it to-Mhemmad
        'Which letter did Mona say that Mary thought that Faatme sent to Mhemmad?'

Second, in both strategies questioning into an island is fully acceptable. This observation is illustrated using relative clause islands (61–62), but can be extended to wh-islands and adjunct clauses.[12]

(61)   *Lebanese Arabic*

  a. miin šəfte l-kalb yalli ʕaDD-o?
    who saw.2fs the-dog that bit.3ms-him
    'Who did you see the dog that bit him?'

  b. miin lli šəfte l-kalb yalli ʕaDD-o?
    who that saw.2fs the-dog that bit.3ms-him
    'Who is it that you saw the dog that bit him?'

(62)   *Palestinian Arabic*

  ʔanii binət ʔilli šufti l-ʔasad ʔilli ʔakal-ha?
  which girl that saw.2fs the-lion that ate.3ms-her
  'Which girl did you see the lion that ate her?'

However, resumptive wh-interrogatives and Class II interrogatives differ in important respects. The obvious and most noticeable difference between the two strategies is the presence of the relativizer *yalli/ʔilli/ʔallaði* 'that' in Class II interrogatives.

Another difference between the two types of wh-questions is the fact that *šu/ʔeh* 'what' can participate in a Class II interrogative but cannot appear in a resumptive wh-interrogative, as illustrated in the contrast in (63) in Lebanese Arabic:

(63)   a. *šu Talabət-o laila b-l-maTʕam?
    what ordered.3fs-it Laila in-the-restaurant
    'What did Laila order in the restaurant?'

---

[12] Wahba (1984c) notes that in Class II interrogatives in Egyptian Arabic, the sentence initial wh-word cannot be related to a resumptive clitic inside an island, as illustrated in (i):

(i)   a. *ʔanhi kitaab illi mona teʕraf miin illi saraʔ-uh?
    which book that Mona know.3fs who that stole.3ms-it
    'Which book does Mona know who stole it?'

  b. *miin illi mona teʕraf feen huwwa raaħ?
    who that Mona know.3sf where he went.3ms
    'Who does Mona know where he went?'

That is, in Egyptian Arabic, Class II interrogatives seem to behave like conventional gap wh-interrogatives with respect to island sensitivity. It is interesting to note here that in Egyptian Arabic, unlike in other Arabic dialects, wh-interrogatives with gaps are not a default strategy (see also the discussion at the end of this section and in section 6.5).

b. šu   yalli Talabət-o   laila b-l-maTʕam?
what that ordered.3fs-it Laila in-the-restaurant
'What is it that Laila ordered in the restaurant?'

In addition, it can be noted that whereas *miin/man* 'who' induces default masculine singular agreement features on the resumptive element that is directly related to it, in Class II interrogatives, it can be related to a resumptive pronominal with full number and gender agreement features, as illustrated in (64) from Lebanese Arabic.

(64)   a. miin ʕazamu-u/*a/*un   ʕa-l-ḥafle?
           who invited.3p-him/*her/*them to-the-party
           'Who did they invite to the party?'

        b. miin yalli ʕazamu-u/a/un   ʕa-l-ḥafle?
           Who that   invited.3p-him/her/them to-the-party
           'Who is it that they invited to the party?'

Shlonsky (2002) notes a similar contrast in Moroccan Arabic, when questioning a subject:

(65)   a. škun mša?
           who left.3ms
           'Who left?'

        b. *škun mšat/mšaw?
           who   left.3fs/3p
           'Who left?'

        c. škun lli mša/   mšat/   mšaw?
           Who that left.3ms/ left.3fs/ left.3p
           'Who left?'

Thus, in a conventional gapped wh-interrogative, questioning the subject entails that the verb appears with third person masculine singular (default) agreement in Arabic; this is not the case in a Class II interrogative, as illustrated in (65c).

The differences outlined above seem to suggest that the wh-word in Class II interrogatives is not directly related to the resumptive pronominal inside the sentence. That is, the resumptive element does not occupy the variable position corresponding to the sentence initial wh-word. Shlonsky (2002) claims that, in their structure, Class II interrogatives parallel identificational sentences where the subject is wh-fronted, as can be seen by comparing (66a) and (66b), in Lebanese Arabic.

(66)   a. šu   (huwwe) l-ʔakl   l-yom?
           what (he)   the-food the-day
           'What is on the menu today?'

       b. šu   (huwwe) lli   raħ   teeklu-u l-yom?
           what (he)   that fut.   eat.2p-it the-day
           'What is it that you are going to eat today?'

In both Class II interrogatives and identificational sentences, the "pronominal copula" (Doron 1983) can appear, separating the subject from the predicate. In such cases, the clause introduced by the complementizer *(ya)lli* 'that' (66b) is analyzed as a free relative, like the ones in (67).[13]

(67)   a. salma bitħibb lli   raħ teeklu-u l-yom   *Lebanese Arabic*
           Salma likes.3fs that fut. eat.2p-it the-day
           'Salma likes what you will eat today.'

       b. l-jnuud   Darabu ʔilli ħabasu-u   *Palestinian Arabic*
           the-army hit.3p   that arrested.3p-him
           'The army beat up the one they arrested.'

Shlonsky's (2002) analysis of Class II interrogatives thus accounts for all the differences that can be observed between those constructions and wh-interrogatives involving resumption, namely, the presence of the relativizer in Class II interrogatives, the acceptability of the Arabic equivalent of 'what' in those constructions, and the agreement facts with *miin/man/škun* 'who.' The clause headed by *lli/yalli/ʔilli* 'that' is analyzed by Shlonsky (2002) as a predicate taking a null pronominal as subject and Class II interrogatives are given the structure in (68).[14]

---

[13] In addition to the agreement facts observed with Class II resumptive interrogatives involving *miin* 'who,' the separability of the wh-word from the relativizer *lli* provides evidence that the wh-word in those constructions is not the head of the relative construction. In fact, in restrictive relatives, the head cannot be separated from the relativizer by a pronoun, as illustrated in the contrast between (ia) and (ib):

(i)   a. *šift   l-walad huwwe lli   xazzaʔ l-kteeb
           saw.1s the-child he   that tore.3ms the-book
           'I saw the child that tore up the book.'

       b. miin huwwe lli   xazzaʔ l-kteeb?
           who he   that tore.3ms the-book
           'Who is it that tore up the book?'

[14] See chapter 7 for a different analysis of the relativizer *lli/yalli/ʔilli* 'that.' Here we are following Shlonsky (2002), where the relativizer is analyzed as a complementizer and this aspect of the analysis does not affect the main points we are trying to make about Class II interrogatives.

(68)

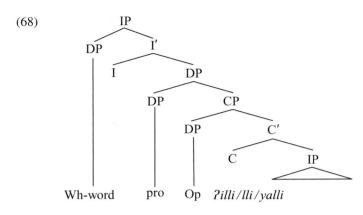

It is the null pronominal element *pro* in [Spec, DP] that agrees with the null operator in [Spec, CP] and with the resumptive element inside the IP. This null pronominal can sometimes be overtly realized as a strong pronoun, as seen in (69).

(69)   a. miin hiyye lli l-ʔasad ʕaDD-a   mbeeriħ?   *Lebanese Arabic*
           who she   that the-lion bit.3ms-her yesterday
           'Who did the lion bite yesterday?'

       b. miin hi ʔilli l-ʔasad ʔakal-ha   mbaariħ?   *Palestinian Arabic*
           who she that the-lion ate.3ms-her yesterday
           'Who did the lion eat yesterday?'

Thus, it seems that resumptive wh-interrogatives and Class II interrogatives are the result of different derivations. They share only a dependency between a wh-word and a resumptive pronominal, but the two constructions differ greatly in how the relation is established between the wh-word and the resumptive. In wh-interrogatives, the resumptive element is directly bound by the wh-word, as a variable is by its corresponding operator. In Class II interrogatives, the relation between the wh-word and the resumptive pronominal is mediated by two predication relations: the first between the null pronominal head of the free relative and the relative CP headed by the relativizer and the second between the two DPs forming the identificational sentence.

Cross-linguistic examination of the two types of resumptive wh-interrogatives provides independent evidence for a separation between the two constructions. In fact Egyptian Arabic uses Class II interrogatives as a common strategy for question formation. All nominal wh-words can enter into this construction in Egyptian Arabic, with the properties discussed earlier in the section (see, however, footnote 12). However, Egyptian Arabic does not make use of the conventional resumptive strategy in forming wh-interrogatives. This is illustrated in the following contrasts provided in Wahba (1984):

(70)   a. miin illi mona šaafit-uh?
           who that Mona saw.3fs-him
           'Who did Mona see?'

        b. *miin mona šaafit-uh?
           who Mona saw.3fs-him
           'Who did Mona see?'

(71)   a. ?anhi walad illi mona šaafit-uh?
           which boy   that Mona saw.3fs-him
           'Which boy did Mona see?'

        b. *?anhi walad mona šaafit-uh?
           which boy   Mona saw.3fs-him
           'Which boy did Mona see?'

The facts in (70) and (71) further confirm that the two resumptive strategies must be independently available in Universal Grammar.

The analysis defended by Shlonsky (2002) makes predictions regarding long extraction in Class II interrogatives that are borne out. In such contexts, extraction of the wh-phrase from an island is prohibited, as the unacceptability of (72a) in Palestinian Arabic and (72b) in Lebanese Arabic indicates.

(72)   a. *miin ma ʕrift-š   weenta (hi) ?illi l-?asad ?akal-ha
           who Neg know.2ms-Neg when   (she) that the-lion ate.3ms-her
           'Who didn't you know when the lion ate?'

        b. *miin ma ʕrəfət   ?eemta (hiyye) lli l-?asad ?akal-a
           who Neg know.2ms when   (she)   that the-lion ate.3ms-her
           'Who didn't you know when the lion ate?'

Whereas in Class II interrogatives the wh-phrase cannot be extracted from inside a wh-island, we have already observed that, in conventional resumptive wh-interrogatives, the sentence initial wh-phrase can be related to a resumptive element embedded within an island.

6.5   wh-in-situ

Having discussed the three strategies of wh-question formation that involve sentence initial wh-words, we now turn to the fourth strategy: the in-situ strategy. In-situ wh-questions have the wh-word occur in the position where we would normally see a non-wh lexical noun phrase. The following sentences from Lebanese Arabic and Egyptian Arabic (Wahba 1984) illustrate this observation:

(73) *Lebanese Arabic*
  a. ħkiito   maʕ miin l-yom?
     talked.2p with who the-day
     'You talked with whom today?'

  b. ħkiito   maʕ saami l-yom
     talked.2p with Sami the-day
     'You talked with Sami today.'

(74) *Lebanese Arabic*
  a. xabbarto ʔayya walad ʕan   l-ħafle?
     told.2p   which child about the-party
     'You told which child about the party?'

  b. xabbarto ha-l-walad   ʕan   l-ħafle
     told.2p   this-the-child about the-party
     'You told this child about the party.'

(75) *Lebanese Arabic*
  a. btibʕud   bayruut ʕan Traablus kam   kilometr?
     be-far.3fs Beirut from Tripoli how many kilometer
     'How many kilometers is the distance between Beirut and Tripoli?'

  b. btibʕud   bayruut ʕan Traablus miit   kilometr
     be-far.3fs Beirut from Tripoli hundred kilometer
     'Beirut is a hundred kilometers away from Tripoli.'

(76) *Egyptian Arabic*
  a. mona nisit   tiktib   ʔeh?
     Mona forgot.3fs write.3fs what
     'What did Mona forget to write?'

  b. mona nisit   tiktib   il-gawab
     Mona forgot.3fs write.3fs the-letter
     'Mona forgot to write the letter.'

6.5.1   *The distribution of wh-words in situ*

In some dialects of Arabic, there are restrictions on which wh-words participate in in-situ wh-questions. Furthermore, the restrictions vary from one dialect to another. In Lebanese Arabic, there is a major division between nominal and adverbial wh-phrases: adverbial wh-phrases generally cannot stay in situ. In fact, they can marginally appear in situ in simplex clauses (77), but only referential adverbial wh-phrases can appear in embedded contexts (78).

(77)   a.? raħ tnaymu-u   ween?
            fut sleep.2p-him where
            'Where are you going to put him to sleep?'

       b.? fall   lee?
            left.3ms why
            'Why did he leave?'

       c.? Sallaħti-i   kiif?
            fixed.2fs-it how
            'How did you fix it?'

(78)   a. ftakarto   ʔənno raħ ynaymu-u   ween?
            thought.2p that   fut sleep.3p-him where
            'Where did you think they were going to put him to sleep?'

       b. *ftakarto   ʔənno fall   lee?
            thought.2p that   left.3ms why
            'Why did you think he left?'

       c. *ftakaro   ʔənno Sallaħti-i   kiif?
            thought.3p that   fixed.2fs-it how
            'How did they think you fixed it?'

As can be seen in (78b–c), the non-referential adverbial wh-words *kiif* 'how' and *lee(š)* 'why' cannot appear in situ in embedded contexts. Unlike adverbial wh-phrases, nominal wh-phrases like *miin* 'who,' *ʔayya NP* 'which NP,' *kam NP* 'how many NP,' and *ʔaddee(š)* 'how much' can be found in situ in embedded contexts in Lebanese Arabic (79).

(79)   a. ftakaro   ʔənno ħkiito   maʕ miin l-yom?
            thought.3p that   talked.2p with who the-day
            'They thought that you talked with whom today?'

       b. ftakaro   ʔənno xabbarto ʔayya walad ʕan   l-ħafle?
            thought.3p that   told.2p   which child about the-party
            'They thought that you told which child about the party?'

       c. btiftikro   ʔənno btibʕud   bayruut ʕan Traablus kam
            think.2p   that   be-far.3fs Beirut from Tripoli how many
            kilometer?
            kilometer
            'How many kilometers do you think is the distance between Beirut and Tripoli?'

d. btiʕtiʔdo ʔənno dafaʕ   ʔaddee(š) ħaʔʔ s-siyyaara?
   think.2p that   paid.3ms how much price the-car
   'How much do you think he paid for the car?'

However, *šu* 'what' cannot be found in situ, neither in simplex contexts (80a) nor in embedded contexts (80b).

(80)   a. *štriito   šu   mn-l-maħall?
            bought.2p what from-the-store
            'You bought what from the store?'

         b. *byiftikro ʔənno štriito   šu   mn-l-maħall?
            think.3p   that   bought.2p what from-the-store
            'They think that you bought what from the store?'

It is interesting to note here that the set of wh-phrases that can occur in situ does not match the set of wh-phrases that can be related to resumptive elements: it contains it. The set of wh-phrases that occur in situ consists of the nominal wh-phrases: *miin* 'who,' *ʔayya NP* 'which NP,' *kam NP* 'how many NP,' and *ʔaddee(š)* 'how much.' The set of wh-words that can be directly related to a resumptive pronominal excludes the measure wh-phrases *kam* NP 'how many NP' and *ʔadde(š)* 'how much.'

Putting *šu* 'what' on the side, we can observe a parallelism between wh-extraction and wh-in-situ: the contrast observed between non-referential adverbial wh-words and referential adverbial wh-words with respect to long-distance extraction is found again in in-situ contexts. What distinguishes in-situ wh-interrogatives from gapped wh-interrogaives in Lebanese Arabic is that the former cannot appear in a discourse out of the blue. Thus consider the minimally contrasting sentences in (81):

(81)   a. ʔe, miin šəfto l-yom?
            yes who saw.2p the-day
            'So, who did you see today?'

         b. ʔe, šəfto   miin l-yom?
            yes saw.2p who the-day
            'So, who did you see today?'

Whereas (81a) can be uttered as a conversation opening, (81b) cannot be uttered in such a context. Example (81b) presupposes the existence of a previous discourse in which the speaker has an indication that his or her addressees met some people on the day in question. Example (81b) is a question about the identity of those people. Therefore one can say that (81b) presupposes the truth of the assertion A = '*you saw someone today.*'

Finally, the wh-in-situ strategy does not have the same properties in all Arabic dialects. We have already observed that Egyptian Arabic uses the in-situ strategy as a default strategy for question formation. Furthermore, Egyptian Arabic puts no restrictions on which wh-words can appear in situ. Thus, unlike Lebanese Arabic, Egyptian Arabic allows its adverbial wh-words to appear in situ in simplex (82), as well as complex wh-interrogatives (83).[15]

(82)   a. saami biruuħ feen   kull yom?
           Sami go.3ms where every day
           'Where does Sami go every day?'

        b. saami ħayruuħ   ʔimta?
           Sami fut.go.3ms when
           'When will Sami go?'

        c. byaʕmilu kida lee?
           do.3p   so   why
           'Why do they do so?'

        d. Tabaxtu   l-muluxiyya   ʔizzay?
           cooked.2p the-mulukhiya how
           'How did you cook the mulukhiya?'

(83)   a. zeinab fakra   saami raħ   feen?
           Zeinab think.3fs Sami went.3ms where
           'Where does Zeinab think Sami went?'

        b. zeinab fakra   saami raħ   ʔimta?
           Zeinab thinking.fs Sami went.3ms when
           'When does Zeinab think Sami left?'

---

[15] The data in (82–83), obtained from our informant, seem to contradict the data in Wahba (1984), where it is claimed that wh-in-situ phrases cannot occur in tensed subordinate clauses (i).

(i)   a. Fariid ħawil   yiʕmil ʔeh?
          Fariid tried.3ms do.3ms what
          'What did Fariid try to do?'

       b. *Fariid iftakar   inn mona ishtarit/bitishtiri/ħatishtiri ʔeh?
          Fariid thought.3ms that Mona bought/buys/will buy   what
          'What did Fariid think that Mona bought/buys/will buy?'

However, all the data Wahba (1984) uses to illustrate this point include the use of *inn* 'that,' the declarative complementizer, which might itself block extraction.

   c. tiftikri   byaʕmilu kida lee?
      think.2fs do.3p   so   why
      'Why do you think they do so?'

   d. tiftikri   byitbuxu l-muluxiya   ʔizzay?
      think.2fs cook.3p the-mulukhiya how
      'How do you think they cook the mulukhiya?'

In addition, in Egyptian Arabic *ʔeh* 'what' (the equivalent of Lebanese Arabic *šu*) is allowed to appear in situ, in simplex (84a) and complex (84b) wh-questions:

(84)   a. saami ħayištiri   ʔeh?
         Sami buy.fut.3ms what
         'What will Sami buy?'

    b. tiftikri   saami ħayištiri   ʔeh?
       think.2fs Sami buy.fut.3ms what
       'What do you think Sami will buy?'

A crucial difference between Egyptian Arabic and Lebanese Arabic in-situ wh-interrogatives is that those constructions in Egyptian Arabic do not carry a presuppositional meaning and can be uttered out of the blue, as the following greeting illustrates:

(85)   ʕamla   ʔeh?
        doing.fs what?
        'How are you doing?'

In effect, Egyptian Arabic does not seem to make extensive use of the gapped wh-interrogatives as a default strategy. While Wahba (1984) reports of several instances of wh-questions involving gaps (86) (generally involving an adverbial wh-word), some native speakers of Egyptian Arabic point out that these sentences sound like translations from Standard Arabic.

(86)   feen itmannit mona tisaafir?
        where hoped.3fs Mona travel.3fs
        'Where did Mona hope to travel?'

6.5.2 Summary and analysis

In this section we have tried to answer the following two basic questions about wh-in-situ interrogatives: (a) which wh-words can remain in situ in Arabic? and (b) what is the distribution of wh-in-situ elements in those languages? The answers to those questions vary across the various dialects of Arabic. Thus,

Standard Arabic does not allow wh-words to remain in situ (except in very restricted contexts[16]), whereas Egyptian Arabic allows all its wh-words to remain in situ in all contexts. In Lebanese Arabic, the picture looks a bit more complicated. All nominal wh-words can remain in situ, except for *šu* 'what.' Adverbial wh-words are split along the "referentiality" dimension: what is referred to as referential adverbial wh-words can remain in situ in simplex as well as complex sentences, whereas non-referential adverbial wh-words are only marginally acceptable in simplex sentences. We have noted that this distinction between non-referential and referential adverbial wh-words is also relevant in the context of the long-distance extraction of wh-words.[17]

Aoun and Li (1993a) propose and argue for an analysis that provides an answer to the first question regarding the nature of the wh-words that may occur in situ. They suggest that wh-words can be classified as either operators or variables. The former need to undergo movement in the syntax, and this is the case in English; the latter can remain in situ, which is the case in Chinese. The authors further note that in Chinese, wh-words can also function as variables in non-question contexts, as illustrated in (87).

(87)   a. Ta gen shei   shuohua ma?
          he with whom speak   Q
          'Did he speak with someone?'

       b. Shenme ta dou yao.
          what   he all want
          'He wants everything.'

       c. Ta bu xihuan shenme
          he not like   what
          'He does not like anything.'

---

[16] One such context is the scholastic context where a teacher is eliciting answers from pupils, as illustrated below:

(i)   yaqra?u l-walad-u   maaðaa?
         reads.3ms the-boy-Nom what
         'What does the boy read?'

[17] The distinction made between referential and non-referential adverbial wh-words was said to hold in English since *when* and *where* have non-wh pronominal counterparts in *then* and *there* respectively. Interestingly, however, in Lebanese Arabic, where the same contrast holds between referential and non-referential adverbial wh-words, it is *ween* 'where,' *leeš/lašu* 'why,' and *kiif* 'how' that have corresponding non-wh pronouns: *hon/honik* 'here/there' and *heek* 'like this/for that reason.' Thus, although we continue to use the terms "referential" and "non-referential," we cannot say that we subscribe to the analysis that underlies it.

In (87a), the wh-word has an existential reading induced by the yes-no question context, in (87b) it has a universal reading induced by the presence of *dou*, a quantificational particle, and in (87c) it has a negative polarity reading. The wh-words in (87) are basically indefinite noun phrases bound to an operator. This is not the case for English wh-words, which cannot occur in any of the contexts in (87).

Ouhalla (1996) points out an empirical and a conceptual drawback in Aoun and Li's analysis of wh-in-situ. First, Iraqi Arabic – and we might add other dialects of Arabic (like Egyptian Arabic and Lebanese Arabic) – allows its wh-words to occur in situ, even though, as in English, none of them can function as variables in the contexts in (87). Thus, wh-words need not be used as indefinite NPs in order for them to occur in in-situ contexts. On a more conceptual level, Ouhalla points out that the ability an NP has to be a bound variable has no relation to its inherent properties. That is, almost all NP types, ranging from anaphors in (88a) to demonstrative NPs (88d), can function as bound variables.

(88)   a. Who loves himself?
        b. Who thinks he is a genius?
        c. Which boy's mother thinks the bastard is a genius?
        d. Every professor thinks that that professor deserves a raise.

Ouhalla (1996) proposes an alternative analysis which can be outlined as follows:

(89)   a. There are two types of wh-words: the bare type and the compound
           type. The compound type shows overt phi-features.
        b. Bare wh-words are long distance A′-anaphors whereas compound
           wh-pronouns are local A′-anaphors.

The assumption in (89a) describes the difference between English or Chinese wh-words on one hand, and those in Iraqi Arabic on the other. Thus, in Iraqi Arabic one observes the occurrence of an overt pronominal element on wh-words such as *šen-o* 'what' and *men-o* 'who.' Those are termed compound wh-words. In English, this pronominal element is assumed to be covert, as *who* and *what* do not show overt phi-features. They are therefore termed bare wh-words. The assumption in (89b) accounts for the distribution of wh-words in situ and for some observed cross-linguistic differences. Thus, in Chinese, where the wh-words do not bear overt phi-features, wh-words in situ appear inside tensed clauses and inside islands: they are long-distance anaphors.

(90)   a. Ta renwei ni   maile   shenme?
           he think   you bought what
           'What does he think you bought?'

b. Ta xiang-zhidao shei maile   shenme?
   he wonder   who bought what
   'What does he wonder who bought?'

The bare wh-word in Chinese can be bound by a [+wh] complementizer across a
tensed clause (90a) or a wh-island (90b). This is not the case in Iraqi Arabic (91).

(91)   a. *mona tSawwarit   Sali ištara   šeno?
           Mona thought.3fs Ali bought.3ms what
           'What did Mona think Ali bought?'

        b. *nasat   mona li-meno tinti   šeno?
           forgot.3fs Mona to-whom to-give.3fs what
           'What did Mona forget to whom to give?'

Given either one of the two analyses outlined above, it remains difficult to explain
the range of facts we observe in the other dialects of Arabic. In fact, in Ouhalla's
analysis, the fact that some languages (like Standard Arabic) do not allow any
of their wh-words to remain in situ remains unexplained. Under Aoun and Li's
assumption that wh-elements in situ need to occur as variables in contexts like
(87) that are different from wh-questions, the contrast between Lebanese Arabic
and Standard Arabic remains unexplained: in both languages the wh-words cannot
occur in the contexts in (87), yet Lebanese Arabic makes use of wh-in-situ, but
Standard Arabic doesn't. In Egyptian Arabic, where wh-words also do not occur
as variables in the contexts in (87), the wh-in-situ strategy is the default strategy
for forming questions. It is clear at this point that more work needs to be done in
order to be able to give a general answer to the questions we put forth at the outset
of this summary.

6.6   Conclusion

In this chapter we have examined the properties of A′-dependencies in
wh-interrogatives. Starting from the observation that the various Arabic dialects
make use of four different strategies to form wh-interrogatives, we investigated
the characteristics of those strategies, with respect to island sensitivity and the
nature of the wh-constituent that they involve.

A major distinction between gapped wh-interrogatives and the other three types
of questions is that there are no restrictions on the type of wh-constituent that can
occur in a gapped wh-interrogative. In addition, whereas gapped wh-interrogatives
are sensitive to islands, resumptive wh-interrogatives are not. We also observed that

the sets of wh-constituents that enter into resumptive interrogatives and Class II resumptive interrogatives are not the same. Thus, whereas *šu* 'what' (in Lebanese Arabic, and its equivalents in other modern varieties of Arabic) is prohibited in resumptive interrogatives, it is allowed to occur in Class II resumptive interrogatives. We discussed possible accounts for the restriction on the type of wh-constituent that can be related to a resumptive and concluded that referentiality (however defined) does not present an adequate answer: amount (quantified) wh-words cannot be related to resumptives in wh-questions, although they can have a referential reading. Finally, the wh-in-situ strategy varies across the Arabic dialects, not only in its availability, but also in terms of the nature of the wh-word that can occur in situ. In Egyptian Arabic, the in-situ strategy is the default strategy for forming questions and all wh-words can occur in situ. In Lebanese Arabic, on the other hand, that is not the case. The set of wh-words that can occur in situ in Lebanese Arabic does not coincide with the set of wh-words that can be related to a resumptive pronoun.

7

Restrictive relatives

7.1   Introduction

In the previous chapter, we focused on the different strategies for forming wh-interrogatives in Arabic and on their different syntactic and interpretive
properties. We discussed the properties of long-distance dependencies between
sentence initial wh-words and their corresponding positions within the sentence.
We observed that the relationship between a wh-word and its corresponding gap
within the sentence is sensitive to islands, whereas this wasn't the case for the
relationship between a wh-word and its corresponding resumptive element. Furthermore, we observed that the resumptive strategy puts restrictions on the nature
of the wh-antecedent, such that only wh-words that correspond to a DP can
be related to a resumptive element. It is also the case that all wh-words that
can be related to a resumptive element are referential, in the sense defined by
Cinque (1990).

This chapter focuses on restrictive relative constructions in Arabic. In restrictive
relative clause formation, it is the resumptive strategy that is the default strategy.
Although gaps can be found in restrictive relatives in Arabic, their distribution is
restricted in various dialects. This allows us to investigate further the properties
of resumption. It will turn out that there are contexts where resumption shares
characteristics of gap constructions in being sensitive to island conditions, and
that referentiality does not adequately constrain the set of possible antecedents of
a resumptive pronoun. In addition, the chapter introduces a new classification of
restrictive relatives in terms of the definiteness of the antecedent (relativized head)
that plays a significant role in the syntax of those constructions.

7.2   Two types of relative clauses

Restrictive relative clauses in Arabic fall into two categories: restrictive
relatives with a definite relativized DP (definite relatives) and restrictive relatives
with an indefinite relativized DP (indefinite relatives).

Definite relatives always occur with the complementizer *allaði*:

(1)   a. Daaʕa   l-kitaabu *(allaði) štaraytu-hu l-baariħata
           lost.3ms the-book that   bought.1s-it yesterday
           'The book that I bought yesterday is lost.'

        b. Turida   l-waladu *(allaði) mazzaqa l-kitaaba
           expelled.3ms the-child that   tore.3ms the-book
           'The boy that tore up the book was expelled.'

Indefinite relatives on the other hand cannot occur with *allaði*; as a matter of fact, indefinite relatives have no complementizer:

(2)   a. ʔufattišu ʕan kitaabin (*allaði) ʔaDaʕtu-hu l-yawma
           look.1s for book   that   lost.1s-it   the-day
           'I am looking for a book that I lost today.'

        b. Taradat   l-muʕallimatu bintan (*allati) Darabat tilmiiðan fi
           expelled.3fs the-teacher.fs girl   that   hit.3fs student in
           S-Saffi
           the-class
           'The teacher expelled a girl that hit a student in the class.'

The complementizer *allaði* is specific to relative constructions. As observed in chapter 2, sentential complements in Arabic are introduced by *ʔanna* or *ʔan*, as illustrated below:

(3)   ʕaadat   l-bintu allati/*ʔan(na) ɣaabat   ʕan
        returned.3fs the-girl that   was-absent.3fs from
        S-Saffi l-bariħata
        the-class yesterday
        'The girl that was absent from class yesterday returned.'

(4)   a. qaalat   l-muʕallimatu ʔanna/*allati l-binta ɣaaʔibatun
           said.3fs the-teacher.fs that   the-girl absent.fs
           'The teacher said that the girl was absent.'

        b. turiidu   l-muʕallimatu ʔan/*allati tufassira   darsa t-taariixi
           want.3fs the-teacher.fs that   explain.3fs lesson the-history
           'The teacher wants to explain the history lesson.'

This state of affairs is found across the Arabic dialects.[1] What unifies the two types of relatives is that they are both generally formed with the resumptive strategy: in constructions with definite relatives and indefinite relatives, the relativized DP is generally related to a resumptive element that occurs within the relative clause. In non-subject positions,[2] the resumptive element is always realized as a clitic (or weak pronoun) (1a) and (2a). Arabic being a null-subject language, it comes as no surprise that there is no overt pronominal in (1b) and (2b) marking the relativized site in subject position (see also chapter 3). As we have observed in the case of wh-interrogatives, the agreement morpheme on the verb may be taken to identify the null pronominal element that serves as a resumptive pronoun in the cases of relativization from subject position.

---

[1] Ouhalla (2004) capitalizes on this difference between relative clauses and sentential complements and argues for two types of relative clauses: the CP-type, found in English and Hebrew, which uses the same complementizer in sentential complements and relative clauses, and the DP-type, found in Semitic, where the relativizer, a nominal element akin to the definite determiner, is different from the sentential complement complementizer.

[2] These non-subject positions include complements of verbs as well as complements of prepositions (i) or nouns (ii).

(i) a. wajadtu kitaaban ʔaxbarat-ni ʕan-hu laila *Standard Arabic*
   found.1s book   told.3fs-me about-it Laila
   fi-l-ʕilliyati
   in-the-attic
   'I found a book that Laila told me about in the attic.'

  b. štarayt l-kteeb yalli ħkiite ʕann-o   *Lebanese Arabic*
   bought.1s the-book that talked.2fs about-it
   mbeeriħ
   yesterday
   'I bought the book that you talked about yesterday.'

(ii) a. štarayt l-kteeb yalli btaʕrfe keetb-o   *Lebanese Arabic*
   bought.1s the-book that know.2fs author-its
   'I bought the book that you know its author.'

  b. taʕarrafnaa ʕala muxriẓin taʕrifu ʔibnu-hu laila *Standard Arabic*
   met.1p on director.ms know.3fs son-his Laila
   'We met a director that Laila knows his son.'

We will illustrate our generalizations using constructions with accusative resumptive clitics. However, these generalizations hold true of resumptive clitics which are complements of prepositions and nouns as well.

7.3   The gap strategy in restrictive relatives

The various Arabic dialects differ in whether they allow gaps in restrictive relatives. In Modern Standard Arabic, gaps are allowed in object positions of definite relatives:

(5)   a. al-kitaabu allaði sayaštari   saami mawžudun fi-l-maktabati
          the-book that buy.fut.3ms Sami exist.ms in-the-bookstore
          'The book that Sami will buy is found at the bookstore.'

       b. raʔaytu l-lawħata   allati qulta   ʔanna-ka   sataštari
          saw.1s the-painting that said.2ms that-you.ms buy.fut.2ms
          'I saw the painting that you said that you will buy.'

Interestingly, Standard Arabic as well as the other dialects of Arabic that allow gaps in restrictive relatives make exclusive use of resumption in indefinite relatives. Thus, the sentence in (5b) contrasts with the one in (6).

(6)   raʔaytu lawħatan qulta   ʔanna-ka   sataštari-*(ha)
       saw.1s painting said.2ms that-you.ms buy.fut.2ms-*(it)
       'I saw a painting that you said that you will buy.'

In some Arabic dialects, such as Lebanese Arabic, gaps are only allowed in the subject position of existential constructions,[3] or in adjunct positions (Choueiri 2002). Thus, consider the following sentences:

(7)   a. (kəll) l-kətub   lli   keen fii   ʕa-T-Taawle Saaro
          (all) the-books that was in-it on-the-table become.3p

          ʕa-r-raff   hallaʔ
          on-the-shelf now
          '(All) the books that there were on the table are now on the shelf.'

---

[3] Carlson (1977) refers to those types of constructions with the name *amount relatives* (AR). However, as Grosu and Landmann (1998) point out, those relative clauses that involve relativization of the subject of existential constructions do not always have an amount reading (i).

(i)   I took with me every book that there was on the table.

The sentence in (i) does not mean that the speaker took as many books (from the library) as there were books (on the kitchen table). In the Lebanese Arabic sentences given in the text, an amount reading does not adequately describe the interpretation of the sentences either. Those sentences imply an identity of substance (the actual objects) as well as an identity of amounts. We will therefore abandon the term *amount relative* in the text.

b. žammaʕt   (kəll) l-kətub   lli   ʕam tʔuulo ʔənno keen
   collected.1s (all) the-books that Asp. say.2p that   was

fii   ʕa-T-Taawle
in-it on-the-table
'I collected (all) the books that you are saying that there were on the table.'

First, it must be noted that neither the particle *fii* (lit. 'in it') nor the PP predicate 'on the table' bear the necessary agreement features to identify a null subject pronoun (see chapter 3). We can then say that the relativized site in (7) clearly corresponds to a gap.[4]

Similarly, adjunct relatives expressing time provide further evidence that gaps are indeed involved in relativization in Lebanese Arabic.[5]

---

[4] This conclusion is further confirmed by the fact that whereas a strong pronoun may optionally appear in the context of pro-drop, as illustrated in (i), it cannot appear in the sentences involving relativization of the subject of an existential construction (ii):

(i)   žamʕiyyit   S-Saliib l-ʔaḥmar ʔaddamit   hdiyye la-l-ḥakiime   lli
     organization the-cross the-red   presented.3fs gift   to-the-doctor.f that

ʔaalo   S-Saḥaafiyye ʔənno **(hiyye)** seeʕadit   l-žarḥa
said.3p the-reporters that   (she)   helped.3fs the-wounded
'The organization of the Red Cross presented a gift to the doctor that the reporters said that (she) helped the wounded.'

(ii)   a. (kəll) l-kətub   lli   ʕam tʔuulo ʔənno keen fii
      (all)   the-books that Asp. say.2p that   was in-it

(*hənne) ʕa-T-Taawle leezim yinḥaTTo ʕa-r-raff
(*them)   on-the-table should put.3p   on-the-shelf
'(All) the books that you are saying that there were (them) on the table should be put on the shelf.'

    b. žammaʕt   (kəll) l-kətub   lli   ʕam tʔuulo ʔənno keen fii
      collected.1s (all) the-books that Asp. say.2p that   was in-it

(*hənne) ʕa-T-Taawle
(*them)   on-the-table
'I collected (all) the books that you are saying that there were (them) on the table.'

The subject position of existential constructions triggers definiteness effects and since personal pronouns are definite, the unacceptability of the sentences in (ii) with a resumptive strong pronoun is not surprising.

[5] Larson (1985) observes, for English, that the headed relative clauses that have a trace in an adjunct position instead of a stranded preposition or a relative adverb are those whose head belongs to the class of *bare-NP adverbs*, NPs that can function adverbially without an accompanying preposition. This generalization also accounts for the difference that can

(8)   raħ nuuSal   Sa-l-ħafle   seeSt lli   bitballiš l-musiiʔa
       fut. arrive.1p to-the-party hour that begin.3fs the-music
       'We will arrive at the party the time that the music begins.'

In addition to cases like (8), a gap can occur in an embedded clause within the relative clause (9).

(9)   a. raħ nuuSal   Sa-l-ħafle   seeSt lli   btiftikro (?? ʔǝnno)
          fut. arrive.1p to-the-party hour that think.2p (?? that)

          raħ bitballiš   l-musiiʔa Ø
          fut. begin.3fs   the-music Ø
          'We will arrive at the party at the time that you think (that) the music will begin.'

       b. ??raħ nǝže   Sa-l-ħafle   seeSt lli   btiʔtinSo   ʔǝnno
          fut.   come.1p to-the-party hour that convince.2p that

          leezim tballiš   l-musiiʔa Ø
          should begin.3fs the-music Ø
          'We will come to the party at the time that you are convinced that the music should begin.'

In (9a), the time adjunct *see Sa(-t)* 'hour' can easily modifiy the higher verb *btiftikro* 'you think' inside the relative clause: under that reading, the time of arrival to the party coincides with the time the hearers think the music will begin, and not the time when the music will actually begin. The latter interpretation – which implies that the adjunct modifies the lower verb *bitballiš* 'begins' – is only available in the absence of the complementizer *ʔǝnno* 'that.' When the embedding verb does not allow complementizer deletion, as in (9b) *btiʔtinSo* 'you are convinced,' the reading that is readily available is the one where the adjunct modifies the higher verb: the time of arrival to the party coincides with the time the hearers are convinced that the music should start. This is what the double question marks indicate in (9b).

be noted between relativized time adverbs and relativized manner adverbs in Lebanese Arabic. Only the former can occur as bare NPs:

(i)   a. wǝSlo   (bi-) seeSǝt-(h)a
          arrived.3p (in-) hour-this
          'They arrived at this hour.'

       b. wǝSlo   (Sa-) s-seeSa Sašra
          arrived.3p (on-) the-hour ten
          'They arrived at ten.'

Thus, the distribution of gaps in definite restrictive relatives in Arabic is restricted: although the gap strategy is not the default strategy for forming restrictive relatives in Arabic, some dialects of Arabic do make use of gaps in those constructions. In Standard Arabic, the gap strategy alternates with the resumptive strategy in direct object positions. In Lebanese Arabic, for instance, the gap strategy is the only strategy available for relativization from adjunct positions and the subject position of existential constructions.

7.4   Gapped relatives and island sensitivity

Like other A'-constructions involving gaps, gapped relatives in Arabic show island sensitivity. Thus, in Standard Arabic, a gap cannot occur in object position if the relativized site is within an adjunct clause (10), a relative clause (11), or a wh-island (12).

(10)   *Adjunct clause*
        *ʕallaqtu l-lawħata   allati saafarti   qabla ʔan ʔaštari
        hung.1s   the-painting that   traveled.2fs before that buy.1s
        'I hung the painting that you traveled before I bought.'

(11)   *Relative clause*
        *raʔaytu l-lawħata   allati taʕrifiina r-rajula allaði ʔištaraa
        saw.1s   the-painting that   know.2fs the-man that   bought.3ms
        'I saw the painting that you know the man that bought.'

(12)   *Wh-island*
        *raʔaytu l-lawħata   allati taʕrifiina man ʔištaraa
        saw.1s   the-painting that   know.2fs who bought.3ms
        'I saw the painting that you know who bought.'

Similarly, in Lebanese Arabic, a gap that corresponds to the subject of an existential construction cannot occur in island contexts (13).

(13)   a. *Adjunct clause*
        *(kəll) l-kətub   lli   narfazto laʔanno keen fii   ʕa-T-Taawle
        (all)   the-books that upset.2p because was   in-it on-the-table

        leezim yinħaTTo ʕa-r-raff
        should put.3p   on-the-shelf
        '(All) the books that you were upset because there were on the table
        should be put on the shelf.'

b. *Wh-island*

    (kəll) l-kətub   lli   baddkun taʕrfo   miin ʔaal   ʔənno
    (all)   the-books that want.2p know.2p who said.3ms that

    keen fii   ʕa-T-Taawle leezim yinħaTTo ʕa-r-raff
    was in-it on-the-table should put.3p   on-the-shelf
    '(All) the books that you want to know who said that there were on
    the table should be put on the shelf.'

c. *Relative clause*

    (kəll) l-kətub   lli   baddkun taʕrfo   S-Sabe lli   ʔaal
    (all)   the-books that want.2p know.2p the-boy that said.3ms

    ʔənno keen fii   ʕa-T-Taawle leezim yinħaTTo ʕa-r-raff
    that   was in-it on-the-table should put.3p   on-the-shelf
    '(All) the books that you want to know the boy who said that there
    were on the table should be put on the shelf.'

In time adjunct relatives, the distribution of the gap is sensitive to islands as
well, as can be seen in the Lebanese Arabic examples in (14).

(14)   a. *Wh-island*

        wSəlna   ʕa-l-ħafle   seeʕt lli   saʔal   saami ʔəza   keeno
        arrived.1p to-the-party hour that ask.3ms Sami whether were.3p

        fallo   ʔahl-o   Ø
        left.3p parents-his Ø
        'We arrived at the party at the time that Sami asked whether his
        parents had left.'

    b. *Adjunct clause*

        wSəlna   ʕa-l-ħafle   seeʕt lli   narfaz   saami laʔanno
        arrived.1p to-the-party hour that upset.3ms Sami because

        keeno   ʔahl-o   fallo Ø
        were.3p parents-his left.3p Ø
        'We arrived at the party at the time that Sami got upset because his
        parents had left.'

    c. *Relative clause*

        wSəlna   ʕa-l-ħafle   seeʕt lli   keeno   l-bolisiyye   ʕam
        arrived.1p to-the-party hour that were.3p the-policemen Asp.

        yilʔaTo   z-zalame lli   Darab   maria Ø
        catching.3p the-man that hit.3ms Maria Ø
        'We arrived at the party at the time that the policemen were catching
        the man that hit Maria.'

The sentences in (14), which illustrate the relativization of the time adjunct *seeʕa* 'hour' from various island contexts, are acceptable only under the reading where the adjunct modifies the higher verb inside the relative. The reading that forces the time adjunct to be construed with the verb inside the relative clause island is unavailable. This shows that time adjunct relatives are indeed sensitive to islands.

If sensitivity to islands is taken as an indication for movement in syntax (Chomsky 1977), then we can say that gapped restrictive relatives in Arabic, like wh-interrogatives involving gaps, are generated by movement in the syntax. That is, the relationship between the gap and its antecedent in the relative clause is a relation created by movement.[6] Thus the representation of restrictive relatives below corresponds to that of wh-interrogatives involving gaps given in chapter 6:

(15)   relativized NP$_i$ ... ... trace$_i$

In the representation in (15), it appears that the relationship between the relativized noun phrase and the trace within the sentence is direct. That is, the trace of movement in (15) is that of the relativized noun phrase itself. This representation thus corresponds to what has been called the "raising" analysis of restrictive relatives. The "raising" analysis has been advocated by several researchers in the field and more recently by Kayne (1994), and it has been discussed in the context of Semitic restrictive relatives in Choueiri (2002) and Ouhalla (2004). An alternative analysis for restrictive relatives is the one argued for in Chomsky (1977), which involves the movement of a null operator coindexed with the relativized noun phrase, as illustrated in (16).

(16)   Relativized NP$_i$ -Op$_i$ ... ... trace$_i$

In (16), the relation between the relativized noun phrase and the trace is mediated by a predication relation, which results in the coindexation of the relativized noun phrase and the null operator *Op*. The data discussed so far conform to both representations in (15–16).

Having discussed the distribution of gaps within restrictive relatives in Arabic, we now turn to the discussion of the default strategy for forming restrictive relatives in Arabic: the resumptive strategy.

---

[6] The relationship between the gap and resumptive strategies and movement is further elaborated on in chapter 9. See also Shlonsky (1992) for a discussion of movement and resumption in the context of restrictive relatives in Hebrew and Arabic.

7.5   The distribution of weak resumptive pronouns in restrictive relatives

Descriptively, a weak resumptive element may appear inside Arabic restrictive relatives in all positions except subject positions and adjunct positions. Illustrative examples of restrictive relatives with weak resumptive pronouns are given below, from Lebanese Arabic and Standard Arabic.

(17)   *Direct object*

    a. mnaʕrif (l-)mara   (lli) raħ yʔeebəl-**a** saami   *Lebanese*
         know-1p (the-)woman (that) will meet-her   Sami   *Arabic*
         'We know the/a woman that Sami will meet.'

    b. ʔaʕrifu l-mumaθilata allati sayuqabilu-**ha** saami *Standard Arabic*
         know.1s the-actress   that fut.meet-her   Sami
         'I know the actress that Sami will meet.'

(18)   *Indirect object*

    a. ʔəža   (l-)mwaZZaf (lli) ʔaaluu-l-**o**   *Lebanese Arabic*
         come.3ms (the-)employee (that) told.3p-to-him

         ʔənno fii   ʔəDraab
         that   there strike
         'An/The employee to whom they told that there was a strike came.'

    b. žaaʔa   (t-)tilmiiðu (allaði) ʔaʕTaytu-**hu**   *Standard Arabic*
         come.3ms (the-)student (that)   gave.1s-him

         l-kitaaba
         the-book
         'The student to whom I gave the book came.'

(19)   *Oblique*

    a. ħDərna (l-)masraħiyyeet (lli)   χabbarna   *Lebanese Arabic*
         saw.1p (the-)plays   (that) told.3ms

         ʕann-**un**   kariim
         about-them Karim
         'We saw (the) plays that Karim told us about.'

    b. qaraʔna (l-)kutuba (allati) ʔaxbarana   *Standard Arabic*
         read.1p (the-)books (that)   told.3ms

         ʕan-**ha**   kariimun
         about-them Karim
         'We read the books that Karim told us about.'

(20)   *Noun complement*

    a. ħDərna (l-)masraħiyye (lli)   byaʕrif   *Lebanese Arabic*
       saw.1p (the-)play   (that) know.3ms

       kariim mmassliin-**a** kəll-un
       Karim actors-it   all-them
       'We saw a/the play that Karim knows all its actors.'

    b. ħaDarna masraħiyyatan yaʕrifu   kariim   *Standard Arabic*
       saw.1p   play   know.3ms Karim

       mumaθθilii-**ha** kulla-hum
       actors-it   all-them
       'We saw a play that Karim knows all its actors.'

In the sentences in (17–20), the relativization site is occupied by a pronominal element that resumes the relative clause head noun. This pronominal element is the same one that resumes wh-words like *miin/man* 'who' and *ʔayy(a) NP* 'which NP' in wh-interrogatives (see chapter 6). In the next sections we investigate the properties of resumption in restrictive relatives in Arabic. We first show that, in those constructions, resumption presents a behavior different from that in wh-interrogatives: in certain given contexts, resumption displays island sensitivity. We then go on to discuss the properties of the relativized noun phrase, which is related to the resumptive element.

7.6   Island sensitivity in restrictive relatives with weak resumptive pronouns

The contrast between resumptive A′-constructions and gapped A′-constructions with respect to island sensitivity is well known in the literature. We have already observed this contrast in wh-interrogatives. Whereas wh-interrogatives involving gaps are sensitive to islands, wh-interrogatives involving resumption are not. In this section we show that resumption is not a unitary phenomenon with respect to island sensitivity and that some resumptive restrictive relatives in Arabic are indeed sensitive to islands.

7.6.1   *The absence of island sensitivity with weak resumptive pronouns*

In general, weak resumptive elements can occur inside islands in restrictive relatives in Arabic, whether definite or indefinite. This observation has been made in the literature dealing with the subject (see, for example, Demirdache

(1991) and Shlonsky (1992) and references cited therein). The paradigms in (21–25) illustrate this generalization for wh-islands, adjunct clauses, and relative clauses respectively.

(21)   *Wh-islands*

    a. mnaʕrif (l-)mara   (lli)   ʕam titseeʔalo miin raħ yʔeebəl-**a**
    know.1p (the-)woman (that) Asp. wonder.2p who will meet.3ms-her
    'We know a/the woman that you are wondering who will meet her.'

    b. naʕrifu   (r-)ražula (allaði) tatasaaʔaluna ʕam-man   sayuqaabilu-**hu**
    know.1p (the-)man (that)   wonder.2p   about-who meet.3ms-him
    'We know a/the man that you are wondering who will meet him.'

(22)   *Adjunct clauses*

    a. mnaʕrif (l-)mara   (lli)   fallayto ʔabl   ma   yʔeebəl-**a**
    know.1p (the-)woman (that) left.2p   before Comp meet.3ms-her
    kariim
    Karim
    'We know a/the woman that you left before Karim met (her).'

    b. ħaDarna (l-)masraħiyyata (allati) ðahabtum lamma ʔaχbara-na
    saw.1p   (the-)play   (that) left.2p   when   told.3ms-us
    kariim ʕan-**ha**
    Karim about-them
    'We saw a/the play that you left when Karim told us about (it).'

(23)   *Relative clauses*

    a. Sawwarna   (l-)mara   (lli)   ħkiito   maʕ r-ražžeel lli
    took.picture.1p (the-)woman that talked.2p with the-man   that
    raħ yʔeebəl-**a**
    will meet-her
    'We took a picture of a/the woman that you talked to the man who will meet (her).'

    b. ħaDarna (l-)masraħiyyata (allati) taʕrifuuna S-Saħaafiyya llaði
    saw.1p   (the-)play   (that) know.2p   the-journalist that
    ʔaχbara-na ʕan-**ha**
    told.3ms-us about-it
    'We saw a/the play that you know the journalist that told us about it.'

It cannot be said, however, that resumptive restrictive relatives in Arabic are not sensitive to islands. In what follows, we present evidence to show that definite relatives generated with a resumptive element are indeed sensitive to islands.[7]

7.6.2 *Abstract noun relativization and island sensitivity*

The first piece of evidence to show that resumptive restrictive relatives are sensitive to islands comes from the relativization of abstract nouns like *sərʕa* 'speed,' *šažeeʕa* 'courage,' *nazeeha* 'integrity,' *narvaze* 'nervousness,' and *Tiibit ʔalb* 'kindness': when they are used as manner adverbials in Lebanese Arabic, these abstract nouns are introduced by an obligatory preposition, as illustrated in (24):

(24)   byištiʁil   saami   *(bi-)

$$\begin{cases} \textit{nazeeha} & \text{`integrity'} \\ \textit{sərʕa} & \text{`speed'} \\ \textit{narvaze} & \text{`nervousness'} \\ \textit{šažeeʕa} & \text{`courage'} \\ \textit{Tiibit ʔalb} & \text{`kindness'} \end{cases}$$

works.3ms Sami *(with-)

Relativization of such adjuncts involves obligatory resumption, as shown in (25).[8]

(25)   a. s-sərʕa   lli   štaʁal   fiy-*(**a**)   saami hiyye l-maTluube
          the-speed that worked.3ms with-*(it) Sami she   the-required
          'The speed with which Sami worked is what is required.'

      b. ʕažabət-ne   š-šažeeʕa   lli   hažam   fiy-*(**a**)   z-zalame
          pleased.3fs-me the-courage that leaped.3ms with-*(it) the-man

          ʕala l-ħarame
          on   the-thief
          'The courage that the man leaped with on the thief pleased me.'

      c. btəʕžəb-ne   Tiibt   l-ʔalb/   n-nazeeha   lli   biʕaamil
          please.3fs-me goodness the-heart/ the-integrity that treat.3ms

          fiy-*(**a**)   l-ʔəsteez   tleemiz-o
          with-*(it) the-teacher.m students-his
          'The kindness/integrity that the teacher treats his students with pleases me.'

---

[7] This observation is a new one for the various Arabic dialects where it has been observed that resumption always alleviates island violations (see, for example, Aoun and Choueiri 1996; Demirdache 1991).

[8] The preposition *bi* 'with' which introduces the abstract NPs in (24) is realized as *fi(y)* with a weak pronominal element.

    d. n-narvaze   lli byiħke fiy-*(**a**)   saami maʕ l-zbuneet
      the-nervousness that talk.3ms with-*(it) Sami with the-clients

      bithaššəl-un
      drives-away.3fs-them
      'The nervousness that Sami speaks with to the clients drives them
      away.'

In (25), all the prepositional phrases inside the relative, which contain the resumptive element, modify a verb, expressing manner. The resumptive element can be related to the relative clause external head across sentence boundaries. Again, the absence of these resumptive elements yields unacceptable sentences, as indicated in (26):

(26)   a. s-sərʕa   lli   ftakarto   ʔənno saami byištiʁil   fiy-*(**a**)
        the-speed that thought.2p that   Sami works.3ms with-*(it)

        hiyye l-maTluube
        she   the-required
        'The speed with which you think that Sami works is the required one.'

    b. ʕažabət-ne   š-šažeeʕa   lli   ʔəlto   ʔənno hažam
        pleased.3fs-me the-courage that said.2p that   leaped.3ms

        fiy-*(**a**)   z-zalame ʕala l-ħarame
        with-*(it) the-man   on   the-thief
        'The courage that you said that the man leaped with on the thief
        pleased me.'

    c. btəʕʕəb-ne   Tiibt   l-ʔalb/   n-nazeeha   lli   ʔannaʕtuu-ne
        please.3fs-me goodness the-heart/ the-integrity that convinced.2p-me

        ʔənno biʕaamil fiy-*(**a**)   l-ʔəsteez   tleemiz-o
        that   treat.3ms with-*(it) the-teacher.m students-his
        'The kindness/integrity that you convinced me that the teacher treats
        his students with pleases me.'

    d. n-narvaze   lli   χabbartuu-ne ʔənno byiħke   fiy-*(**a**)
        the-nervousness that told.2p-me   that   talk.3ms with-*(it)

        saami maʕ l-zbuneet raħ bithaššəl-un
        Sami with the-clients fut. drives-away.3fs-them
        'The nervousness that you told me that Sami speaks with to the
        clients will drive them away.'

Interestingly, however, the resumptive elements corresponding to the manner adverbs cannot be related to the relative clause external head across island boundaries. When the abstract noun is relativized from a position inside an adjunct clause, a wh-clause, or a relative clause, the resulting sentences are unacceptable, although a resumptive element appears in the relativized site (27–29).

(27)   *Adjunct clauses*

    a. *s-sərʕa lli   btinbəSTo laʔanno saami byištiʁil   fiy-**a**   hiyye
        the-speed that pleased.2p because Sami works.3ms with-it she

        l-maTluube
        the-required
        'The speed with which you are pleased because Sami works is the required one.'

    b. *ʕažabət-ne   š-šažeeʕa lli   tfeežaʔto   lamma hažam
        pleased.3fs-me the-courage that surprised.2p when   leaped.3ms

        fiy-**a**   z-zalame ʕala l-ħarame
        with-it the-man on   the-thief
        'The courage that you were surprised when the man leaped with on the thief pleased me.'

    c. *btəʕžəb-ne Tiibt   l-ʔalb/ n-nazeeha lli   nbaSaTTo
        please.3fs-me goodness the-heart/ the-integrity that pleased.2p

        laʔanno biʕaamil fiy-**a**   l-ʔəsteez   tleemiz-o
        because treat.3ms with-it the-teacher.m students-his
        'The kindness/integrity that you were pleased because the teacher treats his students with pleases me.'

    d. *n-narvaze   lli   btiddeeyaʔo laʔanno byiħke fiy-**a**   saami
        the-nervousness that bothered.2p because talk.3ms with-it Sami

        maʕ l-zbuneet raħ bithaššəl-un
        with the-clients fut. drives-away.3fs-them
        'The nervousness that you are bothered because Sami speaks with to the client will drive them away.'

(28)   *Wh-islands*

    a. *s-sərʕa lli   btaʕrfo miin byištiʁil   fiy-**a**   hiyye l-maTluube
        the-speed that know.2p who works.3ms with-it she   the-required
        'The speed with which you know who works is the required one.'

b. *ʕažabət-ne   š-šažeeʕa   lli   btaʕrfo   miin   hažam   fiy-**a**
   pleased.3fs-me the-courage that know.2p who leaped.3ms with-it

   ʕala l-ħarame
   on   the-thief
   'The courage that you know who leaped with on the thief pleased me.'

c. *btəʕžəb-ne   Tiibt   l-ʔalb/   n-nazeeha   lli   btaʕrfo   miin
   please.3fs-me goodness the-heart/ the-integrity that know.2p who

   biʕaamil fiy-**a**   t-tleemiz
   treat.3ms with-it the-students
   'The kindness/integrity that you know who treats the students with
   pleases me.'

d. *n-narvaze   lli   btaʕrfo   miin byiħke   fiy-**a**   maʕ l-zbuneet
   the-nervousness that know.2p who talk.3ms with-it with the-clients

   raħ bithaššəl-un
   fut. drives-away.3fs-them
   'The nervousness that you know who speaks with to the clients will
   drive them away.'

(29)   *Relative clauses*

a. *s-sərʕa lli   btaʕrfo   l-mwaZZaf   lli   byištiʁil   fiy-**a**   hiyye
   the-speed that know.2p the-employee that works.3ms with-it she

   l-maTluube
   the-required
   'The speed with which you know the employee who works is the
   required one.'

b. *ʕažabət-ne   š-šažeeʕa   lli   btaʕrfo   z-zalame lli
   pleased.3fs-me the-courage that know.2p the-man   that

   hažam   fiy-**a**   ʕala l-ħarame
   leaped.3ms with-it on   the-thief
   'The courage that you know the man who leaped with on the thief
   pleased me.'

c. *btəʕžəb-ne   Tiibt   l-ʔalb/   n-nazeeha   lli   btaʕrfo
   please.3fs-me goodness the-heart/ the-integrity that know.2p

   l-ʔəsteez   lli   biʕaamil fiy-**a**   t-tleemiz
   the-teacher that treat.3ms with-it the-students
   'The kindness/integrity that you know the teacher who treats the
   students with pleases me.'

d. *n-narvaze   lli btaʕrfo š-šaʁʁiil   lli byiħke
   the-nervousness that know.2p the-employee that talk.3ms

   fiy-**a**   maʕ l-zbuneet raħ bithaššəl-un
   with-it with the-clients fut. drives-away.3fs-them
   'The nervousness that you know the employee who speaks with to the
   clients will drive them away.'

The data concerning the relativization of abstract nouns like *sərʕa* 'speed,' *šažeeʕa* 'courage,' *nazeeha* 'integrity,' *narvaze* 'nervousness,' *and Tiibit ʔalb* 'kindness' provide the first indication that the presence of resumptive elements in (Lebanese) Arabic definite relatives may not always coincide with the absence of island sensitivity.

7.6.3   The relativization of idiomatic NP chunks

Another piece of evidence that shows that resumptive constructions in Lebanese Arabic are selectively sensitive to islands comes from the relativization of idiomatic NP chunks.[9]

The expression equivalent to *take a nap* in English is *ʔaχad ʁaTTa* in Lebanese Arabic. That this expression is an idiomatic expression can be seen from the fact that the noun *ʁaTTa*, which is a nominalization from the verb *ʁaTT* 'to sleep,' has no independent meaning in Lebanese Arabic.

(30)   a. *l-ʁaTTa baʕd D-Duhr   bitfiid
          the-nap   after the-noon help.3fs
          'The nap in the afternoon helps.'

       b. n-nawme baʕd D-Duhr   bitfiid
          the-sleep after the-noon help.3fs
          'The nap in the afternoon helps.'

(31)   *waSaf-l-e   l-ħakiim   ʁaTTa baʕd D-Duhr
        prescribe.3ms-to-me the-doctor nap   after the-noon
        'The doctor prescribed a nap in the afternoon.'

As shown by the unacceptability of (30a) and (31), the noun *ʁaTTa* cannot take on the meaning 'nap' when it occurs by itself. In fact it has no meaning at all and

---

[9] There is no systematic study of the behavior of idiomatic NP chunks in relativization in Arabic. However, the discussion of the example in the text is sufficient to make the point about the absence of uniformity in the behavior of resumptive constructions with respect to island constraints.

the sentences are totally unacceptable. This interpretation of ʁaTTa as 'nap' is contextualized and conditioned by the presence of the light verb ʔaχad 'to take' in (32):[10]

(32)   saami ʔaχad   ʁaTTa baʕd l-ʁada
        Sami took.3ms nap   after the-lunch
        'Sami took a nap after lunch.'

Interestingly, the idiomatic NP chunk ʁaTTa cannot be pronominalized:

(33)   a. *saami ʔaχad   ʁaTTa baʕd l-ʁada   bas laila ma
           Sami   took.3ms nap   after the-lunch but Laila Neg

        ʔaχadit wəḥde/-a
        took.3fs one/-it
        'Sami took a nap after lunch but Laila didn't take one/it.'

The unacceptability of (33) indicates that the idiomatic meaning 'take a nap' is not available when the NP ʁaTTa is replaced by a(n) (indefinite) pronoun: the contextualized occurrence of one instance of the idiomatic NP chunk ʁaTTa with which the (indefinite) pronoun can be anaphoric is not enough to salvage the sentence. Briefly put, ʁaTTa cannot enter into coreference relations with pronouns, whether indefinite like wəḥde 'one' or not, like the pronominal clitic -a.

However, the NP ʁaTTa can be relativized, and in such a case, a resumptive element is required in the relativization site:

(34)   a. l-ʁaTTa yalli ʔaχad-*(a)   saami baʕd l-ʁada   feedit-o
           the-nap that took.3ms-her Sami after the-lunch helped.3fs-him
           'The nap that Sami took after lunch helped him.'

        b. l-ʁaTTa yalli waSaf-l-e   l-ḥakiim ʔənno
           the-nap that prescribed.3ms-to-me the-doctor that

        ʔeeχəd-*(a) baʕd l-ʁada   feedit-ne
        take.1-it   after the-lunch helped.3fs-me
        'The nap that the doctor prescribed to me to take it after lunch helped me.'

---

[10] The idiomatic meaning 'to take a nap' appears also (and only) in the expression ʁaTT ʁaTTa where the idiomatic NP chunk appears in the context of a cognate verb. The generalizations concerning ʔaχad ʁaTTa in the text apply to the idiomatic expression ʁaTT ʁaTTa.

In both (34a) and (34b), the relativized idiomatic NP chunk is obligatorily related to a weak resumptive pronominal, which appears attached to the verb. As we saw in cases of relativization of abstract nouns functioning as manner adjuncts, the relativization of the idiomatic NP chunk *ʁaTТa* is sensitive to islands, even in the presence of resumptive elements in the relativization site:

(35)   a. *Adjunct clause*
         *l-ʁaTТa yalli narvazit zeina laʔanno ʔaχad-**a**   saami
         the-nap that upset.3fs Zeina because took.3ms-her Sami

         ʔabl l-ʁada   feedit-o
         before the-lunch helped.3fs-him
         'The nap that Zeina was upset because Sami took after lunch helped him.'

      b. *Wh-clause*
         *l-ʁaTТa yalli badda taʕrif   zeina ʔəza ʔaχad-**a**
         the-nap that want.3fs know.3fs Zeina whether took.3ms-her

         saami ʔabl l-ʁada   feedit-o
         Sami before the-lunch helped.3fs-him
         'The nap that Zeina wants to know whether Sami took before lunch helped him.'

      c. *Relative clause*
         *l-ʁaTТa yalli btaʕrif   zeina S-Sabe lli ʔaχad-**a**   ʔabl
         the-nap that know.3fs Zeina the-boy that took.3ms-her before

         l-ʁada   feedit-o
         the-lunch helped.3fs-him
         'The nap that Zeina knows the boy that took before lunch helped him.'

Thus, when the idiomatic NP chunk *ʁaTТa* is related to a resumptive element within an adjunct clause, a wh-clause, or a relative clause, the result is unacceptable. The relativization of idiom chunk NPs provides us then with an additional context where the presence of a weak resumptive element does not coincide with the absence of island sensitivity.

The facts from (Lebanese) Arabic discussed in this section indicate that, for cases of relativization of certain adjuncts and idiomatic NP chunks, resumption obeys island conditions, such as the wh-clause constraint, the complex NP constraint, and the adjunct clause constraint. Therefore, one can conclude that resumption in restrictive relatives appears to be selectively sensitive to islands. This depends on the nature of the relativized head.

A remark is in order here about the parallelism between adjuncts and idiomatic NP chunks, which has been discussed in the literature by Rizzi (1990).[11] In addition to the parallelism detected in the context of relativization, extraction of idiomatic NP chunks from wh-islands is on a par with the extraction of adjuncts; it is strongly disallowed:

(36)   a. ??Who do you wonder whether we believe we can help t?
         b. *How do you wonder whether we believe we can help Bill t?

(37)   *Lebanese Arabic*
         a. ?? ?ayya miškle   baddak   taʕrif   [kiif [raħ nħill t t]] ?
            which   problem want.2ms know.2ms [how [fut.solve.1p t t]]
            'Which problem do you want to know how we will solve?'

         b. *kiif baddak   taʕrif   [?ayya miškle   [raħ nħill t t]]?
            how want.2ms know.2ms [which problem [fut.solve.1p t t]]
            'How do you want to know which problem we will solve?'

What manner adjuncts and idiomatic NP chunks have in common is that they are non-referential noun phrases. We have already observed that idiomatic NP chunks cannot be coreferent with pronouns in discourse (the relevant example is repeated in (38)):

(38)   *saami ?aχad   ʁaTTa baʕd l-ʁada   bas laila ma
         Sami   took.3ms nap   after the-lunch but Laila Neg

         ?aχadit **wəħde/-a**
         took.3fs one/-it
         'Sami took a nap after lunch but Laila didn't take one/it.'

---

[11] Additional evidence that idiomatic NP chunks in Lebanese Arabic differ from selected arguments comes from the fact that a typical object of the verbs *?aχad* 'take,' *?akal* 'ate,' or *taʕma* 'fed' can be questioned using the wh-words *šu* 'what' or *?ayya NP* 'which NP,' as illustrated in (ia):

(i)   a. šu/   ?ayya bluze ?aχadte
            what/ which shirt took.2fs
            'What/Which shirt did you take?'

         b. kam   ʁaTTa ?aχadte l-yom
            how.many nap   take.2fs the-day
            'How many naps did you take today?'

When the verb *?aχad* 'take,' which enters into the idiomatic expression *?aχad ʁaTTa* 'take a nap,' occurs with the wh-word *šu* 'what,' the idiomatic meaning is not available any more. The only possible way to question the idiomatic NP chunk in that expression is by using *kam* 'how much/many,' as illustrated in (ib).

The same generalization holds for the manner adjuncts discussed in section 7.6.2. Thus, whereas the first part of the sentence in (39) is totally acceptable in isolation, the whole discourse, with the relevant interpretation of the pronoun in the second sentence, is unacceptable:

(39)   *byištiʁil   saami   bi- { *nazeeha* 'integrity' / *sərʕa* 'speed' / *narvaze* 'nervousness'. w kəll
       works.3ms   Sami   with *šažeeʕa* 'courage' / *Tiibit ʔalb* 'kindness' } and all

       ššaʁʁiile   byištiʁlo   fiy-a   kameen
       worker.p   work.3p   with-it   too
       'Sami works with integrity/speed/nervousness/courage/kindness.
       And all the workers work with it too.'

The generalization here is that only referential NPs, which can corefer with pronouns in discourse, can be resumed by a weak pronoun in island contexts.

As we have discussed in chapter 6, in Cinque (1990), referentiality is equated with the ability to refer to a specific member of a pre-established set, and therefore, recalls Pesetsky's (1987) notion of d-linking. Cinque (1990) further points out that referential NPs can enter into coreference relations and can undergo long wh-movement. In this section, we have observed that only referential relativized NPs can be resumed by a weak pronominal element occurring inside different island contexts. That is, in the context of restrictive relatives, island contexts seem to impose the referential reading on the antecedent of a resumptive element, while non-island contexts don't.

Kroch (1989), in a discussion of amount quantification in the context of wh-interrogatives, arrives at a similar conclusion. A question like (40a) is associated with two different presuppositions, one corresponding to the non-referential reading of the wh-interrogative (40b), and the other to the referential reading (40c).

(40)   a. How many books did the editor publish this year?
        b. There is an amount of books such that the editor published that
           amount this year.
        c. There is a set of books such that the editor published that set this year.

However, in the context of long wh-movement, the only presupposition associated with the wh-interrogative is the one that corresponds to the referential reading, as illustrated in (41).

(41)   a. How many books did Bill ask whether the company was interested in
           publishing?
        b. There was a set of books for which Bill asked whether the company
           was interested in publishing them.

Kroch claims that the reason why the presupposition that corresponds to the non-referential reading is absent in the context of long wh-movement is pragmatic: that is, while it is well-formed, it is odd and renders the question unusable in most contexts. Thus a wh-interrogative which can plausibly have only a non-referential reading is unacceptable.

(42)   a. *How much money was John wondering whether to pay?
        b. There was a sum of money about which John was wondering
           whether to pay it.

The presupposition in (42b) is odd because it states that there is a uniquely identified sum of money and that John was wondering whether to pay that sum.

As we have seen in chapter 6, in Lebanese Arabic wh-interrogatives, the resumptive element cannot have a non-referential antecedent wh-word. In restrictive relatives, however, this requirement seems to be relaxed a little: a resumptive pronominal can have a non-referential antecedent as long as the resumptive pronominal does not occur within an island. In restrictive relatives, several types of islands seem to impose the referential reading on the antecedent of a resumptive pronominal. The analysis argued for by Kroch (1989) cannot be extended to account for all those cases and it is therefore still unclear why islands force a referential reading on the antecedent of a resumptive pronominal (see section 7.7.2 for further elaboration).

7.7   Indefinite relatives, idiom chunks, and abstract noun relativization

We have already observed the distinction between indefinite and definite relatives in Arabic. It has already been noted that indefinite relatives do not make use of a relativizer and, in dialects that make use of the gap strategy in relativization, indefinite relatives make exclusive use of the resumptive strategy. Now we turn to another distinction between the two types of relatives having to do with the nature of the relativized noun phrase.

7.7.1 Resumption in indefinite relatives and the nature of the antecedent

Interestingly, the relativization of abstract nouns used as manner adjuncts and idiom chunks cannot result in an indefinite relative. Thus, the sentences in (43) contrast with the sentences in (44), and (45) contrasts with the sentence in (46).

(43) a. l-maTluub   huwwe s-sərʕa   lli   štaʁal   fiy-a   saami
         the-required he   the-speed that worked.3ms with-it Sami
         'What is required is the speed with which Sami worked.'

      b. l-maTluub   huwwe s-sərʕa   lli   ftakarto   ʔənno saami
         the-required he   the-speed that thought.2p that   Sami

         byištiʁil   fiy-a
         works.3ms with-it
         'What is required is the speed with which you think that Sami works.'

(44) a. *l-maTluub   huwwe sərʕa   štaʁal   fiy-a   saami
         the-required he   speed worked.3ms with-it Sami
         'What is required is a speed with which Sami worked.'

      b. *l-maTluub   huwwe sərʕa   ftakarto   ʔənno saami byištiʁil
         the-required he   speed thought.2p that   Sami   works.3ms

         fiy-a
         with-it
         'What is required is a speed with which you think that Sami works.'

As seen in (44a–b), when the relativized head is an abstract noun interpreted as a manner adverbial, it cannot be related to a resumptive element inside the sentence. Similarly, an idiomatic chunk appearing as the head of an indefinite relative yields unacceptable sentences.

(45) a. l-ʁaTTa yalli ʔaχad-*(a)   saami baʕd l-ʁada   feedit-o
         the-nap that took.3ms-her Sami after the-lunch helped.3fs-him
         'The nap that Sami took after lunch helped him.'

      b. l-ʁaTTa yalli waSaf-l-e   l-ħakiim ʔənno
         the- nap that prescribed.3ms-to-me the-doctor that

         ʔeeχəd-*(a) baʕd l-ʁada   feedit-ne
         take.1s-it   after the-lunch helped.3fs-me
         'The nap that the doctor prescribed to me to take it after lunch helped
         me.'

(46)   a. *feedit   ʁaTTa ʔaχad-**a**   saami baʕd l-ʁada
        helped.3fs nap   took.3ms-her Sami after the-lunch
        'A nap that Sami took after lunch helped.'

    b. *feedit-ne   ʁaTTa waSaf-l-e   l-ħakiim   ʔənno
        helped.3fs-me nap   prescribed.3ms-to-me the-doctor that

        ʔeeχəd-**a** baʕd l-ʁada
        take.1s-it after the-lunch
        'A nap that the doctor prescribed to me to take it after lunch helped
        me.'

Thus, indefinite relatives, which we have already observed use only the resumptive strategy, also force the relativized head to be referential. Hence the relativized head of an indefinite relative can be neither an abstract adjunct noun phrase nor an idiomatic chunk, since those can only have a non-referential reading.

7.7.2   Restrictive relatives and movement

A question can be put forth at this point as to what indefinite relatives and island contexts have in common that they impose a referential reading on the antecedent of a resumptive pronominal. An answer that is discussed in Choueiri (2002) relates this observation to movement in the context of resumption within restrictive relatives.[12] Choueiri (2002) argues that the derivation of definite relatives differs greatly from that of indefinite relatives and that only the former involve movement. Building on work by Aoun and Choueiri (1996), Choueiri's (2002) proposal is that definite relatives have two possible representations available to them, given in (47a) and (47b), whereas only one representation, given in (48) is available to indefinite relatives. Definite relatives, as indicated in (47) can either be generated by movement (47a) or they can be base-generated (47b); Indefinite relatives can only be base-generated (48).

(47)   a. Definite Relativized-NP_i . . . . trace$_i$
        b. Definite Relativized-NP_i . . . . pro$_i$

(48)   Indefinite Relativized-NP_i . . . . pro$_i$

The referential reading is associated with the representation that involves a pronoun (*pro*) in the variable site. Since indefinite relatives have only that

---

[12] For a discussion of movement in the context of relativization and resumption in Semitic, see Borer (1984), Aoun and Choueiri (1996), and Aoun and Li (2003).

representation, it is no surprise that they allow only the referential reading. The representation in (47b) is the only one available in island contexts and therefore those contexts will allow only the referential reading in definite relatives as well. The representation in (47a) is derived by movement, and there the relativized noun phrase is associated with a trace. This is the only representation available for the relativization of adjuncts and idiomatic chunks as well as the subject of existential constructions. Given the relations between movement and island sensitivity, it comes as no surprise that the latter category of relatives is sensitive to islands.

In chapter 9, we investigate further the relationship between resumption and movement in Arabic. However a few more words need to be said about the discussion in the literature dealing with Semitic languages on the relation between resumption and movement in relativization. There, it is mainly argued that resumption stands in opposition to movement and that resumption involves base-generation. This is the position held in Shlonsky (1992), where it is further argued that resumption is a last resort strategy that languages make use of when (wh-)movement fails. Demirdache (1991) argues for a different position, where resumptive restrictive relatives do involve movement, albeit covert movement.

Based on the observation that resumption in Semitic is not sensitive to islands, Demirdache (1991) argues that resumptive relatives in Arabic represent a case of "relativization in situ," parallel to what is observed in wh-in-situ constructions. That is, the resumptive element in restrictive relatives is an operator that occurs in the variable position in syntax, but is later moved for interpretation, in LF. If island sensitivity constrains only overt movement, then the absence of island sensitivity in restrictive relatives is also accounted for. In a comparative study of Hebrew and Palestinian Arabic restrictive relatives, Shlonsky (1992) follows another approach to resumption, assuming that resumptive constructions are base-generated and do not involve movement at all. The assumption is supported by the distribution of resumption in Hebrew restrictive relatives, where it can generally be said that resumptive pronouns are available, when movement (gaps) is disallowed.[13] In Palestinian Arabic, however, as in all Arabic dialects, the resumptive strategy is the default strategy even when relativizing from positions like the direct object positions, which readily allow movement in wh-questions, for instance. In order to account for the Palestinian Arabic data under the assumption that resumption is a last resort strategy available when movement is not, Shlonsky (1992) suggests that *illi*, the Palestinian Arabic relativizer, marks its specifier as an A-position.

---

[13] However, in Hebrew, gaps alternate with resumptive pronouns in direct object and embedded subject positions. Shlonsky (1992) provides an analysis for those facts as well.

Thus, movement to the specifier position of *illi* is a type of A-movement and is therefore very local. Only the subject closest to *illi* (the highest subject) can move to its specifier, otherwise, movement from any other position will be blocked by the highest subject; a case of minimality. This analysis can easily carry over to other dialects of Arabic that use an equivalent relativizer to *illi,* and it correctly predicts that the only gap that is allowed in Palestinian Arabic is in the highest subject position.

We will observe in chapter 9 that the relationship between resumption and movement is more complex than is argued in Shlonsky (1992) and Demirdache (1991). However, it is already clear that both analyses cannot account for the observed facts in Lebanese Arabic, where it can be argued that resumptive restrictive relatives involve overt movement in the contexts of idiomatic chunks and adjunct relativization, which show island sensitivity.

7.8   Conclusion

In this chapter we have examined in detail the distribution of weak resumptive pronominal elements in restrictive relatives in various Arabic dialects. We first noted that resumption is the default strategy for forming restrictive relatives in the various dialects of Arabic, although the gap strategy is still available to some and in some contexts.

Based on the facts observed, we came to three major conclusions. First, restrictive relatives in Arabic need to be separated into two categories: definite relatives and indefinite relatives. Definite relatives are introduced by a relativizer, whereas indefinite relatives are not. The relativized noun phrase in definite relatives is definite, while it is indefinite in indefinite relatives. More importantly, it is only definite relatives that allow the gap strategy; indefinite relatives always involve resumption. Definite relatives allow the relativized noun phrase to be non-referential, while this is not the case for indefinite relatives.

Second, the gap strategy in restrictive relatives, as in wh-interrogatives, shows island sensitivity. However, we have observed that the resumptive strategy in restrictive relatives is also sensitive to islands when the antecedent of the resumptive element is a non-referential noun phrase. If island sensitivity is related to movement, this observation indicates that resumptive restrictive relatives can also be generated by movement.

Third, the relationship between resumption and referentiality is not as straightforward as has been noted in the literature. That is, it is not the case that resumptive pronominal elements can have only referential antecedents. We have seen that this constraint is imposed on the antecedent of a resumptive element in restrictive relatives only when this element occurs inside an island.

An issue that we have not tackled in this chapter is that of the structure of restrictive relatives in Arabic. This issue is a problematic one and is still under debate in the literature dealing with the topic of relativization (see among others Kayne 1994; Bianchi 1999; Borsely 1997; and Ouhalla 2004 for Semitic).[14]

---

[14] Ouhalla (2004) proposes, based on data from Semitic, a new typology for restrictive relatives: DP vs. CP relatives. CP relatives use the sentential complementizer to introduce relatives, as we can observe in Hebrew, for instance:

(i)　　a. ha-yeled še　rina　ohevet oto
　　　　　the-boy　that Rina loves　him
　　　　　'The boy that Rina loves.'

　　　　b. amarti le-david　še　oto　rina　ohevet
　　　　　said.I　to-David that him Rina loves
　　　　　'I said to David that Rina loves him.'

It can easily be observed that the same element that introduces the restrictive relative in the sentence in (ia) functions also as a complementizer in (ib). This is not the case in the various dialects of Arabic, as observed at the outset of this chapter. In Arabic, the relativizer is akin to a definite determiner (see Fassi Fehri 1982; Aoun and Choueiri 1996; Choueiri 2002). Apart from the morphological similarity between the definite determiner *(a)l-* in Arabic and the relativizer *lli/illi/yalli/ (a)l-laði,* its presence in definite relatives and its absence in indefinite relatives recalls the presence of the definite determiner in definite noun phrases and its absence in indefinite noun phrases, as illustrated in (ii).

(ii)　　a. l-kteeb　l-binne
　　　　　the-book the-brown
　　　　　'The brown book.'

　　　　b. kteeb binne
　　　　　book brown
　　　　　'A brown book.'

This difference in the categorical identity of the relative clauses together with the assumption that in Semitic noun phrases N moves to D drive the representation that Ouhalla gives for Semitic relatives, where the relative clause is generated as a left specifier of N and the relativized noun phrase is a head generated in N later moving to D. It is not clear whether this analysis is the one to be adopted for all definite relatives, even those that involve a non-referential relativized noun phrase. In such cases, it is not clear how the island sensitivity can be captured, since Ouhalla's analysis does not involve movement of the relativized NP. We leave this issue open for future discussions.

8

Clitic-left dislocation and focus constructions

8.1   Introduction

It has become clear by now that the relationship between referentiality and resumption is more complex than has been observed in the literature. It is not the case, for instance, that the antecedent of a resumptive element must be referential. This was an important conclusion arrived at in the investigation of restrictive relatives in Arabic (see chapter 7). In this chapter, which examines two different A′-constructions – clitic-left dislocation and focus fronting – we will see a confirmation for that conclusion in the context of clitic-left dislocation. By comparing and contrasting the properties of clitic-left dislocation and focus fronting, we also begin the investigation of the syntax of the left periphery in Arabic.

The chapter starts with an investigation of clitic-left dislocation. We focus on the distribution of clitic-left dislocated elements with respect to other elements of the left periphery, notably wh-elements. We then investigate the relationship between clitic-left dislocated elements and the resumptive pronominal they are related to within the sentence. The second part of the chapter deals with focus fronting. Here we also examine the distribution of the focus fronted elements with respect to other elements in the left periphery, notably wh-elements and clitic-left dislocated elements. We then turn to the relationship between focus fronted elements and the gap to which they are related inside the sentence. Finally, we examine various analyses of focus fronting that try to account for the differences between those constructions and clitic-left dislocation, as well as for the parallelisms observed between focus fronting and gapped wh-interrogatives.

8.2   Clitic-left dislocation in Arabic

8.2.1   The distribution of clitic-left dislocated NPs

Clitic-left dislocation (henceforth CLLD) is characterized by the presence of a lexical noun phrase in the left peripheral domain of a clause and a weak pronominal element related to it, inside the clause. Typical examples of this construction in Arabic are given in (1).

(1)   a. naadia šeef-a   saami mbeeriħ   *Lebanese Arabic*
          Nadia saw.3ms-her Sami yesterday
          'Nadia, Sami saw her yesterday.'

       b. at-tilmiiðat-u   ra?aa-ha   saami l-baariħa   *Standard*
          the-student.fs-Nom saw.3ms-her Sami the-yesterday   *Arabic*
          'The student, Sami saw her yesterday.'

In Standard Arabic, the dislocated noun phrase typically appears with Nominative Case marking, as shown in (1b). In Lebanese Arabic, the CLLDed noun phrase in matrix contexts can be found either before elements of the complementizer phrase (2a) or after them (2b).

(2)   a. naadia šu   ?aalət-la   l-mʕallme?
          Nadia what told.3fs-her.Dat the-teacher.fs
          'Nadia, what did the teacher tell her?'

       b. šu   naadia ?aalət-la   l-mʕallme?
          what Nadia told.3fs-her.Dat the-teacher.fs
          'What Nadia did the teacher tell her?'

In Standard Arabic, the only possible position for the dislocated phrase is preceding the elements of the complementizer phrase (3–4).

(3)   a. naadia mataa ra?aa-ha   saami?
          Nadia when saw.3ms-her Sami
          'Nadia, when did Sami see her?'

       b. *mata naadia ra?aa-ha   saami?
          when Nadia saw.3ms-her Sami
          'Nadia, when did Sami see her?'

(4)   a. zayd-un   hal qaabalta-hu?
          Zayd-Nom Q   met.2ms-him
          'Zayd, did you meet him?'

b. *hal zayd-un   qaabalta-hu?
Q   Zayd-Nom met.2ms-him
'Zayd, did you meet him?'

In embedded contexts, however, the dislocated noun phrase in Lebanese Arabic can only occur after the complementizer, as the contrast between (5a) and (5b) shows.

(5)   a. fakkart   ʔənno naadia šeef-a   kariim mbeeriħ
          thought.1s that   Nadia saw.3ms-her Karim yesterday
          'I thought that Nadia, Karim saw her yesterday.'

       b. *fakkart   naadia ʔənno šeef-a   kariim mbeeriħ
          thought.1s Nadia that   saw.3ms-her Karim yesterday

In embedded contexts in Standard Arabic, the dislocated NP can also appear after the complementizer. In such cases, however, the dislocated NP is assigned Accusative Case by the complementizer, as can be seen in (6).[1]

(6)   zaʕamtu   ʔanna r-risaalat-a   al-walad-u   kataba-ha
       claimed.1s that   the-letter-Acc the-boy-Nom wrote.3ms-it
       'I claimed that the letter, the boy wrote it.'

8.2.2   *Clitic-left dislocation and left dislocation*

Cinque (1977, 1990) distinguishes between clitic-left dislocation and left dislocation (LD), a construction also called *hanging topic*. LD, as Cinque defines it, is a root clause phenomenon and only one LDed phrase is allowed per sentence. As observed in section 8.2.1, CLLD can occur in many embedded contexts. In addition to (5a) and (6), the facts from Lebanese Arabic in (7) illustrate this observation.

---

[1] As seen in chapter 2, the finite clause complementizer in Standard Arabic assigns Accusative Case to the NP that obligatorily follows it. Further evidence that the complementizer *ʔanna* assigns Accusative Case to the adjacent NP comes from the fact that if the dislocated NP does not immediately follow the complementizer, it appears with Nominative Case marking, as illustrated in (i):

(i)   zaʕamtu   ʔanna al-walad-a   r-risaalat-u   kataba-ha
       claimed.1s that   the-boy-Acc the-letter-Nom wrote.3ms-it
       'I claimed that the boy, the letter, he wrote it.'

(7) a. ma mnaʕrif ʔəza ha-l-kteeb raħ yleeʔuu-l-o mtaržim
Neg know.1p whether this-the-book fut find.3p-to-it translator
'We don't know whether, this book, they will find a translator for it.'

b. š-šaxS l-waħiid lli zeina ʕarrafnee-ha ʕal-ee
the-person the-only that Zeina introduce.1p-her to-him

Təliʕ ma biħibb r-raʔS
turned-out.3ms Neg like.3ms the-dance
'The only person that Zeina, we introduced her to him turned out not to like dancing.'

Furthermore, there can be more than one clitic-left dislocated NP in a given clause (8a) or sentence (8b):

(8) a. kariim zeina ʕarrafnee-ha ʕal-ee
Karim Zeina introduced.1p-her to-him
'Karim, Zeina, we introduced her to him.'

b. kariim ma mnaʕrif ʔəza zeina ʕarrafuw-a ʕale-eh
Karim Neg know.1p whether Zeina introduced.3p-her to-him
'Karim, we don't know whether Zeina, they introduced her to him.'

c. kariim ʔəlnee-lo ʔənno zeina šeef-a saami
Karim told.1p-him.Dat that Zeina saw.3ms-her Sami

mbeeriħ
yesterday
'Karim, we told him that Zeina, Sami saw her yesterday.'

This situation is impossible in LD contexts, as illustrated by topicalization in English (9).

(9)   *Mary, John, she likes him.

Cinque adds that CLLD is characterized by the fact that any phrase can be CLLDed. In Arabic, however, only noun phrases can be clitic-left dislocated, as there are no clitics that correspond to another type of phrase.[2]

---

[2] Cinque also mentions that in CLLD in Italian there is obligatory connectivity between the dislocated phrase and the IP internal position, with respect to Binding Theory, for instance, as illustrated in (ia) for Principles A and B:

8.2.3   The nature of the CLLDed element

In addition to the restriction of CLLDed elements to noun phrases in Arabic, there are additional constraints imposed on the nature of those elements. Thus, CLLDed noun phrases cannot be indefinite, as the contrast between (10) and (11) shows:

(10)   a. *qaSiidat-un ʔallafa-ha   ʕomar   *Standard Arabic*
           poem-Nom   wrote.3ms-it Omar
           'A poem, Omar wrote it.'

        b. *ʔaSiide ʔallaf-a   ʕomar   *Lebanese Arabic*
           poem   wrote.3ms-it Omar
           'A poem, Omar wrote it.'

(11)   a. al-qaSiidat-u   ʔallafa-ha   ʕomar   *Standard Arabic*
           the-poem-Nom wrote.3ms-it Omar
           'The poem, Omar wrote it.'

        b. l-ʔaSiide ʔallaf-a   ʕomar   *Lebanese Arabic*
           the-poem wrote.3ms-it Omar
           'The poem, Omar wrote it.'

Therefore, it comes as no surprise that names (as illustrated in (8) and elsewhere) and demonstrative noun phrases (12), as well as strong pronouns (13), which are also definite, may be clitic-left dislocated.

(12)   a. haaða l-kitaab-u   qaraʔtu-hu munðu   *Standard Arabic*
           this   the-book-Nom read.1s-it   from

           muddat-in
           while-Gen
           'This book, I read it a while ago.'

(i)   a. A *lei/se stessa Maria non ci   pensa
           of her/herself   Maria not there thinks
           'Of herself, Maria does not think.'

        b. S-Sabe lli   naadia htammit fi-i   ʕaTit-o   širweel
           the-boy that Nadia cared.3fs in-him gave.3fs-him pants
           'The boy that Nadia took care of, she gave him pants.'

In (ib), coreference between *Nadia* and the subject of the main clause is possible. The possibility of having the coreference reading indicates that (ib) does not violate Principle C, which prohibits names to be bound. This indicates that in Lebanese Arabic connectivity for Binding Theory in CLLD constructions is not obligatory. For further discussion on this issue see chapter 9.

b. hayda l-kteeb   ?riit-o   bi-nhar   *Lebanese Arabic*
   this   the-book read.1s-it in-day
   'This book, I read it in a day.'

(13) a. huwa ra?aytu-hu fi-l-madiinat-i   *Standard Arabic*
         him saw.1s-him in-the-city-Gen
         'Him, I saw him in the city.'

      b. huwwe šift-o   bi-s-sinama   *Lebanese Arabic*
         he   saw.1s-him in-the-movies
         'Him, I saw him at the movies.'

In addition to definite noun phrases, some quantified phrases can be CLLDed:
universally quantified phrases like *kəll NP* 'every/each NP,' as well as *ʕiddit NP*
'many/several NP' and *?aɣlabiyyit NP* 'most NP' from Lebanese Arabic, can all
occur as clitic-left dislocated elements.

(14) *Standard Arabic*
      a. kull-u   sayyaaraat-in yuriiduuna ?an yaɣsiluu-ha
         every-Nom car.fs-Gen   want.3p   that wash.3p-it
         'Every car, they want to wash it.'

      b. qaala   ʕomar ?inna kull-a   s-sayyaaraat-i
         said.3ms Omar that every-Acc the-cars-Gen

         ?istaqdamuu-ha   min ?almaania
         brought.3p-them from Germany
         'Omar said that all the cars, they brought them from Germany.'

(15) *Lebanese Arabic*
      a. kəll təlmiize baddun ylabsuw-a   maryul
         every student.fs want.3p dress.3p-her uniform
         'Every student, they want her to wear a uniform.'

      b. ʕomar ?aal   ?ənno kəll   s-siyyaaraat žeebuw-un
         Omar said.3ms that every the-cars   brought.3p-them

         min almaania
         from Germany
         'Omar said that all the cars, they brought them from Germany.'

(16)   *Lebanese Arabic*
    a. Siddit zuwwar šarrabit-un   l-mama   Pahwe
        many visitors made-drink.3fs-them the-mother coffee

        Pabl   ma   fallo
        before Comp left.3p
        'Many visitors, Mom made them drink coffee before they left.'

    b. Paγlabiyyit l-wleed   byeexduw-un Sa-l-matħaf
        most   the-children take.3p-them to-the-museum
        'Most of the children, they take them to the museum.'

In light of those facts, one is hard pressed to answer the question as to what brings together definite NPs with such quantifiers as *kəll* 'every/each,' *Səddit* 'several/many,' and *Paγlabiyyit* 'most,' While it is clear that the definite article, the universal quantifier, and *Paγlabiyyit* 'most' are strong determiners (Milsark 1977) in that they cannot occur in the subject position of there-existential constructions (17), *Səddit NP* 'several/many NP,' like indefinite noun phrases, can (18).

(17)   *Lebanese Arabic*
    a. *fii Paγlabiyyit l-wleed   bi-S-Saff
        in-it most   the-children in-the-classroom
        'There are most of the children in the classroom.'

    b. *fii kəll   walad bi-S-Saff
        in-it every child in-the-classroom
        'There is every child in the classroom.'

    c. *fii kəll l-wleed   bi-S-Saff
        in-it all   the-children in-the-classroom
        'There are all the children in the classroom.'

    d. *fii l-walad   bi-S-Saff
        in-it the-child in-the-classroom
        'There is the child in the classroom.'

(18)   *Lebanese Arabic*
    a. fii   walad/wleed bi-S-Saff
        in-it child/children in-the-classroom
        'There is/are a child/children in the classroom.'

    b. fii   Səddit   wleed bi-S-Saff
        in-it many/several children in-the-classroom
        'There are many/several children in the classroom.'

Thus, it is not the strength of the determiner that determines whether a noun phrase can be CLLDed or not.

To complicate the picture further, it can be observed that NPIs like *wala NP* 'no NP' in Lebanese Arabic can also be CLLDed (19).[3]

(19)   wala siyyara ʔaalo   ʔənno žeebuw-a   min almaania   *Lebanese*
       no   car   said.3p that   brought.3p-it from Germany   *Arabic*
       'No car, they said that they brought it from Germany.'

In contrast with *wala NP* 'no NP,' bare negative noun phrases like *ma ħada* or *maši* cannot be clitic-left dislocated:

(20)   a. *ma ħada šeefit-o   zeina ʕam bizaʕbir
           no one saw.3fs-him Zeina Asp. cheat.3ms
           'No one, Zeina saw him cheating.'

       b. *maši žeebit-o   lina min d-dikkeen
           nothing brought.3ms-it Lina from the-store
           'Nothing, Lina brought it from the store.'

We have already observed (see chapters 6 and 7) that the relationship between referentiality and resumption is a complex one. In wh-interrogatives, all wh-words that can occur directly related to a resumptive pronominal are referential (although the reverse is not true). In restrictive relatives however, referentiality only constrains the relativized noun phrase that is related to a resumptive element within an island. In the context of CLLD as well, we see that referentiality does not adequately delimit the set of noun phrases that can be CLLDed. Recall that referentiality, understood as in Cinque (1990), is relevant for binding relations in the following way: only referential noun phrases can enter into coreference relations. We can clearly observe that some NP types, which can be CLLDed, cannot enter into coreference relations with a pronoun. On one hand, the universal quantifier *kəll* 'every/each,' when used with a singular NP cannot enter into coreference relations (21a) and neither does the negative noun phrases *wala NP* 'no NP' (21b).[4]

---

[3] The Lebanese Arabic *wala NP* 'no NP' is clearly negative and can only be used in negative contexts. The equivalent in Standard Arabic, the NPI *ʔayyu NP*, is not inherently negative, since it can also function as a wh-phrase (see chapter 6) and it cannot be CLLDed. For the purposes of the present discussion, we will abstract away from the issue of whether *wala NP* 'no NP' is to be classified as a negative quantifier phrase rather than an NPI.

[4] *ma ħada* 'no one' and *maši* 'nothing,' which cannot be CLLDed, do not enter into coreference relations with pronouns, as can be seen in (i):

(21)   a. *šəft kəll walad$_i$ maʕ ʔahl-o   w   l-mʕallme
             saw.1s each child   with parents-his and the-teacher.fs

             šeefit-o$_i$ baʕdeen
             saw.3fs-him later
             'I saw each child with his parents and the teacher saw him later.'

         b. *ma šəft   wala walad$_i$ maʕ ʔahl-o   w   l-mʕallme
             Neg saw.1s no   child   with parents-his and the-teacher.fs

             šeefit-o$_i$ baʕdeen
             saw.3fs-him later
             'I didn't see any child with his parents and the teacher saw him later.'

However, indefinite NPs, which cannot be CLLDed, can enter into coreference
relations, as illustrated in (22).

(22)   wiSlit   siyyara$_i$ min almaania bas ma   raħ ʔištri-a$_i$
         arrived.3fs car.fs   from Germany but Neg fut. buy.1s-it
         'A car arrived from Germany but I will not buy it.'

Similarly, the noun phrase introduced by *kam* 'few,' which can also enter into
coreference relations with a pronoun (23a), cannot be CLLDed (23b), as the data
from Lebanese Arabic indicate.[5]

(23)   a. žeebo   kam siyyara min almaania w   beeʕuw-un
             brought.3p few car   from Germany and sold.3p-them

             b-l-baleeš
             in-the-free
             'They brought a few cars from Germany and sold them for peanuts.'

         b. *kam siyyara žeebuw-a/un   min almaania
             few   car   brought.3p-it/them from Germany
             'Few cars, they brought them from Germany.'

   (i)   a. *ma ħada$_i$ ʔiža   w   šifne-e$_i$ baʕdeen
              no one   came.3ms and saw.1p-him afterwards
              'No one came and we saw him afterwards.'

           b. *maši$_i$ bifiid   bas baʕml-o$_i$ kill   yom
              nothing be-useful.3ms but do.1s-it every day
              'Nothing is useful but I do it every day.'

5 Recall, from chapter 6, that *kam NP* '(how) many NP,' which can also function as a wh-
   phrase, cannot be related to a resumptive element in a wh-interrogative. We have shown
   there as well that *kam NP* '(how) many NP' has a referential reading as a wh-phrase.

It is interesting to note as well that the set of NPs that can be CLLDed is more restricted than the set of NPs that can occur as preverbal subjects. Thus, while indefinite NPs and *kam NP* 'few NP' cannot occur as preverbal subjects, *ma ħada* and *maši* can (23):[6]

(24)   a. *kam walad rikib/rikbo   b-l-baS
            few   child   rode.3ms/rode.3p in-the-bus
            'Few children rode the bus.'

       b. *walad/wleed rikib/rikbo   b-l-baS
            child/children rode.3ms/rode.3p in-the-bus
            'A child/Children rode the bus.'

       c. ma ħada Ɂiža
            no   one   came.3ms
            'No one came.'

       d. maši   bifiid
            nothing be-useful.3ms
            'Nothing is useful.'

The table in (25) summarizes the facts discussed so far in section 8.2.3:

(25)

NP-type	Occurs in CLLD	Occurs as preverbal subject	Enters into coreference relations
Kəll NP-pl 'all the NP'	√	√	√
Kəll NP-sg 'every/each NP'	√	√	*
wala NP 'no NP'	√	√	*
Ɂaʁlabiyyit NP 'most NP'	√	√	√
ʕiddit NP 'many/several NP'	√	√	√
Definite NP	√	√	√
ma ħada 'no one'/ *maši* 'nothing'	*	√	*
Bare indefinite NP	*	*	√
Kam NP 'few NP'	*	*	√

The major conclusions that we can draw from those facts are: (a) a confirmation that preverbal subjects are not CLLDed elements (see also chapter 3); (b) the

---

[6] The sentence in (i) is only acceptable as a question, and in such cases the verb is in the masculine singular:

   (i)   kam   walad rikib   b-l-baS
               how-many child rode.3ms in-the-bus
               'How many children rode the bus?'

notion of referentiality (or d-linking) is not a defining characteristic of CLLDed NPs. We have suggested in chapter 6 that the wh-words which can be directly related to a resumptive pronominal element are those that form a DP. Applying this proposal in the context of CLLD, it would entail that *ma ħada* 'no one' and *maši* 'nothing,' as well as bare indefinite noun phrases, are not DPs. More work needs to be done in this area to arrive at a proper definition of the nature of elements that can be related to resumptive pronominals.

8.2.4   *The distribution of pronominal clitics inside CLLD constructions*

The pronominal clitic related to the CLLDed element can be a direct object clitic, a dative clitic, or a genitive clitic. Direct object clitics are attached to the verb, as illustrated in (26) and (27a); dative clitics are also attached to the verb (27b).

(26)   ar-risaalat-u   qaraʔa-ha   saami l-yawm-a   *Standard Arabic*
        the-letter-Nom read.3ms-it Sami   the-day-Acc
        'The latter, Sami read it today.'

(27)   a. naadia šeef-a   saami mbeeriħ   *Lebanese Arabic*
           Nadia saw.3ms-her Sami   yesterday
           'Nadia, Sami saw her yesterday.'

        b. fakkart   ʔənno ʕomar ħəkyət-lo   zeina ħkeeye
           thought.1s that   Omar   told.3fs-him Zeina story
           'I thought that Omar, Zeina told him a story.'

The clitic can also be a genitive clitic attached to a preposition or an adnominal clitic attached to the head noun. This is illustrated in the Lebanese Arabic examples in (28a) and (28b) respectively.

(28)   a. sməʕt   ʔənno naadia ltaʔa   fiy-a   ʕomar mbeeriħ
           heard.1s that   Nadia met.3ms in-her Omar   yesterday
           'I heard that Nadia, Omar met her yesterday.'

        b. sməʕte   ʔənno ʕomar ʔriina   kteeb-o
           heard.2fs that   Omar   read.1p book-his
           'You heard that Omar, we read his book.'

The relation between the left peripheral NP and the pronominal clitic can violate island conditions in Arabic. We exemplify this observation in Lebanese Arabic using the adjunct clause condition (29), the complex NP island condition (30), and the wh-island condition (31).

(29)   *Adjunct clause*
       sməʕt   ʔənno naadia rəħt   mən duun ma   təħke   maʕ-a
       heard.1s that   Nadia left.2ms without   Comp talk.2ms with-her
       'I heard that Nadia, you left without talking to her.'

(30)   *Complex NP island*
       sməʕt   ʔənno ha-l-kteeb   ħkiit   maʕ l-walad yalli
       heard.1s that   this-the-book talked.2ms with the-boy that

       katab   ʕal-ee
       wrote.3ms on-it
       'I heard that this book, you talked with the boy that wrote on it.'

(31)   *Wh-island*
       sməʕt   ʔənno naadia byaʕrfo miin šeef-a
       heard.1s that   Nadia know.3p who saw.3ms-her
       'I heard that Nadia, they know who saw her.'

As those examples clearly illustrate, CLLD constructions in Arabic consistently violate island conditions. These data are consistent with what we have seen in chapter 6 with resumptive wh-interrogatives. Here as well, this generalization can lead to the conclusion that CLLD constructions in Arabic are generated without any movement. That is, it can be argued that the peripheral noun phrase in those constructions is base-generated in its surface position and coindexed with a pronominal clitic occupying an argument position inside the sentence (see, among others, Ouhalla 1994b).

8.3   Focus constructions in Arabic

CLLD in Arabic can be distinguished from another construction involving a left peripheral phrase, but a gap instead of a pronominal element within the sentence; that is the focus fronting construction.

Focus constructions have not been discussed by many students of Arabic syntax, generally because their study sits at the edge of syntax and pragmatics, and traditionally focus has been dealt with in the context of rhetoric rather than grammar.[7] Here, we will examine the syntax of focus constructions in Arabic, contrasting them especially with CLLD.

---

[7] Among the major analyses of focus constructions in Arabic, we can count Bakir (1980), Moutaouakil (1989), Ouhalla (1994b), and Shlonsky (2000). Our discussion in this section relies mainly on Ouhalla (1994b) and Shlonsky (2000).

Focus constructions in Arabic need not involve fronting. Thus, a phrase can be focused in situ (32), or displaced to a left peripheral position in the sentence (33).

(32)   a. šariba   zayd-un   ŠAY-AN   *Standard Arabic*
          drank.3ms Zayd-Nom tea-Acc
          'Zayd drank TEA.'

       b. šərib   zayd ŠAY   *Lebanese Arabic*
          drank.3ms Zayd tea
          'Zayd drank TEA.'

(33)   a. ŠAY-AN šariba   zayd-un   *Standard Arabic*
          tea-Acc drank.3ms Zayd-Nom
          'It was tea that Zayd drank.'

       b. ŠAY šərib   zayd   *Lebanese Arabic*
          tea drank.3ms Zayd
          'It was tea that Zayd drank.'

It is argued that the two types of focus constructions are not equivalent in discourse (Moutaouakil 1989): whereas in-situ focus phrases can function as new information focus, fronted focus phrases can only be understood contrastively, that is, in contrast with pre-existing information, which they deny (Ouhalla 1994b). Thus, only the sentences in (32) represent felicitous answers to the questions in (34).

(34)   a. maaðaa šariba   zayd-un?   *Standard Arabic*
          what   drank.3ms Zayd-Nom
          'What did Zayd drink?'

       b. šu   šərib   zayd?   *Lebanese Arabic*
          what drank.3ms Zayd
          'What did Zayd drink?'

As Ouhalla (1994b) further points out, the contrastive focus reading can be shown by the use of a negative continuation for the sentences in (33), as illustrated in (35).

(35)   a. ŠAY-AN šariba   zayd-un   laa ʕaSiir-an   *Standard Arabic*
          tea-Acc drank.3ms Zayd-Nom not juice-Acc
          'It was tea that Zayd drank, not juice.'

       b. ŠAY šərib   zayd miš ħalib   *Lebanese Arabic*
          tea drank.3ms Zayd not milk
          'It was tea that Zayd drank, not milk.'

In the remainder of this chapter, our discussion will address the properties of fronted focus phrases. How they differ from CLLDed phrases and how they interact with them provide clues as to the mapping of the left periphery in Arabic.

8.3.1   The distribution of fronted focused phrases

As observed earlier, focus fronting is characterized by the presence of a phrase in the left peripheral domain of a clause, which is related to a gap inside the clause. Typical examples of this construction in Arabic are given in (36).

(36)   a. naadia šeef   saami   *Lebanese Arabic*
          Nadia saw.3ms Sami
          'Nadia, Sami saw.'

        b. al-kitaab-a   wažada   muḥammad-un   *Standard Arabic*
           the-book-Acc found.3ms Muhammad-Nom
           'The book, Muhammad found.'

When the sentence initial focused phrase is a direct object, it appears with Accusative Case marking in Standard Arabic, as seen in (36b) above. That is, the case marking on the fronted focus phrase matches that of the corresponding gap.

In embedded contexts, focus phrases, like CLLDed noun phrases, must follow the complementizer (37–38).[8]

(37)   a. ʔaðunnu ʔanna fi baɣdaad-a   ḥaSala   l-ʔittifaaq-u
          think.1s that   in Baghdad-Acc happened.3ms the-agreement-Nom
          'I think that in Baghdad, the agreement took place.'

---

[8] Shlonsky (2000) notes the unacceptability of the sentence in (ib), which contrasts with (ia):

(i)   a. zaSamtu   ʔanna r-risaalat-a   kataba-ha   l-walad-u
            claimed.1s that   the-letter-Acc wrote.3ms-it the-boy-Nom
            'I claimed that the letter, the boy wrote it.'

        b. *zaSamtu   ʔanna r-risaalat-a   kataba   l-walad-u
            claimed.1s that   the-letter-Acc wrote.3ms the-boy-Nom
            'I claimed that the letter, the boy wrote.'

Obviously, this observation is contradicted by the data provided in the text.

b. ðanantu   ʔanna kitaab-an qaraʔat zaynab-u   (Ouhalla
   believe.1s that   book-Acc read.3fs Zaynab-Nom   1994b: 70)
   'I believe that, a book, Zaynab read.'

(38)   a. biftikir ʔənno bi-š-šeem   raħ tleeʔe ʔimm-ak   šaraašif
           think.1s that   in-the-Damascus fut. find.3fs mother-you sheets
           'I think that in Damascus, your mother will find sheets.'

        b. biftikir ʔənno kariim ʕarrafit   zeina ʕa-l-mʕallme
           think.1s that   Karim introduced.3fs Zeina to-the-teacher.fs
           'I think that Karim, Zeina introduced to the teacher.'

It is impossible to check whether, in matrix contexts, the focus phrase precedes or follows elements in the complementizer phrase, since focused elements are incompatible with questions, as illustrated in (39) for Standard Arabic and (40) for Lebanese Arabic.

(39)   a. *ʔayna saalim-an qaabala xaalid-un
           where Salim-Acc met.3ms xaalid-Nom

        b. *saalim-an ʔayna qaabala xaalid-un
           Salim-Acc where met.3ms xaalid-Nom

(40)   a. *ween saalim šeefit   zeina
           where Salim saw.3fs Zeina

        b. *saalim ween šeefit   zeina
           Salim   where saw.3fs Zeina

However, in Standard Arabic, focused phrases must follow CLLDed NPs in matrix contexts (41), as observed in Bakir (1980).

(41)   a. faaTimat-u l-wardat-a   ʔaʕTaa-ha   saalim-un
           Fatima-Nom the-rose-Acc gave.3ms-her Salim-Nom
           'Fatima, the rose Salim gave her.'

        b. *l-wardat-a faaTimat-u ʔaʕTaa-ha   saalim-un
           the-rose-Acc Fatima-Nom gave.3ms-her Salim-Nom
           'Fatima, the rose Salim gave her.'

In Lebanese Arabic, focus phrases can either precede or follow CLLDed noun phrases (42).

(42)   a. ʕa kariim zeina ʕarrafnee-ha
           to Karim Zeina introduced.1p-her
           'It is to Karim that we introduced Zeina.'

b. zeina ʕa kariim ʕarrafnee-ha
   Zeina to Karim introduced.1p-her
   'It is to Karim that we introduced Zeina.'

The facts in (41)–(42) obtain whether the focus phrase is found in matrix or embedded contexts. The requirement that focus phrases follow CLLDed NPs in Standard Arabic could be tied to another fact that obtains in the language: focus fronting in Standard Arabic triggers obligatory subject–verb inversion (Ouhalla 1994b) (43). The fact that this generalization does not hold in Lebanese Arabic comes as no surprise (44).

(43)   a. *KITAAB-AN zaynab-u   ʔištarat
            book-Acc   Zaynab-Nom bought.3fs

         b. KITAAB-AN ʔištarat   zaynab-u
            book-Acc bought.3fs Zaynab-Nom
            'It is a book that Zaynab bought.'

(44)   a. KTEEB zaynab štarit
            book   Zaynab bought.3fs
            'It is a book that Zaynab bought.'

         b. KTEEB štarit   zaynab
            book   bought.3fs Zaynab
            'It is a book that Zaynab bought.'

We can thus draw a parallel between focus fronting and wh-interrogatives, since wh-questions in Standard Arabic require subject–verb inversion (45), but they do not do so in Lebanese Arabic (46).

(45)   a. *maaðaa zaynab-u   ʔištarat
            what   Zaynab-Nom bought.3fs

         b. maaðaa ʔištarat   zaynab-u
            what   bought.3fs Zaynab-Nom
            'What did Zaynab buy?'

(46)   a. ʔayya kteeb zaynab štarit
            which book Zaynab bought.3fs
            'Which book did Zaynab buy?'

         b. ʔayya kteeb štarit   zaynab
            which book bought.3fs Zaynab
            'Which book did Zaynab buy?'

Finally, in line with wh-interrogatives and in contrast with CLLD, the number of focused phrases in a given clause is limited to one. Thus, the unacceptability of (47) parallels that of (48), which involves multiple wh-fronting.[9] However, the sentences in (47) contrast with (49a) and (8a) (repeated below as (49b)).

(47)   a. *NAHAAR-AN ZAYNAB-A   zaara   zayd-un   *Standard Arabic*
              day-Acc   Zaynab-Acc visited.3ms Zayd-Nom
              'It was BY DAY that Zayd visited ZAYNAB.'

        b. *BI-N-NHAAR ZAYNAB zaar   zayd   *Lebanese Arabic*
              in-the-day   Zaynab visited.3ms Zayd
              'It was IN THE DAY that Zayd visited ZAYNAB.'

(48)   a. *man man zaara?   *Standard Arabic*
              who   who visited.3ms
              'Who visited whom?'

        b. *min min zaar?   *Lebanese Arabic*
              who   who visited.3ms
              'Who visited whom?'

(49)   a. zayd-un   zaynab-u   ʔaʕTaytu-hu kitaab-a-ha   *Standard*
              Zayd-Nom Zaynab-Nom gave.1s-him book-Acc-her   *Arabic*
              'Zayd, Zaynab, I gave him her book.'

        b. kariim zeina ʕarrafnee-ha   ʕal-ee   *Lebanese Arabic*
              Karim Zeina introduced.1p-her to-him
              'Karim, Zeina, we introduced her to him.'

In section 8.4, we present and discuss Ouhalla's (1994b) analysis of focus constructions, which tries to account for the parallelism between focus fronting constructions and wh-interrogatives and explains the relative ordering of focused and CLLDed elements.

8.3.2   *The nature of the fronted focus phrases*

A clear contrast can be observed between the nature of the fronted focus phrases and that of CLLD NPs: whereas CLLDed NPs cannot be indefinite, as

---

[9] Note that Arabic allows multiple wh-questions as illustrated below:

(i)   a. man zaara   man   *Standard Arabic*
              who visited.3ms who
              'Who visited whom?'

        b. min zaar   min   *Lebanese Arabic*
               who visited.3ms who
              'Who visited whom?'

observed in section 8.2.2, fronted focus NPs can, as illustrated in (50), from both
Standard Arabic and Lebanese Arabic.

(50)   a. qaSiidat-un ʔallafa   ʕomar   *Standard Arabic*
           poem-Nom wrote.3ms Omar
           'A poem, Omar wrote.'

        b. ʔaSiide ʔallaf   ʕomar   *Lebanese Arabic*
           poem   wrote.3ms Omar
           'A poem, Omar wrote.'

Similar facts obtain with *kam NP* 'few NP,' which cannot be CLLDed, but can be
fronted as a focus phrase.[10]

(51)   a. *kam siyyara žeebuw-a/un   min   almaania
           few   car   brought.3p-it/them from Germany
           'Few cars, they brought them from Germany.'

        b. KAM SIYYARA žeebo   min almaania miš ktiir
           few   car   brought.3p from Germany not lot
           'It is few cars that they brought from Germany not a lot.'

    In addition, since no pronominal clitic is involved, focus fronting is not reduced
to NPs, but can affect PPs and VPs, as well as APs (52–54).

(52)   a. baʕd l-ʁada   rəhna   tmaššayna   *Lebanese Arabic*
           after the-lunch went.1p walk.1p
           'After lunch, we went walking.'

        b. ʕinda-ka   yanamu   zayd-un   *Standard Arabic*
           at-you.ms sleep.3ms Zayd-Nom
           'Zayd sleeps at your house.'

---

[10] It comes as no surprise that *ma ħada* 'no one' and *maši* 'nothing' cannot occur as focus
fronted phrases:

(i)   a. *ma ħada zaynab ʕazamit
            no one Zaynab invited.3fs
            'It is no one that Zaynab invited.'

        b. *maši   zaynab ʔakalit
            nothing Zaynab ate.3fs
            'It is nothing that Zaynab ate.'

If in those constructions, the non-focused material is part of the assertion, then a sentence
like (ia), for instance, would be asserting that Zaynab invited someone and then asserting
that it was no one, hence the intuition that by uttering (ia) one would be uttering a
contradiction.

(53)   ʕam yirsum   keen   kariim   *Lebanese Arabic*
        Asp. draw.3ms was.3ms Karim
        'Karim was drawing.'

(54)   a. ħəlwe ktiir keenit l-masraħiyye   *Lebanese Arabic*
           nice.fs very was.3fs the-play
           'Very nice was the play.'

        b. žamiil-an   kaana l-xaatamu ʕala ʔiSbaʕi-ha   *Standard Arabic*
           beautiful-Acc was   the-ring   on finger-her
           'Beautiful was the ring on her finger.'

8.3.3   Focus fronting and island sensitivity

Another contrast that we can observe between focus fronting constructions and CLLD is that focus fronting, unlike CLLD, displays island effects: a left
peripheral focused phrase in Lebanese Arabic may not be related to a gap within
an adjunct clause (55), a complex NP (56), or a *wh*-island (57).

(55)   *Adjunct clause*
        *sməʕt ʔənno naadia rəħte   mən duun ma   tšuufe
        heard.1s that   Nadia left.2fs without Comp see.2fs
        'I heard that Nadia, you left without seeing.'

(56)   *Complex NP island*
        *sməʕt ʔənno ha-l-kteeb   ħkiite   maʕ z-zalame yalli katab
        heard.1s that   this-the-book talked.2fs with the-man that wrote.3ms
        'I heard that this book, you talked with the man that wrote.'

(57)   *Wh-island*
        *sməʕt   ʔənno naadia byaʕrfo ʔayya walad šeef
        heard.1s that   Nadia know.3p which boy   saw.3ms
        'I heard that Nadia, they know which boy saw.'

The paradigm above shows that, unlike CLLD, focus fronting is sensitive to
islands. This observation places focus fronting on a par with other A′-constructions
involving gaps, like wh-interrogatives, for instance (see chapter 6).

8.4   Analyses of focus fronting and CLLD in Arabic

Summing up what needs to be accounted for with respect to CLLD and
focus fronting in Arabic, we have the following generalizations:

(58) a. Focus phrases, when fronted, are related to gaps inside the sentence, while CLLDed phrases are related to a pronominal clitic.
      b. Focus constructions are sensitive to island constraints, while CLLD constructions are not.
      c. There can be only one focused phrase in a given clause, while there are no such limitations on the number of CLLDed elements in a given clause.
      d. A fronted focus phrase bears the case marking of its corresponding gap, whereas a CLLDed phrase generally bears Nominative Case.
      e. Focus fronting, unlike CLLD, triggers subject–verb inversion in Standard Arabic.
      f. In Standard Arabic, focus phrases must follow CLLDed elements. This does not extend, however, to some of the other modern dialects of Arabic, like Lebanese Arabic, for instance.

Furthermore, Ouhalla draws a parallel between focus fronting and wh-questions based on the generalizations in (58a), (58d), and (58e). It can also be noted that wh-interrogatives as well as focus fronting constructions are sensitive to islands (58b). In addition, the first three of the generalizations in (58) apply across the dialects of Arabic; however, there is dialectal variation with respect to the last three generalizations.

Based on the parallelism between wh-questions and focus fronting, Ouhalla argues for a movement analysis of focus fronting. The contrasts between focus fronting constructions and CLLD constructions are accounted for by a base-generation analysis for CLLD. Ouhalla (1994b) assumes that focus fronting constructions involve the generation of a designated projection between CP and TP – he calls it FP, for focus phrase – which hosts elements marked for focus. This projection is headed by an abstract head F, bearing the [+F] feature, which on a par with the [+Q(uestion)] feature on C, needs to be identified. The identification of the [+F] feature is done either by moving a phrase bearing the [+F] feature to the specifier position of FP or by merging a head bearing the [+F] feature with the head of FP, a process that Ouhalla refers to as *morphological identification*. Thus, sentences like those in (33), repeated below as (59), would have the following derivation:

(59) a. ŠAY-AN šariba   zayd-un   *Standard Arabic*
         tea-Acc drank.3ms Zayd-Nom
         'It was tea that Zayd drank.'

      b. ŠAY šərib   zayd   *Lebanese Arabic*
         tea drank.3ms Zayd
         'It was tea that Zayd drank.'

If FP is projected, then the phrase *šay-an/šay* 'tea,' generated in the canonical object position bearing the [+F] feature, moves to [Spec, FP] for identification of the [+F] feature on F. If FP is not projected, there would be no reason to move, and hence the focus marked element remains in situ, as illustrated in (32), repeated below as (60).

(60) a. šariba   zayd-un   ŠAY-AN   *Standard Arabic*
          drank.3ms Zayd-Nom tea-Acc
          'Zayd drank TEA.'

      b. šərib   zayd ŠAY   *Lebanese Arabic*
          drank.3ms Zayd tea
          'Zayd drank TEA.'

Standard Arabic, according to Ouhalla, has a set of *muʔakkidaat*, particles that can be analyzed as focus markers (FM). When one of these particles is merged with the head of FP, the result is that the focus phrase remains in situ and movement is again prohibited in those constructions (61).

(61) laqad šariba   zayd-un   šay-an
      FM   drank.3ms Zayd-Nom tea-Acc
      'Zayd DID drink tea.'

Ouhalla (1994b), citing Moutaouakil (1989), further points out that sentences involving focus markers like *laqad* in (61) "convey information which contradicts the information possessed by the addressee, and, therefore, are instances of contrastive focus" (p. 75). In such contexts as well, a parallel can be drawn between focus fronting and question formation in Arabic: Standard Arabic possesses question particles that morphologically identify the sentence as a yes-no question without disturbing the canonical word order of the sentence, as illustrated in (62).

(62) hal raʔat   mona zayd-an?
      QM saw.3fs Mona Zayd-Acc
      'Did Mona see Zayd?'

Under a movement analysis of focus fronting, the presence of a gap, the sensitivity to island constraints, and the case properties of the fronted focus phrase are readily accounted for. The analysis of focus fronting along the lines of Ouhalla (1994b) also explains the restriction on the number of focus phrases in a given clause. Since focus fronting is triggered by the identification of the [+F] feature in FP, once this feature is identified, the motivation behind the movement disappears and hence further movement is prohibited (Procrastinate; Chomsky 1995).

Shlonsky (2000:331) offers a different analysis to account for the number restriction on focus phrases in Arabic. He bases his analysis on the prohibition in (63).

(63)   A focus cannot be embedded under another focus.

Shlonsky's (2000) account is put forth to explain the incompatibility observed between questions and focus fronting ((39) and (40) are repeated below as (64) and (65)).

(64)   *Standard Arabic*
        a. *?ayna saalim-an qaabala xaalid-un
           where   Salim-Acc met.3ms xaalid-Nom

        b. *saalim-an ?ayna qaabala xaalid-un
           Salim-Acc where met.3ms xaalid-Nom

(65)   *Lebanese Arabic*
        a. *ween saalim šeefit   zeina
           where Salim saw.3fs Zeina

        b. *saalim ween šeefit   zeina
           Salim   where saw.3fs Zeina

If question formation is a specific instance of focalization, then the constraint in (63) accounts for the data in (64–65). However, as Ouhalla (1994b) points out, the constraint in (63) is too strong and would rule out sentences like those in (66), where a focus phrase clearly co-occurs with a question in an embedded clause.

(66)   a. KARIIM sa?alit   ʕan šu ħəke   musa
           Kariim asked.3fs about what spoke.3ms Moussa
           'It was Karim she asked about what Moussa said.'

        b. badna   naʕrif   ʕa-min KARIIM ʕarrafo
           want.1p know.1p to-who Karim introduced.3p
           'We want to know to whom it was that Karim was introduced.'

Thus it can be observed that the incompatibility of questions with focus and the uniqueness restriction on focus phrases holds at the level of the clause and not the whole sentence. Ouhalla's (1994b) account of those restrictions relies on Tsimpli's (1990 and 1995) analysis of Modern Greek. The analysis relies on the assumption that root clauses lack a CP, and the category C is claimed to be a selected category. Thus, in root clauses FP is the highest functional projection, and focus phrases as well as wh-elements move to its specifier position. The incompatibility between wh-questions and focus fronting then reduces to the fact that both wh-elements and fronted focus phrases target the same position, namely [Spec, FP].

The contrasts observed between focus fronting and CLLD are argued to be the result of the difference in how focus fronting constructions and CLLD constructions are derived. Whereas focus fronting involves movement to a specifier position, CLLD, according to Ouhalla, involves base-generation of the CLLDed phrase in a position adjoined to the highest functional projection in the clause and related to a pronominal clitic in the sentence.[11] This base-generation analysis of CLLD readily accounts for the case properties of CLLDed elements and for the absence of island effects in those constructions. Furthermore, the uniqueness requirement does not apply in the context of CLLD since those constructions do not involve a designated position in the tree structure. Since base-generation and adjunction are free, the number of CLLDed elements does not have to be limited to one. Ouhalla's analysis also accounts for the relative ordering of fronted focus elements and CLLDed elements. Since the latter are adjoined to FP, and fronted focus phrases land in [Spec, FP], it follows that CLLDed elements will always precede fronted focus phrases.

Shlonsky (2000) further proposes a constraint that accounts for subject–verb inversion in fronted focus constructions. Following Bakir (1980), he claims that the verb in focus constructions needs to be adjacent to the element bearing the focus feature. Hence, the verb in those constructions must move to F, in order to be adjacent to the fronted focus phrase in [Spec, FP]. This adjacency requirement explains why wh-questions trigger subject–verb inversion as well, if wh-questions are taken to be a subclass of focus constructions. It is, however, interesting to note that this analysis applies only to Standard Arabic, where the adjacency requirement is observed, and not to Lebanese Arabic, where fronted focus phrases can be separated from the verb and where there is no relative ordering between CLLDed elements and fronted focus phrases.

Whereas Ouhalla's (1994b) analysis of focus fronting captures the generalizations concerning those constructions, his analysis of CLLD constructions faces problems in accounting for the dialectal variations observed with respect to those constructions. First, it rules out the possibility of having the fronted focus phrase precede the CLLDed material, a case we have observed in Lebanese Arabic, and more importantly, it presents CLLD constructions as a unified class by claiming

---

[11] Ouhalla uses the term *topic* to refer to what we have been calling CLLD, but for consistency we will continue to refer to *topics* as *CLLDed elements*. Furthermore, it would be more accurate to refer to the adjunction site of the topic/CLLDed element as FP since it has been observed that, in embedded clauses, the topic/CLLDed element follows the complementizer and hence clearly does not adjoin to the highest functional projection of the clause, which would be CP, in those cases.

that all those constructions are base-generated. We will see in chapter 9 that CLLD constructions, although involving resumption, can be generated by movement, and therefore Ouhalla's (1994b) analysis for those constructions is not sufficient to account for the range of data we can observe in the various dialects of Arabic.

8.5   Conclusion

In this chapter we have examined two A'-constructions in Arabic: CLLD and focus fronting. By comparing and contrasting their properties, we were able to conclude first that focus fronting constructions share many properties with gapped wh-interrogatives: both construction types involve a gap within the sentence, which is related to a phrase in the left periphery. Both are triggered by the need to identify a feature – [+F] – generated on the head of a functional projection – FP – located between CP and TP. Following Ouhalla (1994b), we suggested that the sentence initial phrase in both types of constructions targets the same position, [Spec, FP], which explains why focus fronted phrases and fronted wh-phrases do not co-occur in simple sentences. Furthermore, both focus fronting constructions and wh-interrogatives are sensitive to islands.

CLLD, unlike focus fronting, involves resumption. Whereas only one phrase can be fronted as a focus phrase, more than one phrase can be CLLDed in a given sentence. Like resumptive wh-interrogatives, CLLD shows no island sensitivity, and the notion of referentiality does not adequately constrain the set of noun phrases that can be CLLDed. We have also observed that, in some dialects of Arabic (for instance, Standard Arabic), there are requirements imposed on the relative ordering of CLLDed and focus fronted phrases. This requirement is absent in other dialects of Arabic (for instance, Lebanese Arabic). In chapter 9, we further investigate this requirement and evaluate the various analyses that have been put forth to account for it.

9

The syntax of the Arabic left periphery

9.1 Introduction

In the previous chapter we examined briefly the interaction between CLLD and focus fronting in Arabic. The following generalization was uncovered:

(1)   *Interaction between CLLD and focus fronting*
        In Standard Arabic, focus phrases must follow CLLDed elements. This
        does not extend however to some of the other modern dialects of
        Arabic, like Lebanese Arabic, for instance.

In Ouhalla (1994b), the relative ordering between fronted focus phrases and CLLDed phrases in Standard Arabic was attributed to the positions that each type of phrase occupies in the tree structure: while fronted focus phrases target [Spec, FP], CLLDed phrases are base-generated adjoined to FP. It was also noted that while Ouhalla's analysis accounted for the facts of Standard Arabic, it couldn't be extended to Lebanese Arabic, where the restriction on the relative ordering between fronted focus elements and CLLDed elements does not apply.

In this chapter, we take a closer look at the ordering of focused and CLLDed elements in the left periphery of the Arabic sentence. In order to provide a more adequate analysis for the relative ordering of these elements in the A′-domain, we need to expand the data paradigms to include more complex sentences. Following Shlonsky (2000) and Rizzi (1997), we propose a "split-CP" analysis of the left periphery where both focused elements and CLLDed elements have designated positions: fronted focused elements target [Spec, FP], as in Ouhalla (1994b), whereas CLLDed elements target [Spec, TopP], the specifier of topic phrases, which are projected at several points in the structure. We also show that in order to account for the observed cross-dialectal difference between Standard Arabic and Lebanese Arabic, we have to appeal to the derivational history of the sentence (Aoun and Benmamoun 1998).

9.2   Revisiting focus fronting and CLLD

The contrast between Standard Arabic and Lebanese Arabic with respect to the relative ordering of fronted focus phrases and CLLDed phrases was illustrated in chapter 8 ((41) and (42) from chapter 8 are repeated below).

(2)   a. faaTimat-u   al-wardat-a   ?aʕTaa-ha   saalim-un
           Fatima.Nom the-rose.Acc gave.3ms-her Salim.Nom
           'Fatima, the rose Salim gave her.'

       b. *al-wardat-a faaTimat-u ?aʕTaa-ha   saalim-un
           the-rose.Acc Fatima.Nom gave.3ms-her Salim.Nom
           'Fatima, the rose Salim gave her.'

(3)   *Lebanese Arabic*
       a. ʕA KARIIM zeina ʕarrafnee-ha
           to Karim   Zeina introduced.1p-her
           'It is to Karim that we introduced Zeina.'

       b. zeina ʕA KARIIM ʕarrafnee-ha
           Zeina to Karim   introduced.1p-her
           'It is to Karim that we introduced Zeina.'

It is clear that Ouhalla's (1994b) adjunction analysis of CLLD does not adequately account for the ordering possibilities between CLLDed elements and focus elements in Lebanese Arabic, since it predicts the ordering in Standard Arabic to be the only one available.

Interestingly, Shlonsky (2000), following Rizzi (1997), proposes a cartography of the left periphery that can easily accommodate the Lebanese Arabic data. Thus, according to Shlonsky (2000), the traditional CP projection may be better viewed as several distinct heads, ordered as in (4).

(4)   ForceP > TopP > FP > TopP > FinP

ForceP is the projection where the (illocutionary) force of the sentence is marked. That is, the head of ForceP marks the sentence as an assertion, a question, etc. FinP stands for TP; it is where the tense features are projected. As can be further noted, the focus phrase (FP) is sandwiched between two topic phrases (TopP), which are the projections that typically host CLLDed elements. Thus, a sentence structure that adheres to the ordering in (4) will have available two potential sites for CLLDed elements, for instance. In the Lebanese Arabic sentences in (3), it can be said that while (3a) instantiates a representation where TopP precedes FP,

(3b) instantiates a representation where the CLLDed NP occupies the specifier position of the lower TopP.

In light of the contrast in (2), this account immediately raises the question of why the lower TopP cannot be instantiated in Standard Arabic. Shlonsky's (2000) answer to that question is given in the form of a constraint that states that focus phrases need to be adjacent to the verb (see also Bakir 1980). This adjacency requirement also accounts for subject–verb inversion in Standard Arabic wh-questions under the assumption that those constructions are a subclass of focus constructions. What we can add here in order to make Shlonsky's analysis fit with the Lebanese Arabic data in (3) is that this adjacency requirement is not at work in Lebanese Arabic. This would be consistent with what we observe in wh-questions in Lebanese Arabic, where subject–verb inversion is not required (5).

(5)   a. ʔeemta kariim šeef   mona?
            when   Karim saw.3ms Mona
            'When did Karim see Mona?'

       b. ʔeemta šeef   kariim mona?
            when   saw.3ms Karim Mona
            'When did Karim see Mona?'

However, a closer look at the interaction between CLLD and focus fronting in Lebanese Arabic shows that the story does not end with the adjacency requirement. More specifically, Aoun and Benmamoun (1998) show that, despite the absence of an adjacency requirement between a fronted focus phrase and the verb in Lebanese Arabic, there are still contexts where a focused phrase cannot precede a CLLDed phrase. That is, the data in (2) and (3) cannot be accounted for by appealing to this adjacency requirement.

It turns out that, in Lebanese Arabic, focus fronting across a CLLDed NP is possible only if the CLLDed NP is not separated from its corresponding clitic by an island (6–7).

(6)   nəkte (sməʕte   ʔənno) naadia (sməʕte   ʔənno) xabbaruw-a
        joke   (heard.2fs that)   Nadia (heard.2fs that)   told.3p-her
        'A joke, (you heard that) Nadia, (you heard that) they told her.'

(7)   ʕan   l-mudiir   (sməʕte   ʔənno) naadia (sməʕte   ʔənno)
        about the-director (heard.2fs that)   Nadia (heard.2fs that)

        ħəkuu-la
        talked.3p-her.Dat
        'About the director, (you heard that) Nadia, (you heard that) they talked to her.'

The constructions in (6–7) significantly contrast with ones in which the focused phrase is fronted across a CLLDed NP related to a clitic within a complex NP island (8), an adjunct clause (9), or a wh-island (10).[1]

(8)   *Complex NP Islands*

    a. *nəkte (sməʕte   ʔənno) naadia xabbaro S-Sabe yalli
       joke   (heard.2fs that)   Nadia told.3p the-boy that

       byaʕrəf-a
       know.3ms-her
       'A joke, Nadia, they told the boy that knows her.'

    b. *ʕan s-safra (sməʕte   ʔənno) naadia xabbaro r-rəžžeel yalli
       about the-trip (heard.2fs that)   Nadia told.3p the-man that

       zaar-a
       visited.3ms-her
       'About the trip, (you heard that) Nadia, they told the man that visited her.'

(9)   *Adjunct clauses*

    a. *farD   (sməʕte   ʔənno) naadia xabbaruu-ne ʔabl   ma
       homework (heard.2fs that)   Nadia told.3p-me   before Comp

       šəft-a   ʔənno l-mʕallme   ʕəTyit t-tlemiiz
       saw.1s-her that   the-teacher.fs gave.3fs the-students
       'Homework, (you heard that) Nadia, they told me before I saw her, that the teacher gave the students.'

    b. *ʕan l-faḥS   (sməʕte   ʔənno) naadia xabbaruune ʔabl
       about the-exam (heard.2fs that)   Nadia told.3p-me before

       ma   šəft-a   ʔənno l-mʕallme   ḥəkyit
       Comp saw.1s-her that   the-teacher.fs talked.3fs
       'About the exam, (you heard that) Nadia, they told me before I saw her that the teacher talked.'

---

[1] Although the link between the fronted focus phrase and its trace, and the one between the CLLDed element and its corresponding clitic, cross paths in (10), the unacceptability of those sentences cannot be attributed to a prohibition against crossing given that in the sentences in (8–9), the links between the fronted elements and their corresponding gap or resumptive clitic do not cross.

(10)   *Wh-islands*

    a. *l-mudiir   (sməʕte ʔənno) naadia saʔalto ʔəza
       the-principal (heard.2fs that)   Nadia asked.2p whether

       l-ʔisteez šaħaT-a
       the-teacher dismissed.3ms-her
       'The principal, (you heard that) Nadia, you asked whether the teacher
       dismissed her.'

    b. *mən l-mudiir   (ʔəlte   ʔənno) naadia badkun taʕrfo
       from the-principal (said.2fs that)   Nadia want.2p know.2p

       šu   ʕaTuw-a
       what gave.3p-her
       'From the principal, (you said that) Nadia, you want to know what
       they gave her.'

Summing up, fronted focus phrases do not display a uniform behavior with respect to their interaction with CLLDed NPs. Focus fronting across a CLLDed NP related to a clitic within an island is consistently ruled out (11b). On the other hand, focus movement across a CLLDed NP that is not separated from its corresponding clitic by an island is possible (11a).

(11)   a. ... (Focus-NP/PP)$_i$ ... CLLDed-NP$_j$ ... V+Clitic$_j$ ... t$_i$ ...

        b. *... (Focus-NP/PP)$_i$ ... CLLDed-NP$_j$ ... [$_{Island}$ ... clitic$_j$ ...] ... t$_i$

It can also be pointed out that the contrast observed in (6–10) obtains regardless of whether the CLLDed NP and the focused phrase occur within the same clause or in separate clauses.

In contrast with focus fronting, CLLD across another CLLD phrase, a focused phrase, or a wh-phrase is acceptable, as illustrated in the sentences in (12).

(12)   a. kariim sməʕt   ʔənno naadia ʔaʕʕaduw-a ħadd-o
       Karim heard.2ms that   Nadia seated.3p-her near-him
       'Karim, you heard that Nadia, they seated her near him.'

    b. naadia saʔalo   ʔayya rəžžeel xabbarto-(u) ʕann-a
       Nadia asked.3p which man   told.2p-(him) about-her
       'Nadia, they asked which man you told (him) about her.'

    c. naadia ʔaalo   ʔənno maʕ kariim ħkiito   ʕann-a
       Nadia said.3p that   with Karim talked.2p about-her
       'Nadia, they said that, with Karim, you spoke about her.'

This is also true if the lower CLLDed phrase or the wh-phrase are related to a resumptive element inside an island (13).

(13)   a. kariim sməʕt   ʔənno naadia fallo   bala   ma
           Karim heard.2ms that   Nadia left.3p without Comp

           yʔaʕʕduw-a   ħadd-o
           seated.3p-her near-him
           'Karim, you heard that Nadia, they left before they seated her near
           him.'

        b. naadia saʔalo   ʔayya rəžžeel ziʕil   laʔanno xabbarto-(u)
           Nadia asked.3p which man   upset.3ms because told.2p-(him)

           ʕann-a
           about-her
           'Nadia, they asked which man was upset because you told (him)
           about her.'

The schemata in (14) represent the data given in (12)–(13).

(14)   a. CLLDed-NP$_i$ . . . CLLDed-NP$_j$ . . . pro$_j$ . . . pro$_i$
        b. CLLDed-NP$_i$ . . . Wh$_j$ . . . t$_j$/pro$_j$ . . . pro$_i$
        c. CLLDed-NP$_i$ . . . Top$_j$ . . . t$_j$ . . . pro$_i$

What we have seen here shows that the facts about the interaction between focus fronting and CLLD in Lebanese Arabic are more complicated that they first appear to be: CLLDed elements can co-occur with focused phrases, only if the CLLDed element precedes the focus, or, in case the focused phrase precedes the CLLDed element, the latter must be related to a resumptive outside an island.

9.3   A minimality account

To account for the complex interaction observed between focus fronting and CLLD in Lebanese Arabic, Aoun and Benmamoun (1998) cast their analysis within Chomsky's Minimalist Program and, relying on the availability of movement in CLLD constructions, they offer an account of the interaction between focus fronting and CLLD in terms of minimality (Rizzi 1990; Chomsky 1995).

9.3.1   Two representations for CLLD constructions

Aoun and Benmamoun (1998) point out that CLLD constructions that do not involve islands could actually correspond to two different representations: one where the clitic is coindexed with a lexical NP that can later undergo movement (15a), and another where the clitic is coindexed with a null pronominal that is related to a base-generated CLLDed NP (15b). This latter configuration gives rise to standard resumptive constructions where a preposed NP binds a pronominal clitic within an island (16).

(15)   a. CLLDed-NP$_j$ . . . t$_i$-X+clitic . . .
        b. CLLDed-NP$_j$ . . . *pro$_i$*-X+clitic . . .

(16)   CLLDed-NP$_j$ . . . [$_{Island}$ . . . *pro$_j$* − X+clitic . . .]

Aoun and Benmamoun argue that (15a) is a representation that must be added to the inventory of representations available to resumptive constructions. This representation patterns with the standard gap strategy (17), in that they both involve movement to the left periphery.

(17)   *Constructions with the gap strategy*
        XP$_i$ . . . t$_i$ . . .

The representation in (17) is available to standard A′-constructions involving gaps. Representation (15a) differs from (17) only in that the moved element in the former is coindexed with a pronominal element, the clitic. This distinction is attributed to the presence of a Cl(itic) P(rojection) in (15a) but not in (17) (Sportiche 1998:244–307). A lexical NP generated in the specifier position of ClP may not remain there. Borrowing Sportiche's analysis of clitic constructions in Romance, Aoun and Benmamoun attribute this generalization to a generalized Doubly Filled Specifier/Head Filter that applies at the level of ClP. In that case, the lexical NP has to vacate this specifier position, leaving a gap.

To argue for the existence of (15a) as a representation for resumptive constructions, Aoun and Benmamoun make use of reconstruction. Assuming that reconstruction is a property of chains generated by movement (Hornstein 1984; Barss 1986; Chomsky 1993), they show that it applies in CLLD constructions that can be given the representation in (15a). Furthermore, as expected, CLLDed NPs related to a clitic within an island – which have the representation in (15b) – don't display reconstruction effects.

9.3.2   *Reconstruction effects in CLLD*

CLLD constructions are shown to display reconstruction effects in the context of pronominal binding. Aoun and Benmamoun provide the following contrast to illustrate this point:[2]

(18)   a. **təlmiiz-[a]$_i$ š-šiTaan**   btaʕrfo ʔənno [kəll mʕallme]$_i$
           student-her the-naughty know.2p that   every teacher

        ʔaaSaSət-o
        punished.3fs-him
        'Her naughty student, you know that every teacher punished him.'

---

[2] The same facts illustrated in (18b) using an adjunct clause can be shown using other types of islands, like wh-islands or complex NP islands.

b. *təlmiiz-[a]ᵢ š-šiTaan   fallayto ʔabl   ma   [kəll mʕallme]ᵢ
   student-her   the-naughty left.2p   before Comp. every teacher
   tʔaaSəs-o
   punish.3fs-him
   'Her naughty student, you left before every teacher punished him.'

In (18a), the quantifier phrase (QP) *kəll mʕallme* 'every teacher' can bind the pronoun within the CLLDed NP *təlmiiza š-šiTaan* 'her naughty student.' Assuming that bound pronouns must be c-commanded at LF by the operators that bind them (Chomsky 1976; Higginbotham 1980; Hornstein and Weinberg 1990), the relevant reading in (18a) then follows from the reconstruction of the CLLDed NP containing the bound pronoun below the subject QP. As expected, the pronoun in (18b) cannot be interpreted as bound by the QP within the adjunct clause. This is because the CLLDed NP containing the pronoun to be bound is related to a clitic within an island. Since extraction from islands is not possible, the CLLDed NP in (18b) does not reconstruct under the QP since reconstruction is a property of chains created by movement.

Thus, CLLD constructions do not behave uniformly with respect to reconstruction: CLLDed elements that are not separated from their corresponding clitics by an island reconstruct; the others do not. Aoun and Benmamoun (1998) account for this observation by linking it to the presence of movement in constructions that display reconstruction and its absence from those that don't.

9.3.3 Interception in Lebanese Arabic

The facts about the interaction between CLLD constructions and focus movement indicate that when CLLDed elements are separated from their corresponding clitic by an island, focus fronting across those elements is unacceptable in Lebanese Arabic (19).

(19)   a. . . . (Focus-NP/PP)ᵢ . . . CLLDed-NPⱼ . . . V+Cliticⱼ . . . tᵢ . . .
        b. *. . . (Focus-NP/PP)ᵢ . . . CLLDed-NPⱼ . . . [Island . . . cliticⱼ . . .] . . . tᵢ

Aoun and Benmamoun link the contrast observed in (19) to the fact that CLLD constructions do not form a natural class with respect to the availability of movement ((15a) and (15b) are repeated here).

(20)   a. CLLDed-NPⱼ . . . tᵢ-X+clitic . . .
        b. CLLDed-NPⱼ . . . *pro*ᵢ-X+clitic . . .

Thus, Aoun and Benmamoun analyze the difference between the two types of CLLDed elements in their relation to focus fronting in terms of interception. Specifically,

(21)   a. A moved CLLDed NP (20a) reconstructs and therefore does not
            intercept focus fronting (19a).
        b. A base-generated CLLDed NP (20b) cannot reconstruct and
            therefore intercepts focus fronting (19b).

Briefly, Aoun and Benmamoun's analysis takes the derivational history of a CLLD
construction to be the key element for explaining the interaction between CLLDed
and focus fronted phrases.

To illustrate how their analysis works, consider the ill-formed sentence in (22).

(22)   *nəkte sməʕt   ʔənno naadia xabbaro S-Sabe yalli byaʕrəf-a
        joke   heard.2ms that   Nadia told.3p the-boy that know.3ms-her
        'A joke, you heard that Nadia, they told the boy that knows her.'

In (22) focus fronting has applied across a CLLDed NP related to a clitic within a
complex NP island, as given in the representation in (23).

(23)   *[Focus-NP/PP]$_i$ . . . CLLDed-NP$_j$ . . . V . . . [$_{Island}$ . . .
        pro$_j$-V+Clitic] . . . t$_i$

In this context the CLLDed element is base-generated in its surface position. No
reconstruction of the CLLDed element can take place; hence, focus movement is
intercepted.

On the other hand, the well-formed sentences in (24) have the representation
in (25).

(24)   a. nəkte naadia xabbaruw-a
            joke Nadia told.3p-her
            'A joke, Nadia they told her.'

        b. ʕan   l-masraħiyye naadia ħkitii-la
            about the-play   Nadia told.2p-her.Dat.
            'About the play, Nadia, you told her.'

(25)   [Focus-NP/PP]$_i$ . . . CLLDed-NP$_j$ . . . t$_j$-V+Clitic . . . t$_i$

In this representation, the CLLDed NP, derived by movement, binds a trace. At LF,
the CLLDed NP is reconstructed, and thus will not intercept the focused phrase.
The alternative representation (26), in which the CLLDed NP is base-generated
and binds a pronominal, is ill-formed: since it is not derived by movement, the
CLLDed NP cannot reconstruct, and focus movement will be intercepted.

(26)   *[Focus-NP/PP]$_i$ . . . CLLDed-NP$_j$ . . . *pro*$_j$-V+Clitic . . . t$_i$

Two assumptions underlie Aoun and Benmamoun's discussion of the interaction
between CLLD and focus fronting: (a) the surface position of the CLLDed element

is an A′-position. Therefore, if the CLLDed element does not reconstruct, it can intercept another A′-element, namely a focused phrase; the interception of focus fronting by CLLD is the result of a minimality effect (see Rizzi 1990; Chomsky 1993, 1994; Aoun and Li 1993a, b). (b) The position to which the CLLDed element reconstructs is an A-position. In that case, focus fronting is not intercepted; minimality therefore does not apply.

9.3.4   Interception and binding

Aoun and Benmamoun provide further support for their analysis of the interaction between CLLD and focus fronting in terms of interception by examining pronominal binding in those contexts. Consider the following paradigm illustrating the well-known generalization that CLLD extends the binding possibilities of a given sentence (see Zubizarreta 1992 and 1998, among others).[3]

(27)   a. ʕaTit   S-Sabe yalli naadia htammit fi-i   širweel
           gave.3fs the-boy that Nadia cared.3fs in-him pants
           'She gave the boy that Nadia took care of pants.'

        b. **S-Sabe yalli naadia htammit fi-i**   ʕaTit-o   širweel
           the-boy that Nadia cared.3fs in-him gave.3fs-him pants
           'The boy that Nadia took care of him, she gave him pants.'

In (27a), the NP *Nadia* contained within the direct object in its canonical postverbal position cannot be coreferential with the pronominal subject of the main verb

---

[3] The facts in (27b) seem to go against what has been observed in Italian by Cinque (1990) (see also footnote 2, in chapter 8). Recall that in Italian CLLD constructions, there is obligatory connectivity between the CLLDed element and the IP internal position with respect to Binding Theory, as illustrated in (i).

(i)   A *lei/se stessa Maria non ci   pensa
          of her/herself   Maria not there thinks
          'Of herself, Maria does not think.'

In light of Aoun and Benmamoun's proposal, it is possible to deal with the facts illustrated in (i) by claiming that only movement is available in the generation of Italian CLLD. This option is supported by the fact that CLLD constructions in Italian seem to be sensitive to islands (Cinque 1990):

(ii)   *[A casa]ᵢ lo   abbiamo incontrato [PP prima che ci andasse]
          Home   him have.1p met   before that there went-he
          'At home, we met him before he went there.'

Alternatively, if we were to say that base-generation is also available for CLLD constructions in Italian, then the reported connectivity facts would have to be dealt with without appealing to movement.

ʕaTit 'she gave.' Given the hierarchical relation between subjects and objects, this observation can be attributed to a violation of Principle C: the pronominal subject c-commands the name *Nadia* and hence they cannot corefer. In (27b), which involves a preposed CLLDed object however, the coreferential reading is possible. This is taken to indicate that the CLLDed NP in (27b) does not reconstruct. Based on the observation that CLLDed elements that do not reconstruct intercept focus movement, it is expected that in contexts similar to (27), tension will arise between reconstruction and binding.

(28)   širweel **S-Sabe yalli naadia htammit fi-i**   ʕaTit-**o**
         pants   the-boy that Nadia   cared.3fs in-him   gave.3fs-him
         'Pants, the boy that Nadia took care of him, she gave him.'

Example (28) is unacceptable under the reading where *Nadia* is coreferential with the main clause pronominal subject, but acceptable otherwise. Aoun and Benmamoun consider two possibilities for (28): either the CLLDed NP reconstructs or it does not. If it reconstructs, the focused phrase is not intercepted; however, a binding violation occurs if *Nadia* and the pronominal subject are coreferential. On the other hand, if the CLLDed NP does not reconstruct, *Nadia* and the pronominal subject can corefer, but the focused phrase is intercepted. The facts in (27) and (28) are consistent with Aoun and Benmamoun's analysis and hence provide added confirmation for it.

9.4   Interaction between focus fronting and CLLD in Standard Arabic

Recall that in Standard Arabic, unlike Lebanese Arabic, focus fronting across a CLLDed element is always unacceptable. We have seen that in Lebanese Arabic the unacceptability of such sentences is related to the derivational history of the sentence and whether the CLLDed element is generated by movement or not. More precisely, when the CLLDed element is base-generated, moving a focus phrase across it is prohibited. This analysis may be extended to account for the facts observed in Standard Arabic on the assumption that, unlike in Lebanese Arabic, CLLD in Standard Arabic is always base-generated. In that case, CLLD constructions in Standard Arabic will correspond only to the representation where the CLLDed element is related to a pronominal clitic inside the sentence (29).

(29)   *CLLD constructions in Standard Arabic*
         $CLLD_i \ldots \ldots \ldots pro_i+$clitic $\ldots$

Under such an analysis, it is expected that CLLD in Standard Arabic will always intercept focus fronting; and that is what we have observed. Therefore, even if the lower topic projection – the one dominated by the focus phrase – were available in Standard Arabic, a CLLDed element base-generated in its specifier position would intercept a fronted focus phrase.

9.5   Interception: a constraint on the well-formedness of movement chains?

Returning to Lebanese Arabic, the relevant generalizations Aoun and Benmamoun (1998) try to account for with respect to the interaction between CLLDed phrases and fronted focus phrases are expressed in (30).

(30)   a. CLLDed NPs derived by movement display reconstruction effects.
        b. CLLDed NPs derived by movement do not intercept wh-extraction or focus movement.

These generalizations were accounted for as follows. A CLLDed element that has been fronted from the specifier of the clitic projection appears to be (re)located at LF in the position of its trace within the clitic projection, which can be considered an A-position. As a result of reconstruction, at LF there no longer is an A′-element that could intercept the fronting of wh-elements or focused elements. This account crucially assumes that the minimality constraint is a condition on LF representations rather than derivations. Otherwise, A′-extraction across a CLLDed NP would always violate minimality.

By examining the interaction between CLLD and resumptive wh-interrogatives, Aoun and Benmamoun further show that minimality is a constraint on chains resulting from movement. It has already been observed (see chapter 6) that wh-phrases related to resumptive clitics do not obey island constraints, as illustrated in (31).

(31)   ʔayya walad rəħt   ʔabl   ma   tšuuf-o/*Ø
        which boy   went.2ms before Comp see.2ms-him
        'Which boy did you go before you saw him?'

Interestingly, in (32) where the wh-element is related to a resumptive clitic and the CLLDed NP is related to a clitic within an island, interception does not apply.

(32)   ʔayya rəžžeel **naadia** xabbarto l-bənt   yalli šeefət-a   ʔənno
        which man   Nadia   told.2p the-girl that saw.3fs-her that
        raħ təʕəzmu-u
        fut. invite.2p-him
        'Which man, Nadia, you told the girl that saw her that you will invite him?'

That is, even though the CLLD occupies the topic position below the focus phrase where the wh-phrase is located, the sentence in (32) is perfectly acceptable. Given the representations available for constructions involving pronominal clitics, the resumptive element related to the wh-phrase can be taken to indicate the presence of a pronominal in the corresponding clitic projection, and hence the absence of movement in the generation of the sentence in (32). Thus the representation of (32) is as shown in (33).

(33)   wh-NP$_i$ . . . CLLDed-NP$_j$ . . . [$_{CNP}$ . . . pro$_i$-V+Clitic] . . . pro$_i$-V+Clitic . . .

It follows then that, since the CLLDed element does not intercept the relation between the wh-phrase and its corresponding clitic, interception applies only to movement chains. This analysis is confirmed by examining reconstruction in the following wh-questions.

(34)   a.   ʔayya dor mən ʔadwaar-[a]$_i$ **kariim** xabbartu-**u** ʔənno [kəll
              which role of   roles-her   Karim told.2p-him that   every

              mmasle]$_i$ bəthibb təlʕab-o?
              actress   like.3fs play.3fs-it
              'Which one of her roles, Karim, did you tell him that every actress
              likes to play it?'

        b.   *ʔayya dor mən ʔadwaar-[a]$_i$ **kariim** xabbarto r-rəžžeel yalli
              which role of   roles-her   Karim told.2p   the-man that

              byaʕrf-**o**   ʔənno [kəll mmasle]$_i$ bəthibb təlʕab-o?
              know.3ms-him that   every actress   like.3fs play.3fs-it
              'Which one of her roles, Karim, did you tell the man that knows
              him that every actress likes to play?'

The schema in (35) represents the sentences given in (34).

(35)   [$_{wh\text{-}NP}$ . . . pronoun$_i$]$_k$ . . . CLLDed-NP$_j$ . . . t$_j$/pro$_j$-V+Clitic . . .
        [$_{CP}$ QP$_i$ . . . t$_k$/*pro$_k$*-V+Clitic]

In (34a) the bound reading of the pronoun contained within the fronted wh-phrase is available; according to Aoun and Benmamoun's analysis, this is a reconstruction effect. For the bound reading to obtain, the wh-phrase must reconstruct to a position c-commanded by the QP inside the sentence. Thus the wh-phrase must be generated by movement. The relationship between the wh-phrase and its trace is not intercepted by the CLLDed element, since at LF the latter is reconstructed to the A-position – that is, the specifier position of the clitic to which it is related.

In the case that CLLDed element is base-generated in its surface A′-position and cannot reconstruct, it will intercept the relation between the fronted wh-phrase and its trace. In that case, the relation between the wh-phrase and its trace will be intercepted. This is what (34b) illustrates: in (34b) the bound reading that results from reconstruction is not available.

9.6   Interception: a constraint on derivations?

Aoun and Benmamoun's account of the interaction between CLLD and focus fronting leads to the expectation that CLLDed NPs generated by movement should not be intercepted. The reason is that these moved CLLDed NPs reconstruct. This expectation is not borne out: it can be shown that CLLD is not immune to interception. That is, moving a CLLDed NP across another CLLDed NP, or for that matter across a wh-phrase or a fronted focus phrase, is consistently ill-formed, as schematized in (36) and illustrated in the Lebanese Arabic sentences in (37).[4]

(36)   a. *CLLDed-NP$_i$ . . . CLLDed-NP$_j$ . . . t$_j$/pro$_j$ . . . t$_i$
        b. *CLLDed-NP$_i$ . . . Wh$_j$ . . . t$_j$/pro$_j$ . . . t$_i$
        c. *CLLDed-NP$_i$ . . . Top$_j$ . . . t$_j$ . . . t$_i$

(37)   a. *__Saaħəbt-[a]__$_i$ fakkaro   ʔənno *kariim*$_j$ ʕarrafət-o$_j$
            friend.f-her   thought.3p that   Karim introduced.3fs-him

            [kəll mʕallme]$_i$ ʕalay-**a**
            every teacher.f   to-her
            'Her friend, they thought that, Karim, every teacher introduced him to her.'

        b. *__Saaħəbt-[a]__$_i$ saʔalo   ʔayya *rəžžeel*$_j$ ʕarrafət-o$_j$
            friend.f-her   asked.3p which man   introduced.3fs-him

            [kəll mʕallme]$_i$ ʕalay-**a**
            every teacher.f   to-her
            'Her friend, they asked which man every teacher introduced (him) to her.'

        c. *__Saaħəbt-[a]__$_i$ fakkaro   *kariim* ʕarrafit   [kəll mʕallme]$_i$
            friend.f-her   thought.3p Karim introduced.3fs every teacher.f

            ʕalay-**a**
            to-her
            'Her friend, they thought that Karim, every teacher introduced to her.'

---

[4] The representations in (36) differ systematically from those in (14) in that they clearly involve movement of the CLLDed NP.

In these sentences, the QP subject *kəll mʕallme* 'every teacher' in the embedded clause cannot bind the pronoun contained within the CLLDed NP *Saaħəbta* 'her friend': binding the pronoun requires reconstruction of the CLLDed NP, in order for c-command to obtain between the QP subject and the pronoun. Since only elements derived by movement can undergo reconstruction, it follows that the CLLDed NP must have been extracted across the embedded CLLDed NP, the wh-phrase, or the fronted focus phrase. The unavailability of a bound reading in (37a–c) indicates that CLLDed elements that are moved are intercepted. This conclusion is further confirmed by the fact that, in the absence of an intervening A′-element, the bound reading of the pronoun contained within the CLLDed NP is available (38).

(38)   **Saaħəbt-[a]**$_i$ fakkaro   ʔənno ʕarrafət-ne   [kəll mʕallme]$_i$
        friend.f-her   thought.3p that   introduced.3fs-me every teacher.f

ʕalay-**a**
to-her
'Her friend, they thought that every teacher introduced her to me.'

Aoun and Benmamoun argue that the facts in this section would not come as a surprise if minimality is understood as a constraint on syntactic derivations rather than a constraint on LF representations.

In brief, an analysis that considers minimality to be a constraint on LF representations will not account for the fact that a CLLDed element cannot move across another CLLDed element, a wh-element, or a focus phrase. On the other hand, an analysis that considers minimality to be a constraint on derivations will account for the fact that a moved CLLDed element is intercepted by an intervening CLLDed element, a wh-element, or a focus phrase. However, with the derivational account of minimality we lose the explanation for why a CLLDed NP does not always intercept focus fronting in Lebanese Arabic. Therefore, under the assumption that the interception effects observed so far in the interaction between CLLD and focus are to be accounted for as minimality violations, the conclusion is that minimality, whether construed as a constraint on derivations or on LF representations, cannot account for all the generalizations.

Underlying the discussion so far has been the assumption that movement in CLLD constructions is on a par with movement in wh-interrogatives and focus fronting. Aoun and Benmamoun call into question this assumption, suggesting that CLLD movement is a post-spell-out operation taking place in the PF component of the grammar. Assuming that extraction of a CLLDed element is a PF operation, the issue of why such a PF operation does not intercept the extraction of a wh-element or a focus phrase does not arise. Pre-spell-out, the CLLDed element is still in ClP, an A-position, and therefore not in a position that can intercept the movement of a wh-element or a moved phrase. On the other hand, a CLLDed element that binds a pronominal is generated in a dislocated A′-position and intercepts both wh-extraction and focus movement.[5]

This proposal also accounts for the "reconstruction" effects that CLLD constructions display. In a generative model that considers that PF operations do not feed LF operations, the movement of a CLLDed element in the PF component will have no LF import. That is, in the LF component, the PF fronted CLLDed element is located in CIP; hence the "reconstruction" effects. On the other hand, a CLLDed element directly generated in the dislocated A′-position binds a pronominal and will not display "reconstruction."

In addition, since fronted CLLDed elements are intercepted by other CLLDed elements, wh-elements, and fronted focus phrases, it is possible to assume that they are intercepted by elements in an A′-position and that minimality constrains PF-movement as well as movement in syntax proper. Within a minimalist framework, this result can be obtained if minimality is considered to be part of the formulation of the operation Move: minimality applies whenever Move applies, as argued in Chomsky (1995).[6]

9.7   Broad subject constructions revisited

So far we have seen that the left periphery in Arabic comprises at least three projections hierarchically ordered such that a topic phrase which hosts CLLDed elements dominates a focus phrase, which hosts fronted focus phrases (and wh-phrases) and which, in turn, dominates another topic phrase. Both topic phrases seem to be available for CLLD in Lebanese Arabic, except when the CLLD element is related to a resumptive clitic in an island and a focus phrase is fronted to [Spec, FP]. In such contexts, the CLLDed element, if located in the lower TopP, intercepts the focus phrase. In Standard Arabic, where CLLDed elements are always base-generated, the specifier of the lower topic phrase cannot be filled in the context of focus fronting. That is because a base-generated CLLDed element will always intercept focus fronting.

[5] Assuming that CLLD movement takes place in the PF component of grammar means that this type of movement has no LF import. It differs from other syntactic movement operations which result in operator-variable chains, like quantifier raising or wh-movement. The latter affect scope possibilities in the sentence, which CLLD movement does not seem to affect.

[6] The various island effects that constrain this PF movement are to be incorporated in the formulation of Move as well (see Chomsky 1995).

Alexopoulou, Doron, and Heycock (2004) question the existence of two types of CLLD constructions: a type that involves movement and displays reconstruction effects and another type that doesn't. Instead, they argue for the existence of a construction with a left peripheral XP related to a pronominal clitic within the construction that is different from clitic-left dislocation. Those constructions are called *broad subject (BS) constructions* (Doron and Heycock 1999).[7] Typical examples of those in Arabic are given in (39–40).

(39)   *Standard Arabic*
      a. al-baytu   alwaanu-hu   zaahiyatun
         the-house.Nom colors.Nom-it bright.Nom
         'The house, its colors are bright.'

      b. hind-un   šaʕru-ha   Tawiil-un
         Hind-Nom hair.Nom-her long-Nom
         'Hind, her hair is long.'

(40)   *Lebanese Arabic*
      a. l-beet   alween-o fee?ʕa
         the-house colors-it bright
         'The house, its colors are bright.'

      b. hind šaʕr-a   Tawiil
         Hind hair-her long
         'Hind, her hair is long.'

Thus, broad subjects share with CLLDed NPs the relationship to a clitic inside the sentence.[8]

We have observed that Doron and Heycock (1999) present different criteria to show the parallelism between BSs and canonical subjects, such as the possibility of embedding both BSs and canonical subjects under the auxiliary *kaan* (41) (see also chapter 3).

(41)   *Standard Arabic*
      a. kaanat zaynab-u   taquudu s-sayyaarat-a
         was.3fs Zaynab-Nom drive.3fs the-car-Acc
         'Zaynab was driving the car.'

---

[7] We discuss broad subject constructions in chapter 3 of this book.

[8] However, broad subjects differ from CLLDed NPs in that they are neutral with respect to information structure. That is, they can be interpreted either as topics or as foci. Alexopoulou, Doron, and Heycock (2004) take CLLDed NPs to be consistent only with the discourse function topic and thus incompatible with focal stress and a focus interpretation.

b. kaanat   zaynab-u   šaʕru-ha   Tawiil-an
was.3ms Zaynab-Nom hair.Nom-her long-Acc
'Zaynab, her hair was long.'

9.7.1   Broad subjects and CLLD

Taking Romance CLLD as a test case for CLLD, Alexopoulou, Doron, and Heycock (2004) argue for a distinction between broad subjects and CLLDed NPs based on the following criteria. First, whereas downward entailing QPs such as *nessuno* 'no one' or *nessun uomo* 'no man' in Italian cannot occur as CLLDed elements, their Lebanese equivalents can appear as broad subjects. Thus, the Italian sentences in (42) contrast with the Lebanese Arabic sentences in (43).

(42)   a. *Nessuno lo   ho   visto
              no one   him have.1s seen
              'No one, I have seen him.'

         b. *Nessun uomo lo   ho   visto
              no   man   him have.1s seen
              'No man, I have seen him.'

(43)   a. wala walad šaʕr-o   Tawiil
              no   child hair-him long
              'No child, his hair is long.'

         b. ma ħada šaʕr-o   Tawiil
              no one hair-him long
              'No one, his hair is long.'

Alexopoulou, Doron, and Heycock thus argue that the fact that downward entailing QPs such as *ma ħada* 'no one' can appear in contexts like (43b) is a clear indication that such constructions are not CLLD constructions (see also chapter 8).

A second contrast that Alexopoulou, Doron, and Heycock observe between BS constructions and CLLD is with respect to island violations. Whereas CLLD constructions cannot violate island constraints in Romance (Cinque 1990), BS constructions can.[9] The examples cited in Alexopoulou, Doron, and Heycock (2004) are the following:

(44)   a. *A Carlo, ti   parlerò   solo delle persone che gli
              To Carlo you (I) will talk only of-the people that to-him

              piacciono
              appeal
              'To Carlo, I will talk to you only about the people who appeal to him.'

[9] Cinque (1990) has used this observation to distinguish between CLLD and left-dislocation (LD).

b. *A casa, lo   abbiamo incontrato prima che ci   andasse.
To home him (we) have met   before that there (he) went
'Home, we met him before he went there.'

BS constructions on the other hand clearly violate island constraints, as observed in (45).

(45)   bad-kun taʕrfo   ʔayya bint saʔalo   ʔəza   šaʕr-a   Tawiil
        want-2p know.2p which girl asked.3p whether hair-her long
        'You want to know which girl they asked if her hair was long.'

Alexopoulou, Doron, and Heycock conclude that a distinction needs to be made between CLLD constructions and BS constructions. BS constructions are parallel to canonical subject–predicate constructions in that the BS is generated in an A-position, without movement, related to a pronominal element inside the sentence. Hence, BS constructions can freely violate island conditions. CLLDed NPs on the other hand are generated by movement of the CLLDed NP to its surface position by A′-movement. Hence, like other A′-movement constructions CLLD constructions obey island constraints.

Revisiting Aoun and Benmamoun (1998), Alexopoulou, Doron, and Heycock suggest that the two types of CLLD found in Lebanese Arabic are better understood if one takes CLLD constructions that do not involve movement to be instances of BS constructions. Applied to Standard Arabic, this analysis implies that Standard Arabic has BS constructions but no CLLD constructions. Then, only those CLLD constructions identified by Aoun and Benmamoun as unambiguously involving movement are considered as CLLD constructions by Alexopoulou, Doron, and Heycock. Thus, sentences involving a fronted negative quantifier phrase binding a pronominal clitic, as illustrated in (46), would be clear instances of a BS construction since those quantifier phrases cannot participate in CLLD.

(46)   a. wala masraħiyye ʔaalit   zaynab ʔənno badda   tšuuf-a
           no   play   said.3fs Zaynab that want.3fs see.3ms-it
           'No play, Zaynab said that she wants to see it.'

        b. wala waaħad byaʕrfo ʔəza   fallatu-u
           no   one   know.3p whether released.3p-him
           'No one, they know whether they released him.'

Given the distinction that Alexopoulou, Doron, and Heycock make between BSs and CLLDed elements, it comes as no surprise that only those constructions that are classified as CLLD constructions display reconstruction effects, as illustrated in (47).

(47)   a. **tilmiiz-[a]ᵢ š-šiTaan**   ʔaalo   ʔənno [kəll mʕallme]ᵢ
           student-her the-naughty said.3p that   every teacher

        ʔaaSaSət-o
        punished.3fs-him
        'Her naughty student, they said that every teacher punished him.'

      b. ***tilmiiz -[a]ᵢ š-šiTaan**   fallo   ʔabl ma [kəll mʕallme]ᵢ
           student-her   the-naughty left.3p before Comp every teacher

        ʔaaSaSət-o
        punished.3fs-him
        'Her naughty student, they left before every teacher punished him.'

According to Alexopoulou, Doron, and Heycock, the contrast between (47a) and (47b) is attributed to the fact that, in (47a), the left peripheral noun phrase is a CLLDed element generated by movement, whereas in (47b), the left peripheral element is a BS base-generated in its surface position and hence is not subject to reconstruction.

9.7.2   Broad subjects and interception

Alexopoulou, Doron, and Heycock note the contrast between extraction out of a BS construction and extraction out of a CLLD construction as illustrated in (48a) and (48b) respectively.

(48)   a. *nəkte/šu **naadia** xabbaro S-Sabe yalli byaʕrif-a
           joke/what Nadia   told.3p the-boy that know.3ms-her
           'A joke/what, Nadia, (did) they told (tell) the boy that knows her.'

      b. nəkte/šu **naadia** smeʕte   ʔənno xabbaruw-a
           joke/what Nadia   heard.2fs that   told.3p-her
           'A joke/what, Nadia (did) you heard (hear) that they told her.'

This observation, Alexopoulou, Doron, and Heycock attribute to the fact that BSs, unlike CLLD constructions, create islands for extraction. Thus, (48a) parallels (49).

(49)   *addeeš feetħa l-fəstaan ʔalween-o
         how   light.p the-dress colors-its
         'How light are the colors of the dress?'

In (49), as in (48a), a wh-phrase/focus phrase has been extracted out of the predicate of a BS construction, which is unacceptable. Example (48b) is ambiguous in that it can be given two representations: the left peripheral NP following the focus/wh-element can be analyzed as either a BS or a CLLDed NP. In the latter case it wouldn't create an island for extraction and hence movement of the focused element or the wh-element past the CLLDed NP is legitimate.

Confirmation for this analysis comes from the fact that if one substitutes a downward entailing QP for the CLLDed NP in (48b), the sentence becomes unacceptable, as illustrated in (50).

(50)   *nəkte/šu **wala waħad** smeʕte   ʔənno xabbaru-**u**
        joke/what no   one   heard.2fs that   told.3p-him
        'A joke/what, no one (did) you heard (hear) that they told him.'

The unacceptability of (50) is expected under Alexopoulou, Doron, and Heycock's analysis since they assume that downward entailing QPs give rise to BS constructions, but not to CLLD constructions. Hence, when they occur in the left periphery related to a pronominal clitic within the sentence, they block extraction and will constitute islands for movement.

Alexopoulou, Doron and Heycock's claim is that in Aoun and Benmamoun's (1998) analysis, data like (50) are not expected since nothing prevents the downward entailing QP from being analyzed as a CLLDed element generated by PF-movement, and hence the expectation is that, at LF, it is found in its original A-position where it would not intercept the relation between the wh-element or the focus phrase and its trace.[10]

It must be noted however, that in Alexopoulou, Doron, and Heycock's analysis of BS constructions, Aoun and Benmamoun's account for the relation between CLLD and focus in terms of interception cannot be maintained. The reason for this is that, like canonical subjects, BSs are in fact considered to be generated in A-positions and are therefore not expected to interfere in the relationship between an A′-element and its trace. Consequently, the reason why BS constructions, but not CLLD, create islands for extraction is not discussed by Alexopoulou, Doron, and Heycock.

There is also doubt that one should group, under one explanation, sentences like (48a) and sentences like (49). Two reasons militate against such a conclusion. First, there are ways to extract from a BS construction without yielding an unacceptable sentence. Thus, observe the contrast between (51a) and (51b):

---

[10] It could be said however that QPs need to form an operator variable chain, relevant for interpretation at LF and therefore, that negative QPs like *wala waħad* 'no one' in (50) will have to be preposed in the syntax proper, in which case they will intercept focus fronting.

(51)   a. *addeeš feetħa l-fəstaan ʔalween-o
            how   light.p the-dress colors-its
            'How light are the colors of the dress?'

        b. ʔaddeeš l-fəstaan feetħa ʔalween-o
            how   the-dress light.p colors-its
            'How light are the colors of the dress?'

Thus, a BS construction does not seem totally immune to extraction since the wh-word itself can be extracted, leaving the adjective behind. However, sentences involving a CLLDed NP related to a pronominal clitic inside an island always intercepts A′-movement, as was shown earlier.

Furthermore, having noted that BS constructions can occur embedded under *kaan* 'was,' it can easily be checked that a left peripheral NP related to a pronominal clitic within an island cannot occur in such contexts (52).

(52)   *keenit/keeno   **naadia** ʕam bixabbro S-Sabe yalli šeef-**a**
        was.3fs/were.3p Nadia   Asp. tell.3p   the-boy that saw.3ms-her

        nəkte
        joke
        'It was the case that Nadia, they were telling the boy that saw her a joke.'

In sum, data like (43b) and (49) indicate that there is a case for assuming the existence of BS constructions alongside CLLD constructions. However, the argument cannot be made that constructions with left peripheral NPs related to a clitic within an island are in fact BS constructions rather than CLLD generated without movement, since the latter lack defining properties of BS constructions. More research needs to be done in order to identify the position that BSs occupy in the left periphery.

9.8   Conclusion

This chapter was mainly concerned with the interaction of elements in the left periphery of the Arabic sentence. Starting from the observation that in Standard Arabic CLLDed elements must precede focus fronted elements, we refute the analysis that attributes this to the position that each of those elements occupy in the sentence structure. By examining similar facts in Lebanese Arabic, we show that the universal "split CP" structure argued for by Rizzi (1997) is also available in Arabic. However, the explanation for the ordering restrictions between CLLDed and focus elements is shown to be the result of the derivational history of these elements: whereas focus phrases are fronted by movement, CLLD elements can be either derived by PF-movement, or they can be base-generated in their surface position. In the latter case, they intercept focus movement. By contrasting CLLD constructions with BS constructions, we concluded that, whereas BS constructions need to be added to the inventory of "resumptive" constructions in Arabic, they don't coincide with the set of CLLD constructions that are base-generated, as claimed in Alexopoulou, Doron, and Heycock (2004).

References

Abu-Haidar, F. 1979. *A Study of the Spoken Arabic of Baskinta*. Leiden: E. J. Brill.

Ackema, Peter, and Ad Neeleman. 2003. Context-Sensitive Spell-Out. *Natural Language and Linguistic Theory* 21: 681–735.

Alexiadou, Aretemis, and Elena Anagnostopoulou. 1999. EPP without Spec, IP. In *Specifiers: Minimalist Approaches*, eds. David Adger, Susan Pintzuk, Bernadette Plunkett, and George Tsoulas, 93–109. Oxford University Press.

Alexopoulou, Theodora, Edit Doron, and Caroline Heycock, 2004. Broad Subjects and Clitic-Left Dislocation. In *Peripheries: Syntactic Edges and their Effects*, eds. David Adger, Cecile De Cat, and George Tsoulas, 329–358. Dordrecht: Kluwer.

Aoun, Joseph, 1978. Structure interne du syntagme nominal en Arabe: L'Idafa. *Analyses Théories* 2: 1–40.

1986. *Generalized Binding*. Dordrecht: Foris.

Aoun, Joseph, and Elabbas Benmamoun,1998. Minimality, Reconstruction, and PF Movement. *Linguistic Inquiry* 29: 569–592.

1999. Gapping, PG Merger, and Patterns of Partial Agreement. In *Fragments: Studies in Ellipsis and Gapping*, eds. S. Lappin, and E. Benmamoun, 170–187. Oxford University Press.

Aoun, Joseph, Elabbas Benmamoun, and Dominique Sportiche, 1994. Agreement and Conjunction in Some Varieties of Arabic. *Linguistic Inquiry* 25: 195–220.

1999. Further Remarks on First Conjunct Agreement. *Linguistic Inquiry* 30: 669–681.

Aoun, Joseph, and Lina Choueiri, 1996. Resumption and Last Resort. Unpublished manuscript, USC, Los Angeles.

1999. Modes of Interrogation. In *Perspectives on Arabic Linguistics XII*, ed. Elabbas Benmamoun, 7–26. Amsterdam: John Benjamins.

2000. Epithets. *Natural Language and Linguistic Theory* 18: 1–39.

Aoun, Joseph, Lina Choueiri, and Norbert Hornstein, 2001. Resumption, Movement, and Derivational Economy. *Linguistic Inquiry* 32: 371–403.

Aoun, Joseph, and Yen-Hui Audrey Li, 1993a. *Syntax of Scope*. Cambridge, Mass.: MIT Press.

1993b. *Wh*-Elements in Situ: Syntax or LF? *Linguistic Inquiry* 24: 199–238.

2003. *Essays on the Representational and Derivational Nature of Grammar: The Diversity of Wh-Constructions*. Cambridge, Mass.: MIT Press.

Ayoub, Georgine, 1981. Structure de la Phrase en Arabe Standard. Doctoral dissertation, Université de Paris VII, France.

Bahloul, Maher, 1994. The Syntax and Semantics of Taxis, Aspect, Tense and Modality in Standard Arabic. Doctoral dissertation, Cornell University, Ithaca.

Bahloul, Maher, and Wayne Harbert, 1993. Agreement Asymmetries in Arabic. In *Proceedings of WCCFL 11*, ed. Jonathan Mead, 15–31. Stanford: CSLI.

Bakir, Murtadha, 1980. Aspects of Clause Structure in Arabic. Doctoral dissertation, Indiana University, Bloomington.

Barss, Andrew, 1986. Chains and Anaphoric Dependence. Doctoral dissertation, MIT, Cambridge, Mass.

Benmamoun, Elabbas, 1992a. Inflectional and Functional Morphology: Problems of Projection, Representation and Derivation. Doctoral dissertation, USC, Los Angeles.

   1992b. Structural Conditions on Agreement. *Proceedings of the North Eastern Linguistic Society (NELS 22)*, 17–32. University of Massachusetts at Amherst.

   1993. The Status of Agreement and the Agreement Projection in Arabic. *Studies in the Linguistic Sciences* 23: 61–71.

   1996. Negative Polarity and Presupposition in Moroccan Arabic. In *Perspectives on Arabic Linguistics VIII*, ed. Mushira Eid, 47–66. Amsterdam: John Benjamins.

   1997. Licensing of Negative Polarity in Moroccan Arabic. *Natural Language and Linguistic Theory* 15: 263–287.

   2000. *The Feature Structure of Functional Categories: A Comparative Study of Arabic Dialects*. Oxford University Press.

   2003. Agreement Parallelism between Sentences and Noun Phrases: A Historical Sketch. *Lingua* 113: 747–764.

   2006. Licensing Configurations: The Puzzle of Head Negative Polarity Items. *Linguistic Inquiry* 37: 141–149.

Benmamoun, Elabbas, and Heidi Lorimor, 2006. Featureless Expressions: When Morphophonological Markers are Absent. *Linguistic Inquiry* 37: 1–23.

Berman, Ruth, and Alexander Grosu. 1976. Aspects of the Copula in Modern Hebrew. In *Studies in Modern Hebrew Syntax and Semantics*, ed. Peter Cole, 265–284. Amsterdam: North Holland.

Bianchi, Valentina, 1999. *Consequences of Antisymmetry: Headed Relative Clauses*. Berlin: Mouton de Gruyter.

Borer, Hagit, 1984. Restrictive Relatives in Modern Hebrew. *Natural Language and Linguistic Theory* 2: 219–260.

   1996. The Construct in Review. In *Studies in Afroasiatic Grammar*, eds. J. Lecarme, J. Lowenstamm, and U. Shlonsky, 30–61. The Hague: Holland Academic Graphics.

Borsley, Robert, 1997. Relative Clauses and the Theory of Phrase Structure. *Linguistic Inquiry* 28: 629–647.

Brame, Mark, 1970. Arabic Phonology: Implications for Phonological Theory and Historical Semitic. Doctoral dissertation, MIT, Cambridge, Mass.

Brockelmann, C. 1910. *Linguistique Sémitique*. Translated from German by W. Marçais and M. Cohen. Paris: Librairie Paul Geuthner.

Brustad, Kristen, 2000. *The Syntax of Spoken Arabic*. Washington, DC: Georgetown University Press.

Carlson, Gregory, 1977. Amount Relatives. *Language* 53: 520–542.

Carnie, Andrew, 1995. Non-Verbal Predication and Head-Movement. Doctoral dissertation, MIT, Cambridge, Mass.

Caubet, Dominique, 1991. The Active Participle as a Means to Renew the Aspectual System: A Comparative Study in Several Dialects of Arabic. In *Semitic Studies*, ed. Alan S. Kaye, 207–224. Wiesbaden: Otto Harrassowitz.

1993. *L'Arabe Marocain*. Paris: Éditions Peeters.

1996. La Négation en Arabe Maghrébin. In *La Négation en Berbère et en Arabe Maghrébin*, eds. S. Chaker, and C. Caubet, 79–97. Paris: L'Harmattan.

Chomsky, Noam, 1976. Conditions on Rules of Grammar. *Linguistic Analysis* 2: 303–349.

1977. On Wh-movement. In *Formal Syntax*, eds. P. Culicover, T. Wasow, and A. Akmajian, 71–132. New York: Academic Press.

1981. *Lectures on Government and Binding*. Foris, Dordrecht.

1986. *Knowledge of Language: Its Nature, Origin and Use*. New York: Praeger.

1993. A Minimalist Program for Linguistic Theory. In *The View from Building 20*, eds. K. Hale and S. J. Keyser, 1–49. Cambridge, Mass.: MIT Press.

1994. Bare Phrase Structure. *MIT Occasional Papers in Linguistics, volume 5*. Cambridge, Mass.: MIT Department of Linguistics and Philosophy.

1995. *The Minimalist Program*. Cambridge, Mass.: MIT Press.

2000. Minimalist Inquiries: The Framework. In *Step by Step: Essays on Minimalist Syntax in Honor of Howard Lasnik*, eds. Roger Martin, David Michaels, and Juan Uriagereka, 89–155. Cambridge, Mass.: MIT Press.

2001. Derivation by Phase. In *Ken Hale: A Life in Language*, ed. Michael Kenstowicz, 1–52. Cambridge, Mass.: MIT Press.

2004. On Phases. Ms., MIT.

Choueiri, Lina, 2002. Issues in the Syntax of Resumption: Restrictive Relatives in Lebanese Arabic. Doctoral dissertation, USC, Los Angeles.

Cinque, Guglielmo, 1977. The Movement Nature of Left Dislocation. *Linguistic Inquiry* 8: 397–412.

1990. *Types of Ā-dependencies*. Cambridge, Mass.: MIT Press.

1999. *Adverbs and Functional Heads*. Oxford University Press.

Comrie, Bernard, 1976. *Tense*. Cambridge University Press.

Cowell, Mark, 1964. *A Reference Grammar of Syrian Arabic*. Washington, DC: Georgetown University Press.

Déchaine, Rose-Marie, 1993. Predicates Across Categories. Doctoral dissertation, University of Massachusetts, Amherst.

Demirdache, Hamida, 1991. Resumptive Chains in Restrictive Relatives, Appositives, and Dislocation Structures. Doctoral dissertation, MIT, Cambridge, Mass.

Doron, Edit, 1983. Verbless Predicates in Hebrew. Doctoral dissertation, University of Texas at Austin, Austin, Texas.

1986. The Pronominal "Copula" as Agreement Clitic. In *Syntax of Pronominal Clitics*, ed. Hagit Borer, 313–332. New York: Academic Press.

1996. The Predicate in Arabic. In *Studies in Afroasiatic Grammar*, eds. J. Lecarme, J. Lowenstamm, and U. Shlonksy, 77–87. Leiden: Holland Academic Graphics.

Doron, Edit and Caroline Heycock, 1999. Filling and Licensing Multiple Specifiers. In *Specifiers*, eds. David Adger, Susan Pintzuk, Bernadette Plunkett, and George Tsoulas, 69–89. Oxford University Press.

Eid, Mushira, 1983. The Copula Function of Pronouns. *Lingua* 59: 197–207.

1991. Verbless Sentences in Arabic and Hebrew. In *Perspectives on Arabic Linguistics III*, eds. Bernard Comrie and Mushira Eid, 31–61. Amsterdam: John Benjamins.

1993. Negation and Predicate Heads. In *Principles and Prediction*, eds. Mushira Eid and Gregory K. Iverson, 135–152. Philadelphia: John Benjamins.

Eisele, John, 1988. The Syntax and Semantics of Tense, Aspect, and Time Reference in Cairene Arabic. Doctoral dissertation, University of Chicago.

Fassi Fehri, Abdelkader, 1982. *Linguistique Arabe: Forme et Interprétation*. Rabat: Publications de la Faculté des Lettres et Sciences Humaines.

1988. Agreement in Arabic, Binding and Coherence. In *Agreement in Natural Language: Approaches, Theories, Description*, eds. M. Barlow and C. Ferguson, 107–158. Stanford: CSLI.

1993. *Issues in the Structure of Arabic Clauses and Words*. Dordrecht: Kluwer.

1999. Arabic Modifying Adjectives and DP Structures. *Studia Linguistica* 53: 105–154.

2000. Distributing Features and Affixes in Arabic Subject Verb Agreement Paradigms. In *Research in Afroasiatic Grammar 4*, eds. J. Lecarme, J. Lowenstamm, and U. Shlonsky. Amsterdam: John Benjamins.

Ferguson, Charles, 1959. Diglossia. *Word* 15: 325–340.

1983. God Wishes in Syrian Arabic. *Mediterranean Language Review* 1: 65–83.

Fleisch, Henri, 1979. *Traité de Philologie Arabe*. Beirut: Librairie Orientale.

Fox, Danny, 1999. Reconstruction, Binding Theory, and the Interpretation of Chains. *Linguistic Inquiry* 30: 157–196.

Gamal-Eldin, Saad, 1967. *A Syntactic Study of Egyptian Colloquial Arabic*. The Hague: Mouton.

Gary, Judith, and Saad Gamal-Eldin, 1982. *Cairene Egyptian Colloquial Arabic*. Amsterdam: North Holland.

Gelderen, Elly van, 1996. Parametrising Agreement Features in Arabic, Bantu Languages, and Varieties of English. *Linguistics* 34: 753–767.

Gordon, Raymond G., Jr. (ed.) 2005. *Ethnologue: Languages of the World, 15th Edition*. Dallas, Tex.: SIL International. Online version: www.ethnologue.com/

Gray, Louis, 1934. *Introduction to Comparative Semitic Linguistics*. Amsterdam: Philo Press.

Greenberg, Yael, 2002. The Manifestation of Genericity in the Tense Aspect System of Hebrew Nominal Sentences. In *Themes in Arabic and Hebrew Syntax*, eds. Jamal Ouhalla and Ur Shlonsky, 267–298. Dordrecht: Kluwer.

Grimshaw, Jane, 1991. Extended Projections. Unpublished manuscript, Rutgers University, New Brunswick.

Grosu, A., and Landmann, F. 1998. Strange Relatives of the Third Kind. *Natural Language Semantics* 6: 125–170.

Halila, Hafedh, 1992. Subject Specificity Effects in Tunisian Arabic. Doctoral dissertation, USC, Los Angeles.

Hallman, Peter, 2000. The Structure of Agreement Failure in Lebanese Arabic. In *Proceedings of the 19th West Coast Conference on Formal Linguistics*, ed. Roger Billerey, 178–190. Somerville, Mass.: Cascadilla Press.

Harbert, Wayne, and Maher Bahloul, 2002. Postverbal Subjects in Arabic and the Theory of Agreement. In *Themes in Arabic and Hebrew Syntax*, eds. U. Shlonsky and J. Ouhalla, 45–70. Dordrecht: Kluwer.

Hassan, Abbas, 1973. *Al-NaHw Al-Waafii*. Cairo: Dar Al Maarif.

Hazout, Ilan, 1990. Verbal Nouns: Theta Theoretic Studies in Hebrew and Arabic. Doctoral dissertation, University of Massachusetts, Amherst.

1995. Action Nominalizations and the Lexicalist Hypothesis. *Natural Language and Linguistic Theory* 13: 355–404.

Heggie, Lorie, 1988. The Syntax of Copular Structures. Doctoral dissertation, USC, Los Angeles.

Heycock, Caroline, 1995. Asymmetries in Reconstruction. *Linguistic Inquiry* 26: 547–570.

Higginbotham, James, 1980. Pronouns and Bound Variables. *Linguistic Inquiry* 11: 679–708.

Holes, Clive, 1990. *Gulf Arabic*. London: Routledge.

Hornstein, Norbert, 1984. *Logic as Grammar*. Cambridge, Mass.: MIT Press.

Hornstein, Norbert, and Amy Weinberg, 1990. The Necessity of LF. *The Linguistic Review* 7: 129–168.

Hoyt, Frederick, 2002. Impersonal Agreement as a Specificity Effect in Rural Palestinian Arabic. In *Perspectives on Arabic Linguistics XIII–XIV*, eds. Dil Parkinson and Elabbas Benmamoun, 111–141. Amsterdam: John Benjamins.

Iaach, J. 1996. La Négation en Hassaniyya. In *La Négation en Berbère et en Arabe Maghrébin*, eds. S. Chaker and Dominique Caubet, 163–176. Paris: L'Harmattan.

Iatridou, Sabine, 1990. About Agr(P). *Linguistic Inquiry* 21: 551–577.

Jelinek, Eloise, 1981. On Defining Categories: Aux and Predicate in Egyptian Colloquial Arabic. Doctoral dissertation, University of Arizona, Tuscon.

Kayne, Richard, 1994. *The Antisymmetry of Syntax*. Cambridge, Mass.: MIT Press.

Kenstowicz, Michael, 1989. The Null Subject Parameter in Modern Arabic Dialects. In *The Null Subject Parameter*, eds. Osvaldo Jaeggli and Ken Safir, 263–275. Dordrecht: Kluwer.

Khalafallah, Abdelghani, 1969. *A Descritptive Grammar of Saʕiidi Egyptian Colloquial Arabic*. The Hague: Mouton.

Koopman, Hilda, and Dominique Sportiche, 1991. The Position of Subjects. *Lingua* 85: 211–258.

Kroch, Anthony, 1989. Amount Quantification, Referentiality, and Long wh-movement. Unpublished manuscript, University of Pennsylvania Philadelphia.

Kuroda, Sige-Yuki, 1968. English Relativization and Certain Related Problems. *Language* 44: 244–266.

Laka, Itziar, 1990. Negation in Syntax: On the Nature of Functional Categories and Projections. Doctoral dissertation, MIT, Cambridge, Mass.

Larcher, Pierre, 1994. Ma Faʕala vs Lam Yafʕal: Une Hypothesèse Pragmatique. *Arabica* 41: 388–415.

Larson, Richard, 1985. Bare-NP Adverbs. *Linguistic Inquiry* 14: 595–621.

Marantz, Alec. 1984. *On the Nature of Grammatical Relations*. Cambridge, Mass.: MIT Press.

Matar, A. 1976. *Dhawaahir Naadhira fii lahajaat l-xaliij l-'arabii*. Qatar: College of Education.

McCarthy, John, 1979. Formal Problems in Semitic Phonology and Morphology. Doctoral dissertation, MIT, Cambridge, Mass.

1981. A Prosodic Theory of Non-concatenative Morphology. *Linguistic Inquiry* 12: 373–418.

McCarus, Ernest, 1976. A Semantic Analysis of Arabic Verbs. In *Michigan Oriental Studies in Honor of George G. Cameron*, ed. L. L. Orlin, 3–28. Ann Arbor: University of Michigan.

McCloskey, James, 1990. Resumptive Pronouns, Ā-binding and Levels of Representation in Irish. In *Syntax and Semantics 23: Syntax of the modern Celtic languages*, ed. Randall Hendrick, 199–248. San Diego: Academic Press.

1996. Subjects and Subject Positions. In *The Syntax of the Celtic Languages*, eds. R. Borsley and I. Roberts, 241–283. Cambridge University Press.

1997. Subjecthood and Subject Positions. In *Elements of Grammar: A Handbook of Generative Syntax*, ed. L. Haegeman, 197–235. Dordrecht: Kluwer.

2002. Resumption, Successive Cyclicity, and the Locality of Operations. In *Derivation and Explanation in the Minimalist Program*, eds. Samuel David Epstein and T. Daniel Seeley, 184–226. Oxford: Blackwell.

2005. Resumption. In *The Blackwell Companion to Syntax, Volumes I–IV*, eds. Martin Everaert and Henk van Riemsdijk, 94–117. Oxford: Blackwell.

Milsark, Gary, 1977. Toward an Explanation of Certain Peculiarities of the Existential Construction in English. *Linguistic Analysis* 3: 1–29.

Mohammad, Mohammad, 1988. On the Parallelism between IP and DP. In *Proceedings of WCCFL VII*, ed. Hagit Borer, 241–254. Stanford: CSLI.

1989. The Sentence Structure of Arabic. Doctoral dissertation, USC, Los Angeles.

1999. Checking and Licensing Inside DP in Palestinian Arabic. In *Perspectives on Arabic Linguistics XII*, ed. Elabbas Benmamoun, 27–44. Amsterdam: John Benjamins.

2000. *Word Order, Agreement and Pronominalization in Standard and Palestinean Arabic*. Amsterdam: John Benjamins.

Moritz, Luc, and Daniel Valois, 1994. Pied-piping and Specifier–Head Agreement. *Linguistic Inquiry* 25: 667–707.

Mouchaweh, Lina, 1986. De la Syntaxe des Petites Prépositions. Doctoral dissertation, Université de Paris VIII, Paris.

Moutaouakil, Ahmed, 1987. *min qaDaayaa r-raabiT fii l-lugha l-'arabiyya*. Casablanca: 'ocaadh.

1989. *Pragmatic Functions in a Functional Grammar of Arabic*. Dordrecht: Foris.

1993. *al-wathiifa wa l-binya*. Casablanca: 'ocaadh.

Mughazy, Mustafa, 2004. Subatomic Semantics and the Active Participle in Egyptian. Doctoral dissertation, University of Illinois, Urbana-Champaign.

Noyer, Rolf, 1992. Features, Positions and Affixes in Autonomous Morphological Structure. Doctoral dissertation, MIT, Cambridge, Mass.

Ouhalla, Jamal, 1990. Sentential Negation, Relativized Minimality and Aspectual Status of Auxiliaries. *Linguistic Review* 7: 183–231.

1991. *Functional Categories and Parametric Variation*. London: Routledge.

1992. Focus in Standard Arabic. *Linguistics in Potsdam* 1: 65–92.

1993. Negation, Focus and Tense: The Arabic *maa* and *laa*. *Rivista di Linguistica* 5: 275–300.

1994a. Verb Movement and Word Order in Arabic. In *Verb Movement*, eds. D. Lightfoot and N. Hornstein, 41–72. Cambridge University Press.

1994b. Focus in Standard Arabic. *Linguistics in Potsdam* 1: 65–92.

1996. Remarks on the Binding Properties of wh-pronouns. *Linguistic Inquiry* 27: 676–707.

1997. Remarks on Focus in Standard Arabic. In *Perspectives on Arabic Linguistics X*, eds. Mushira Eid and Robert Ratcliffe, 9–45. Amsterdam: John Benjamins.

2001. Parasitic Gaps and Resumptive Pronouns. In *Parasitic Gaps*, eds. David Lightfoot and Norbert Hornstein, 41–72. Cambridge University Press.

2002. The Structure and Logical Form of Negative Sentences in Arabic. In *Themes in Arabic and Hebrew Syntax*, eds. J. Ouhalla and U. Shlonsky, 299–320. Dordrecht: Kluwer.

2004. Semitic Relatives. *Linguistic Inquiry* 35: 288–300.

Owens, Jonathan, 1984. *A Short Reference Grammar of Eastern Libyan Arabic*. Wiesbaden: Otto Harrassowitz.

2007. *A Linguistic History of Arabic*. Oxford University Press.

Palva, Heikke, 1972. *Studies in the Arabic Dialect of the Semi-Nomadic əl-ʕayarma Tribe*. Göteborg: Acta Universitatis Gothorburgensis.

Pesetsky, David, 1987. *Wh*-in-situ: Movement and Unselective Binding. In *The Representation of (In)definiteness*, eds. Eric Reuland and Alice ter Meulen, 98–129. Cambridge, Mass.: MIT Press.

Pesetsky, David and Esther Torrego, 2007. The Syntax of Valuation and the Interpretability of Features. In *Phrasal and Clausal Architecture: Syntactic Derivation and Interpretation*, eds. S. Karimi, V. Samiian, and W. Wilkins, 262–294. Amsterdam: John Benjamins.

Pollock, Jean-Yves, 1989. Verb Movement, UG and the Structure of IP. *Linguistic Inquiry* 20: 365–424.

Rapoport, Tova, 1987. Copular, Nominal, and Small Clauses: A Study of Israeli Hebrew. Doctoral dissertation, MIT, Cambridge, Mass.

Ritter, Elizabeth, 1988. A Head-Movement Approach to Construct State Noun Phrases. *Linguistics* 26: 909–929.

1995. On the Syntactic Category of Pronouns and Agreement. *Natural Language and Linguistic Theory* 13: 405–443.

Rizzi, Luigi, 1990. *Relativized Minimality*. Cambridge, Mass.: MIT Press.

1997. The Fine Structure of the Left Periphery. In *Elements of Grammar*, ed. L. Haegeman, 281–337. Dordrecht: Kluwer.

Ross, John, 1967. Constraints on Variables in Syntax. Doctoral dissertation, MIT, Cambridge, Mass.

Rothstein, Susan, 1995. Small Clauses and Copular Constructions. *Syntax and Semantics* 28: 27–48.

Sells, Peter, 1984. Syntax and Semantics of Resumptive Pronouns. Doctoral dissertation, University of Massachussets, Amherst.

Shlonsky, Ur, 1992. Resumptive Pronouns as Last Resort. *Linguistic Inquiry* 23: 443–468.

1997. *Clause Structure and Word Order in Hebrew and Arabic: An Essay in Comparative Semitic Syntax*. Oxford University Press.

2000. Remarks on the Complementizer Layer of Standard Arabic. In *Research in Afroasiatic Grammar*, eds. J. Lecarme, J. Lowenstamm, and U. Shlonsky, 325–344. Amsterdam: John Benjamins.

2002. Constituent Questions in Palestinian Arabic. In *Themes in Arabic and Hebrew Syntax*, eds. Jamal Ouhalla and Ur Shlonsky, 137–160. Dordrecht: Kluwer.

2004. The Form of Semitic Noun Phrases. *Lingua* 114: 1465–1526.

Siloni, Tali, 1997. *Noun Phrases and Nominalization: The Syntax of DPs*. Dordrecht: Kluwer.

Simone-Senelle, Marie-Claude, 1996. Negation in Some Arabic Dialects of the Thaamah of the Yemen. In *Perspectives on Arabic Linguistics IX*, eds. Mushira Eid and Dilworth Parkinson, 206–221. Amsterdam: John Benjamins.

Soltan, Usama, 2007. On Agree and Postcyclic Merge in Syntactic Derivations: First Conjunct Agreement in Standard Arabic Revisited. In *Perspectives on Arabic Linguistics XIX*, eds E. Benmamoun, 191–216. Amsterdam: John Benjamins.

Sportiche, Dominique. 1998. *Partitions and Atoms of Clause Structure: Subjects, Agreement, Case and Clitics*. London: Routledge.

Suleiman, Yasir, 2003. *The Arabic Language and National Identity: A Study in Ideology*. Washington, D.C.: Georgetown University Press.

Travis, Ann, 1979. Inflectional Affixation in Transformational Grammar: Evidence from the Arabic Paradigm. *Indiana University Linguistics Club Publication no.192*. Bloomington, Indiana.

Travis, Lisa. 1984. Parameters and Effects of Word Order Variation. Doctoral dissertation, MIT, Cambridge, Mass.

Tsimpli, Ianthi-Maria, 1990. The Clause Structure and Word Order of Modern Greek. In *UCL Working Papers in Linguistics 2*, ed. by John Harris, 226–255. London: University College London, Department of Phonetics and Linguistics.

    1995. Focusing in Modern Greek. In *Discourse Configurational Languages*, ed. by Katalin É. Kiss, 176–206. New York: Oxford University Press.

Vanhove, Martine, 1996. The Negation *maašii* in a Yaafi`i Dialect (Yemen). *In Perspectives on Arabic Linguistics IX,* eds. Mushira Eid and Dilworth Parkinson, 195–206. Amsterdam: John Benjamins.

Versteegh, Kees. 1997. *The Arabic Language*. Edinburgh University Press.

Wahba, Wafaa, 1984. *Wh*-constructions in Egyptian Arabic. Doctoral dissertation, University of Illinois, Urbana-Champaign.

    1991. LF-Movement in Iraqi Arabic. In *Logical Structure and Linguistic Structure*, eds. C.-T. J. Huang and R. May, 253–276. Dordrecht: Kluwer Academic Publishers.

Watson, Janet, 1993. *A Syntax of Sanʕani Arabic*. Wiesbaden: Otto Harrassowitz.

Wise, Hilary, 1975. *A Transformational Grammar of Spoken Egyptian Arabic*. Oxford: Basil Blackwell.

Woidich, Manfred, 1968. Negation und Negative Säte in Ägyptisch-Arabischen. Doctoral dissertation, Universität zu München, Munich.

Wright, William, 1889. *A Grammar of the Arabic Language*. Cambridge University Press.

Youssi, Abderrahim, 1992. *Grammaire et Lexique de L'Arabe Marocain Moderne*. Casablanca: Wallada.

Zanuttini, Raffaella, 1997. *Negation and Clausal Structure: A Comparative Study of Romance Languages*. Oxford University Press.

Zubizarreta, Maria Luisa, 1992. The Lexical Encoding of Scope Relations Among Arguments. In *Syntax and Semantics 26: Syntax and the Lexicon*, ed. Eric Wehrli and Tim Stowell, 211–255. San Diego, Calif.: Academic Press.

    1998. *Prosody, Focus, and Word Order*. Cambridge, Mass.: MIT Press.

Index